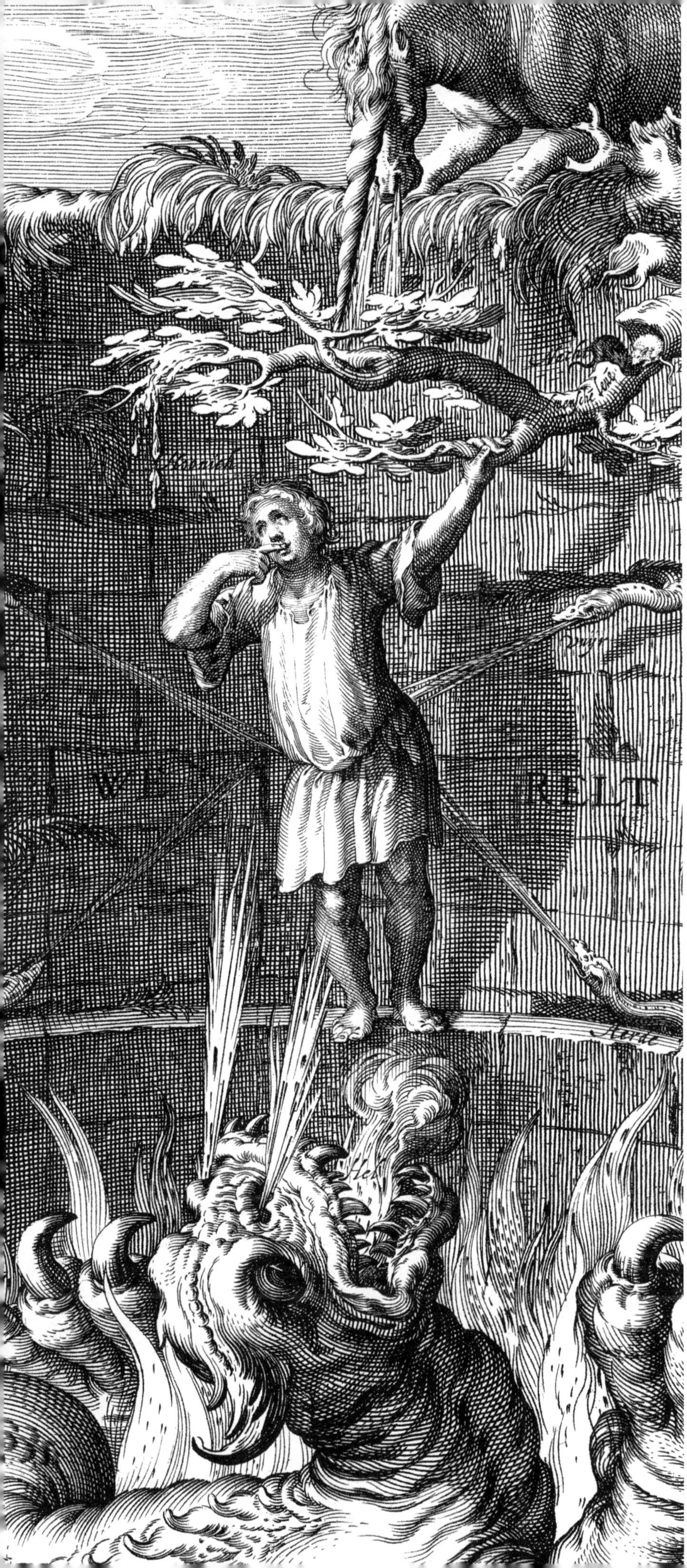

NUMBER ONE

DRAGONS & MYTHICAL CREATURES

AN IMAGE ARCHIVE FOR ARTISTS And DESIGNERS

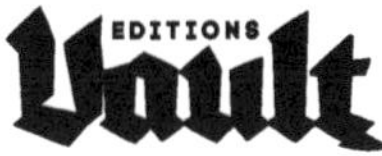

INTRODUCTION

This pictorial archive from Vault Editions is a treasury of 182 engravings and etchings documenting the folklore and fantasy art of the 19th, 18th and 17th-century. Expect to find epic battle scenes of kings, gods and warriors slaying savage dragons, centaurs at war, grotesque and fantastical creatures, scenes from the apocalypse, ferocious serpents, ornaments and heraldry adorned with griffins, unicorns, mermaids and much more.

Features:
Each book comes with a unique download link providing instant access to high-resolution files of all images featured. These images can be used in art and graphic design projects or printed and framed to make stunning decorative artworks. We promise you will love this impressive pictorial archive.

Additionally, each book comes with the Vault Editions Skulls and Anatomy sample pack.

About the author:
This book was curated and authored by the creative director of Vault Editions, Kale James. Kale has published over 20 acclaimed books within the art design space and has worked with brands including Nike, Samsung, Adidas and Rolling Stone. Kale's artwork is published in numerous titles, including No Cure, Semi-Permanent, Vogue and more.

This is an essential resource for any graphic designer, tattooist, fantasy artist, illustrator or collage artist looking to take their artwork to the next level.

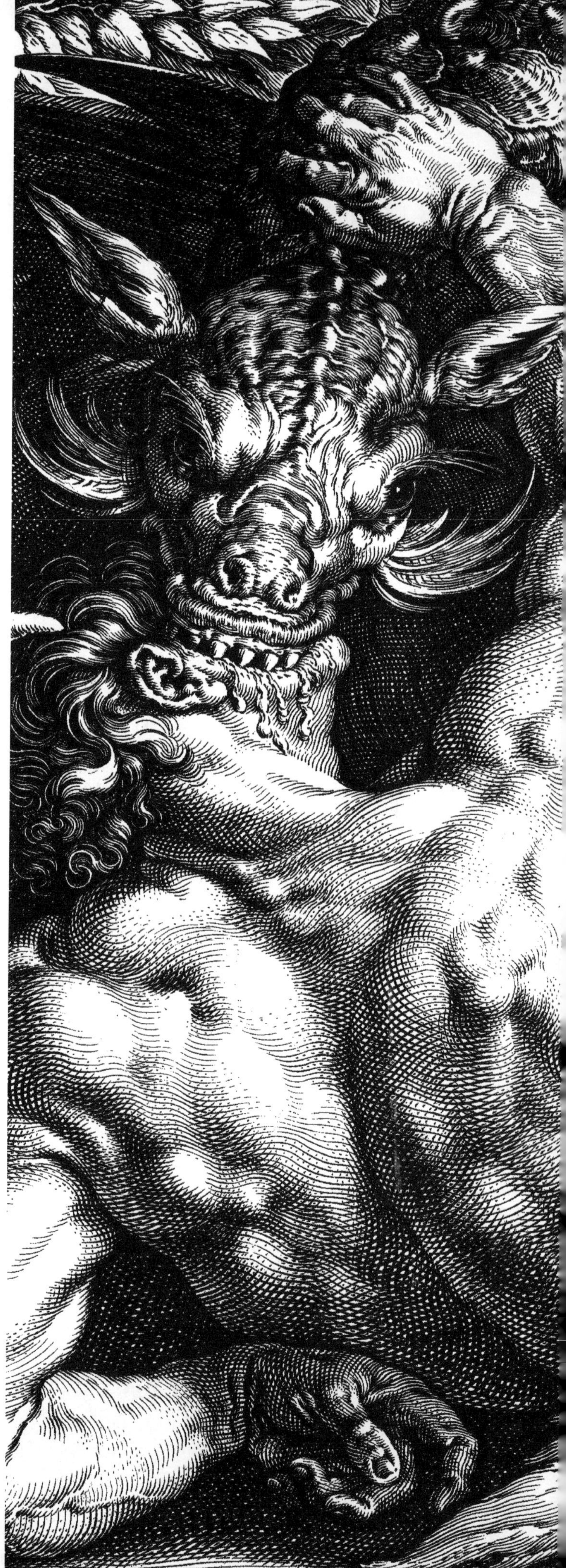

TABLE OF CONTENTS

DOWNLOAD YOUR FILES

Downloading your files is simple. To access your digital files, please go to the last page of this book and follow the instructions.

For technical assistance, please email:
info@vaulteditions.com

Bibliographical Note

This book is a new work created by Vault Editions Ltd.

ISBN: 978-1-925968-50-7

DRAGONS & MYTHICAL CREATURES

VAULT EDITIONS

01

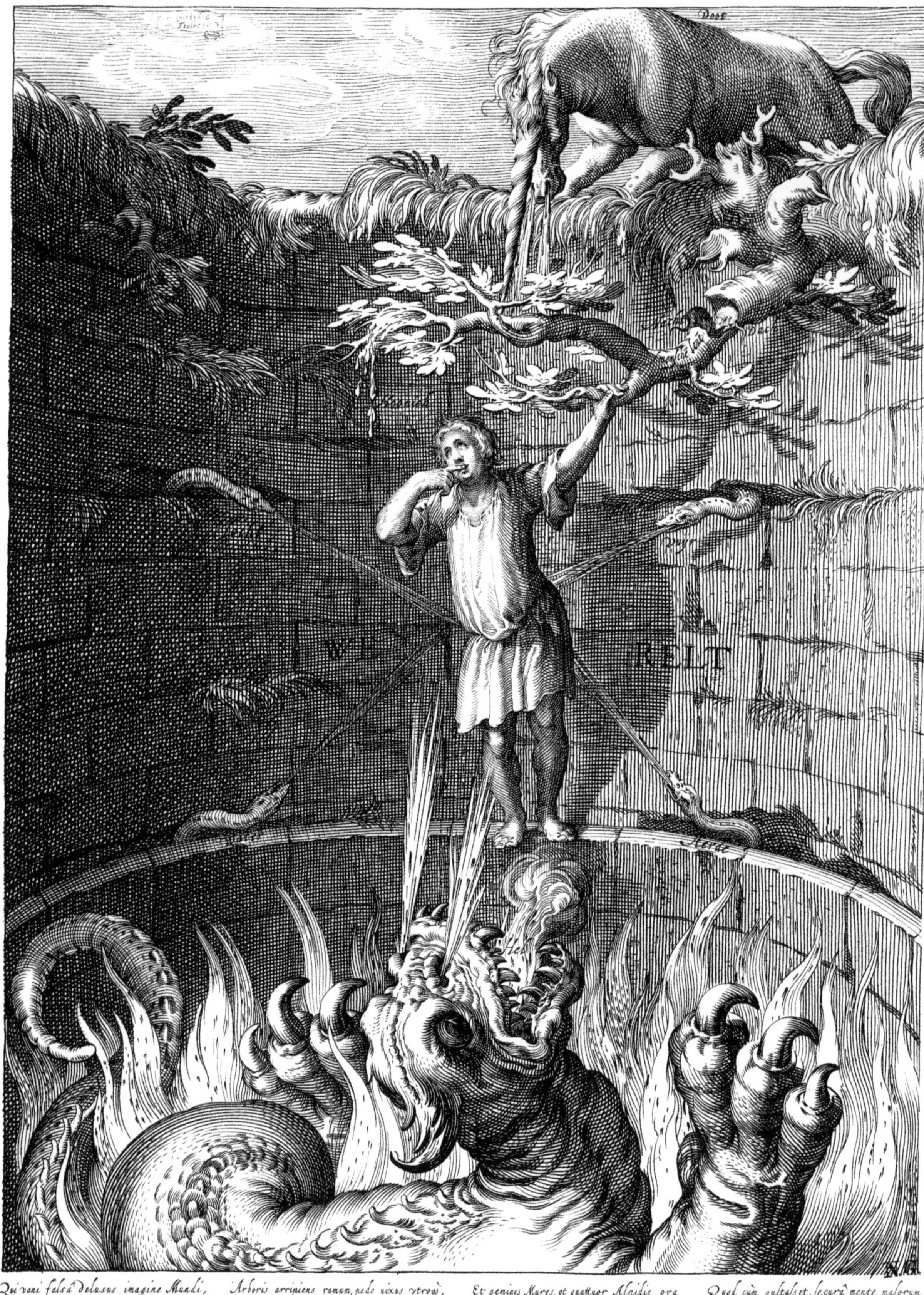

01: Allegory of the World, Boëtius Adamsz. Bolswert, after unknown, 1590 – 1633.

02

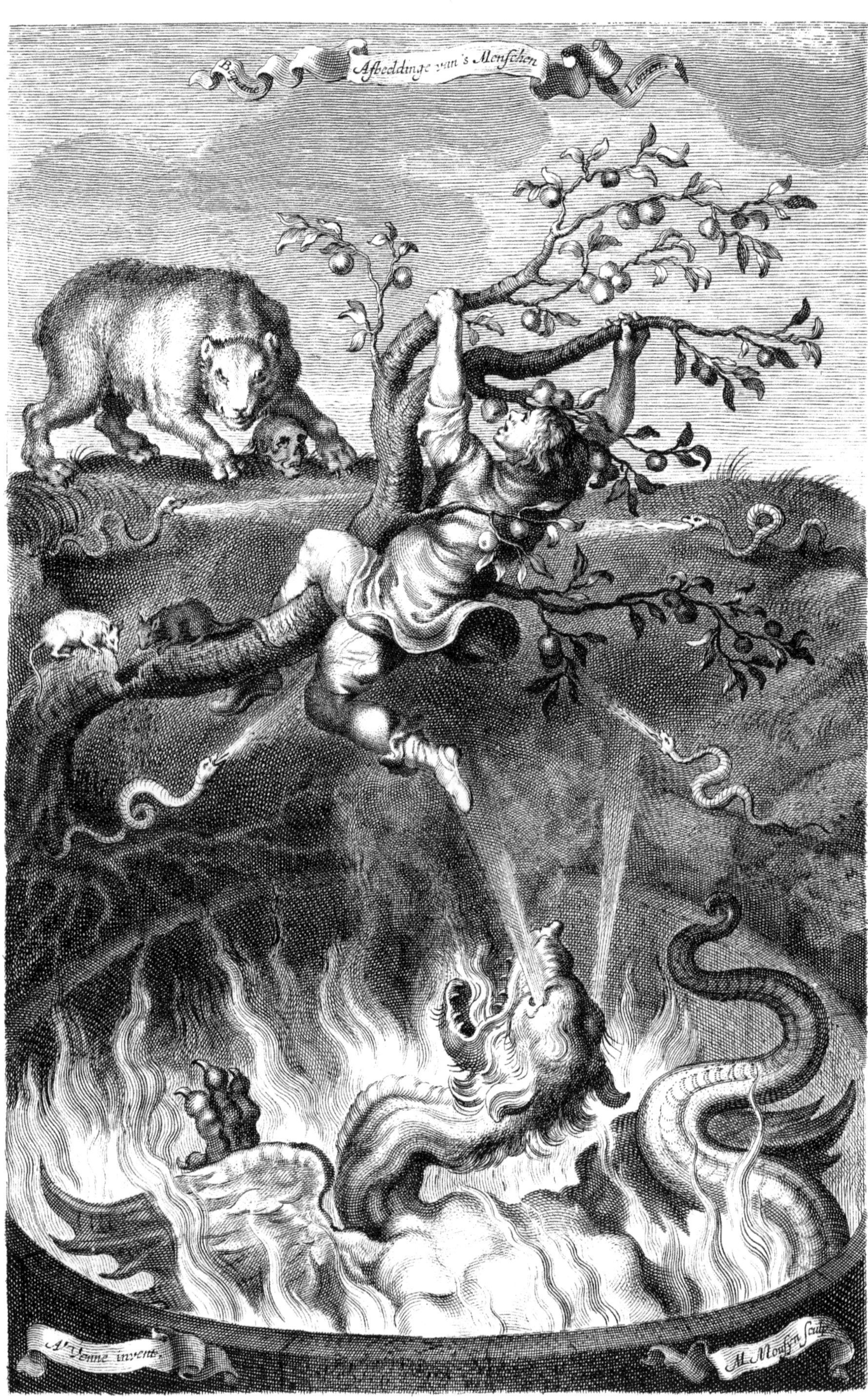

02: Man in apple tree threatens to fall out, Michiel Mosijn, after Adriaen Pietersz. van de Venne, 1640 – 1655.

03

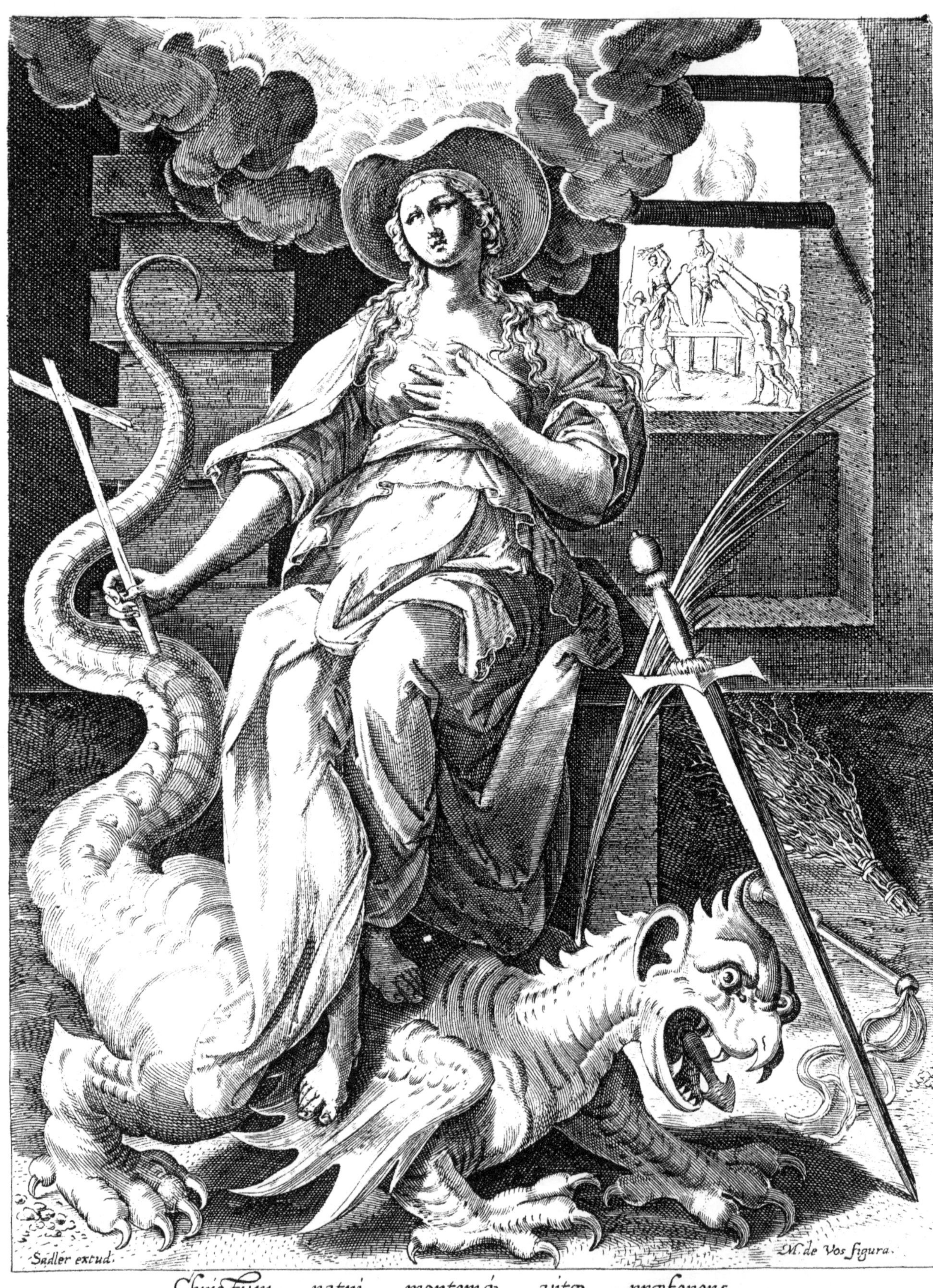

03: Saint Margaret, Johann Sadeler, after Maerten de Vos, 1583 – 1587.

04

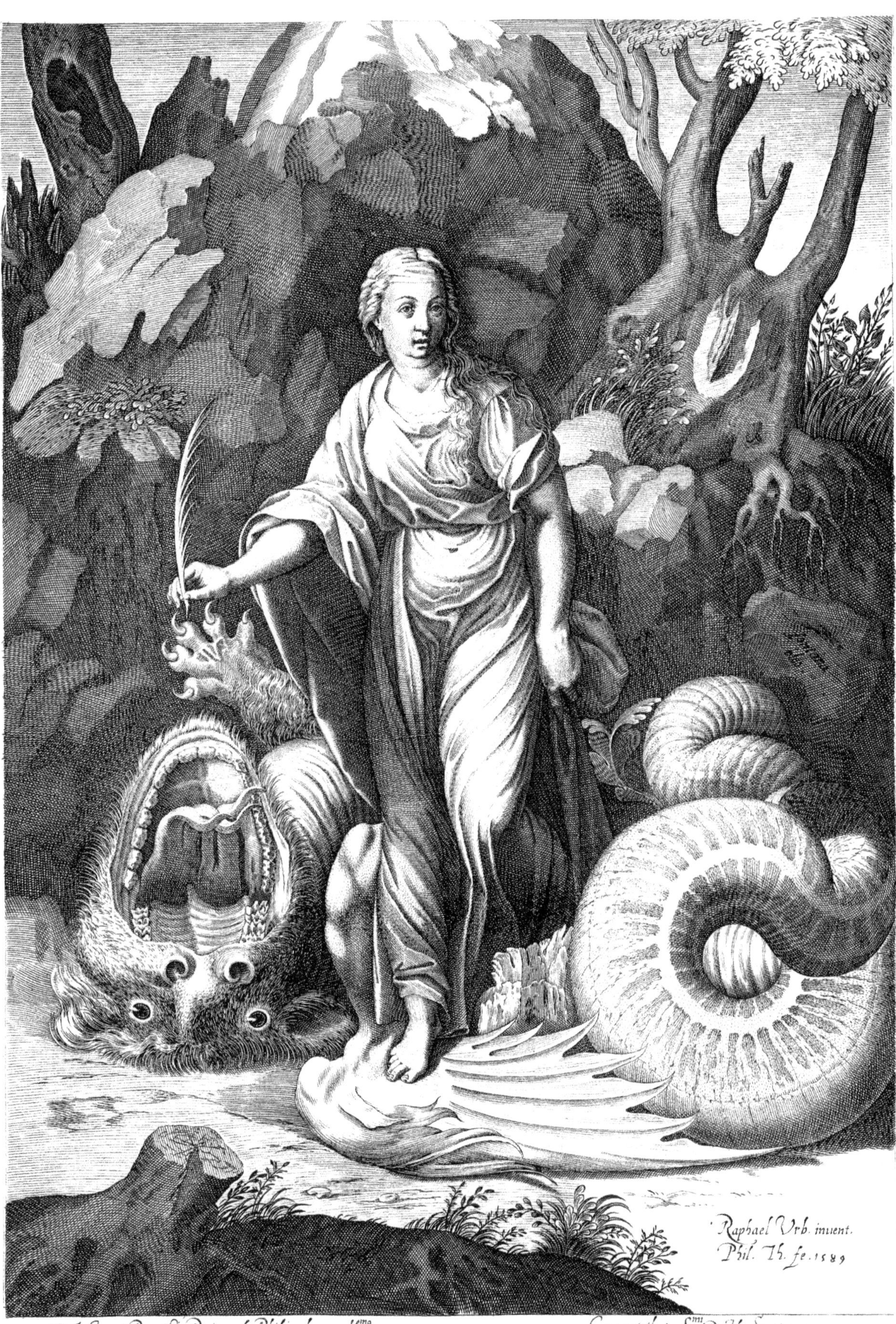

04: Saint Margaret of Antioch, Philippe Thomassin, after Raphael, after Giulio Romano, 1589.

05

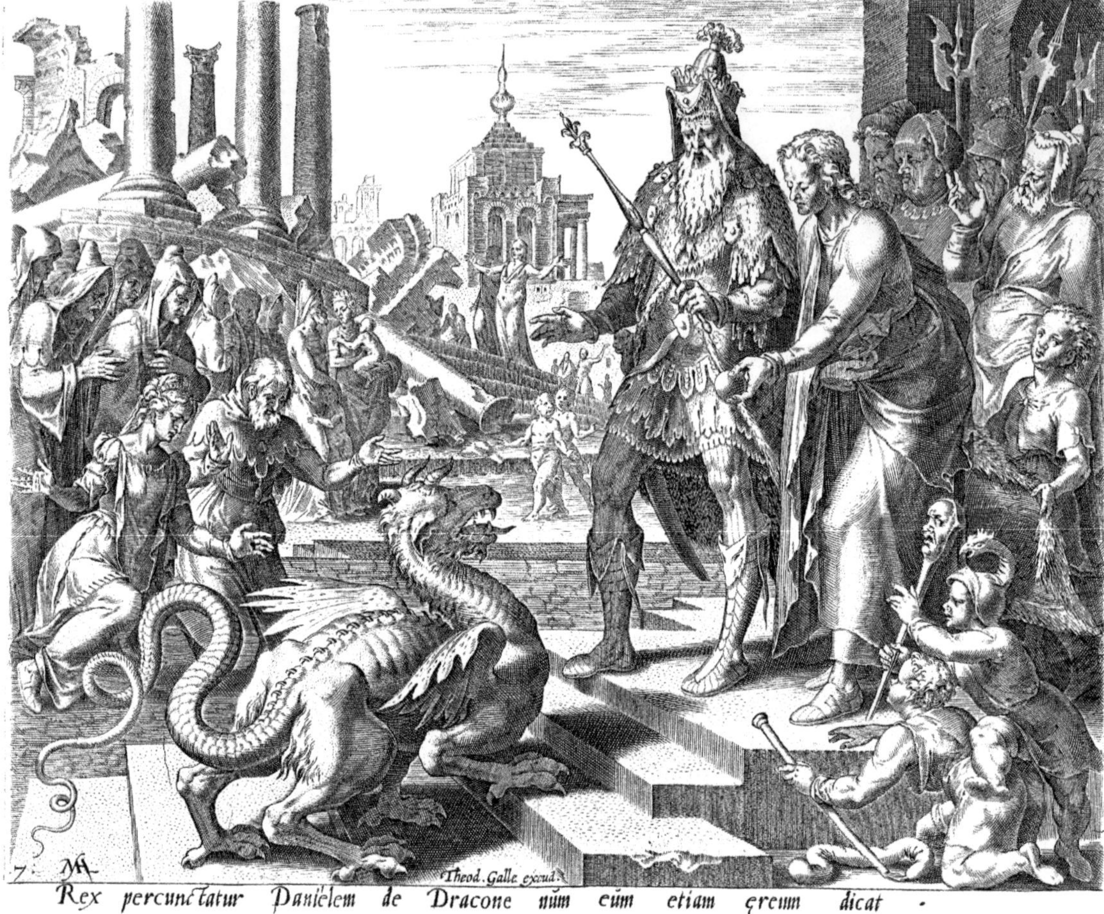

06

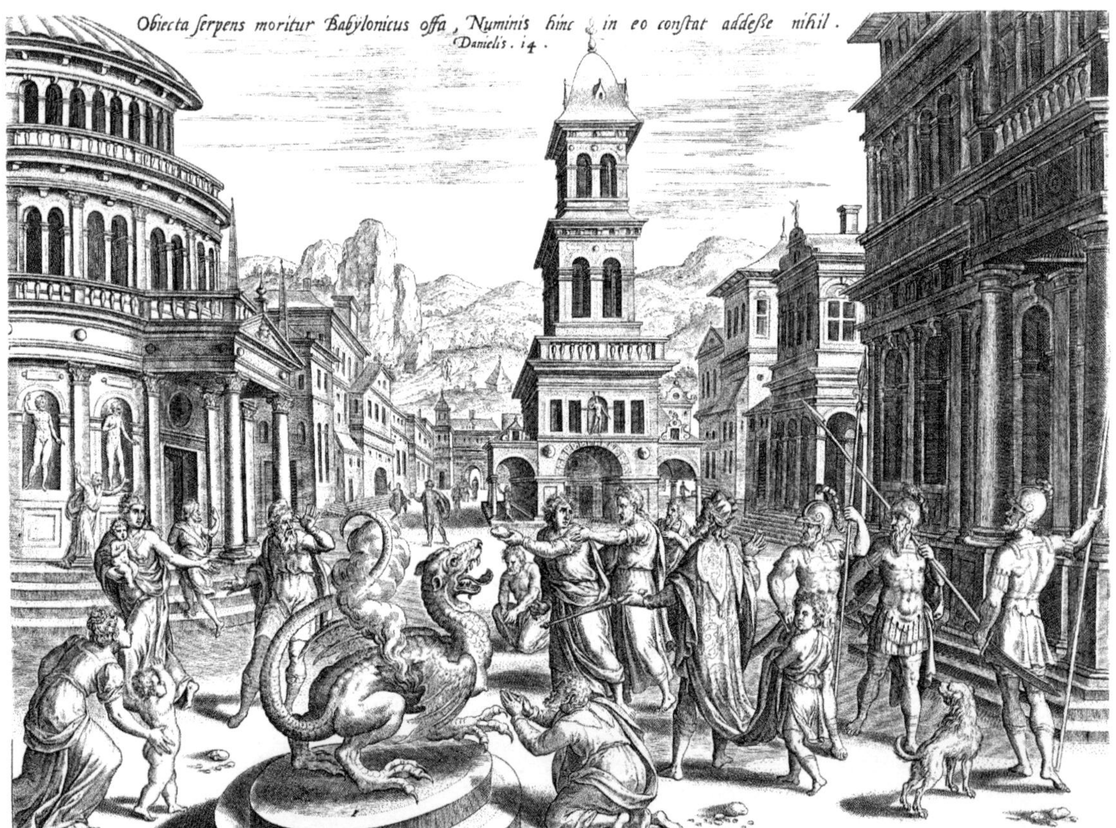

05: Daniel feeds the dragon, Philips Galle, after Maarten van Heemskerck, 1601 – 1633.

06: Daniel and the dragon, Johannes or Lucas van Doetechum, after Hans Vredeman de Vries, 1585.

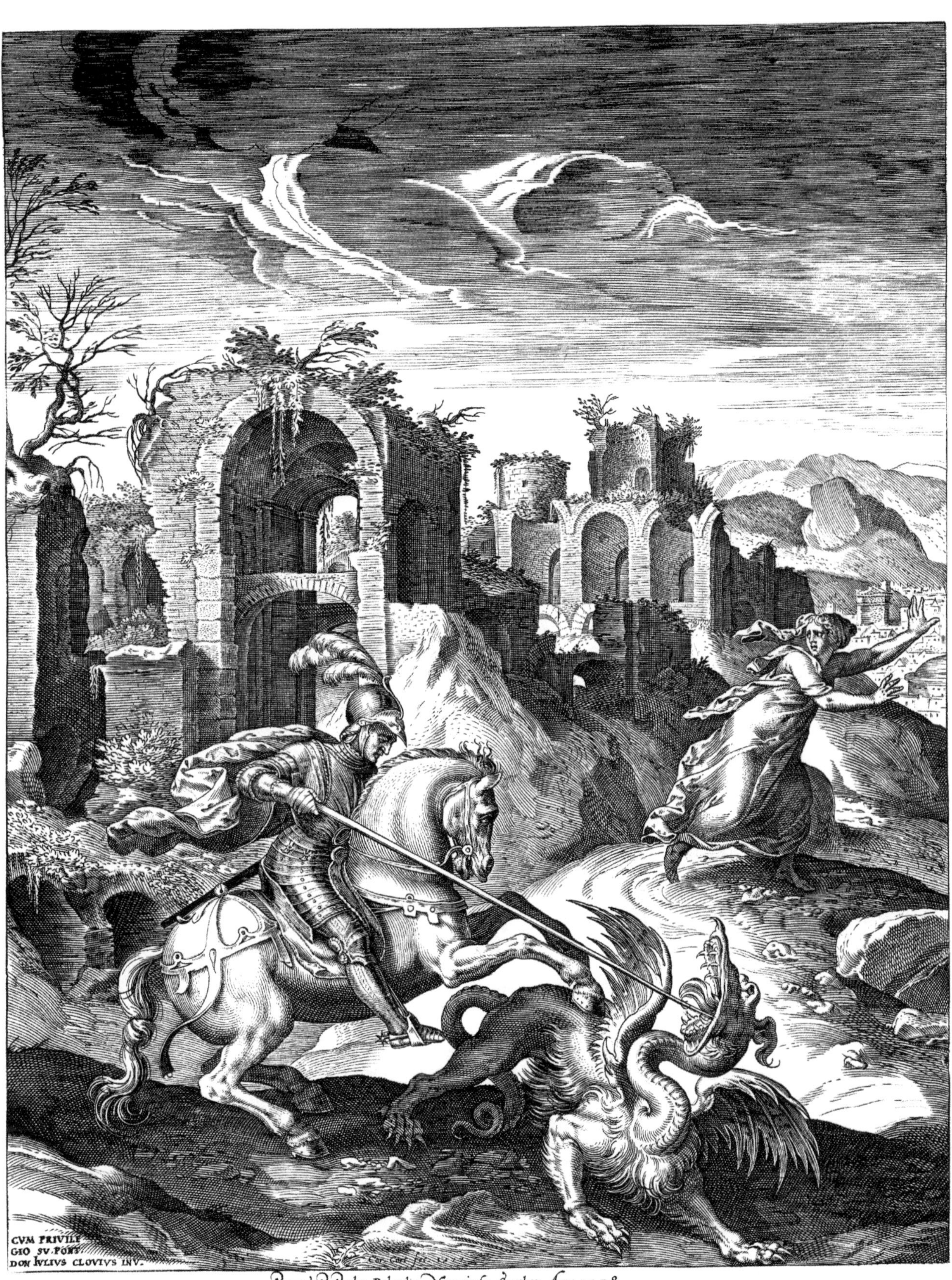

07: George Slaying the Dragon, Cornelis Cort, after Giulio Clovio, 1578

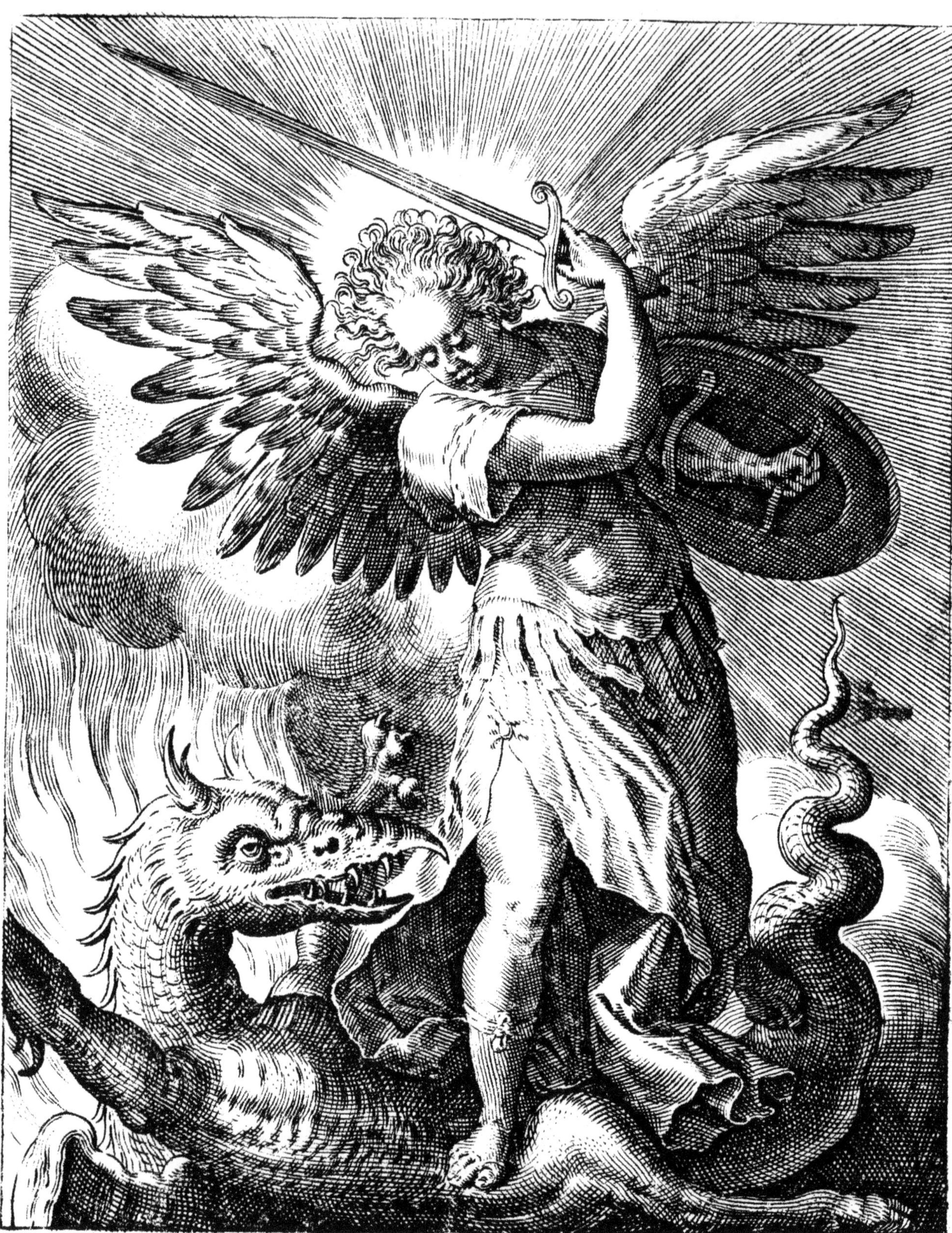

08: Archangel Michael Slays the Dragon, Raphaël Sadeler (I), 1617.

09

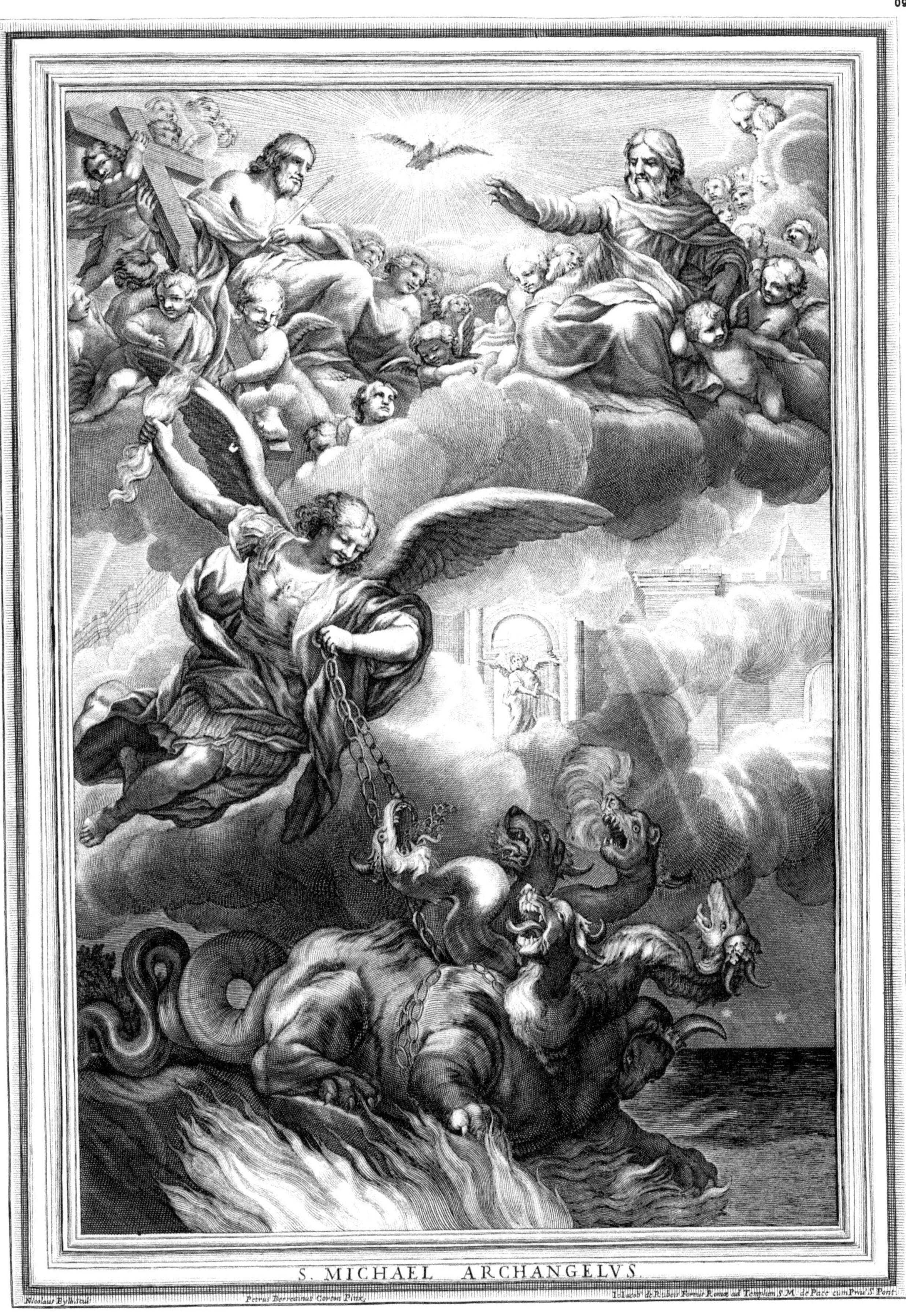

09: Archangel Michael, Nicolo Billy, after Pietro da Cortona, 1637 – 1691.

10

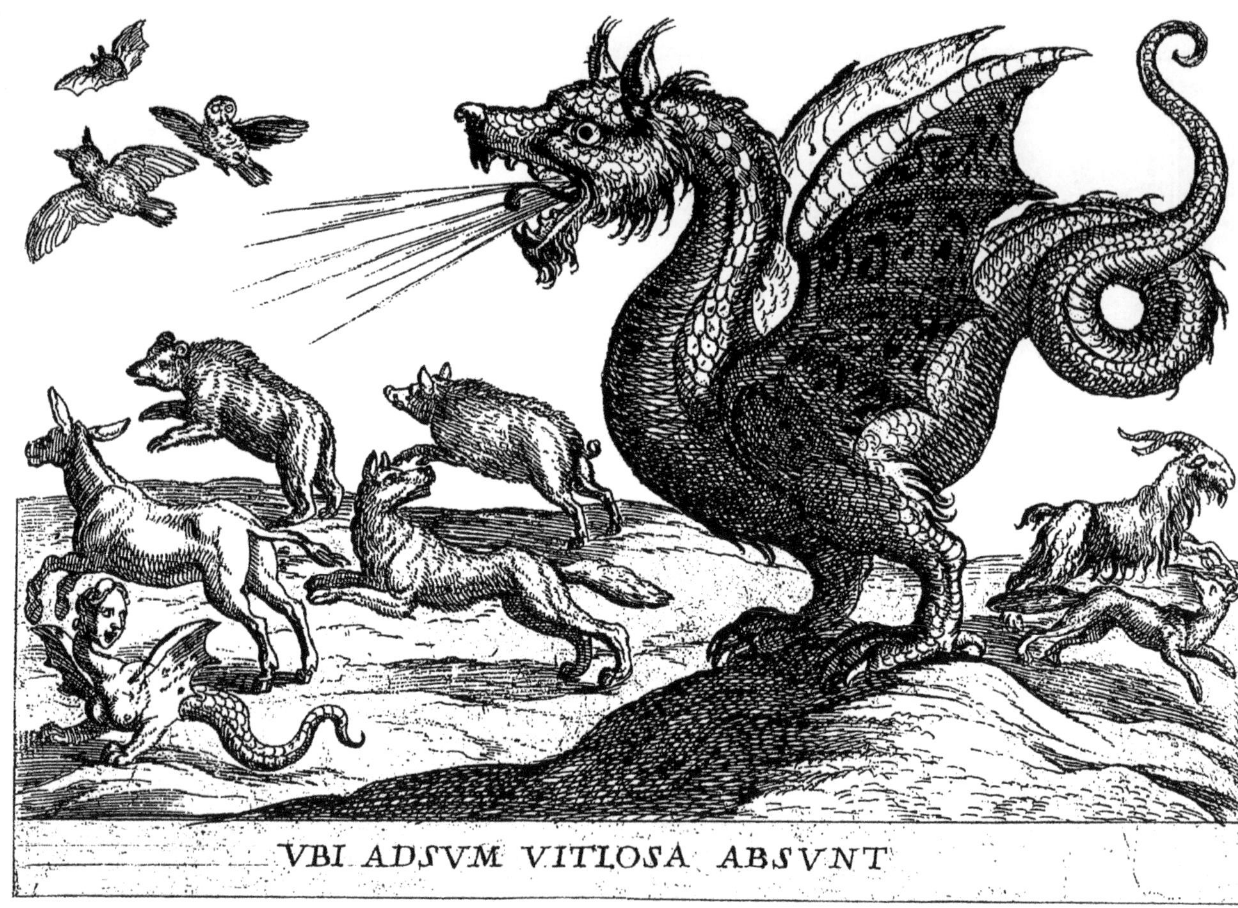

11

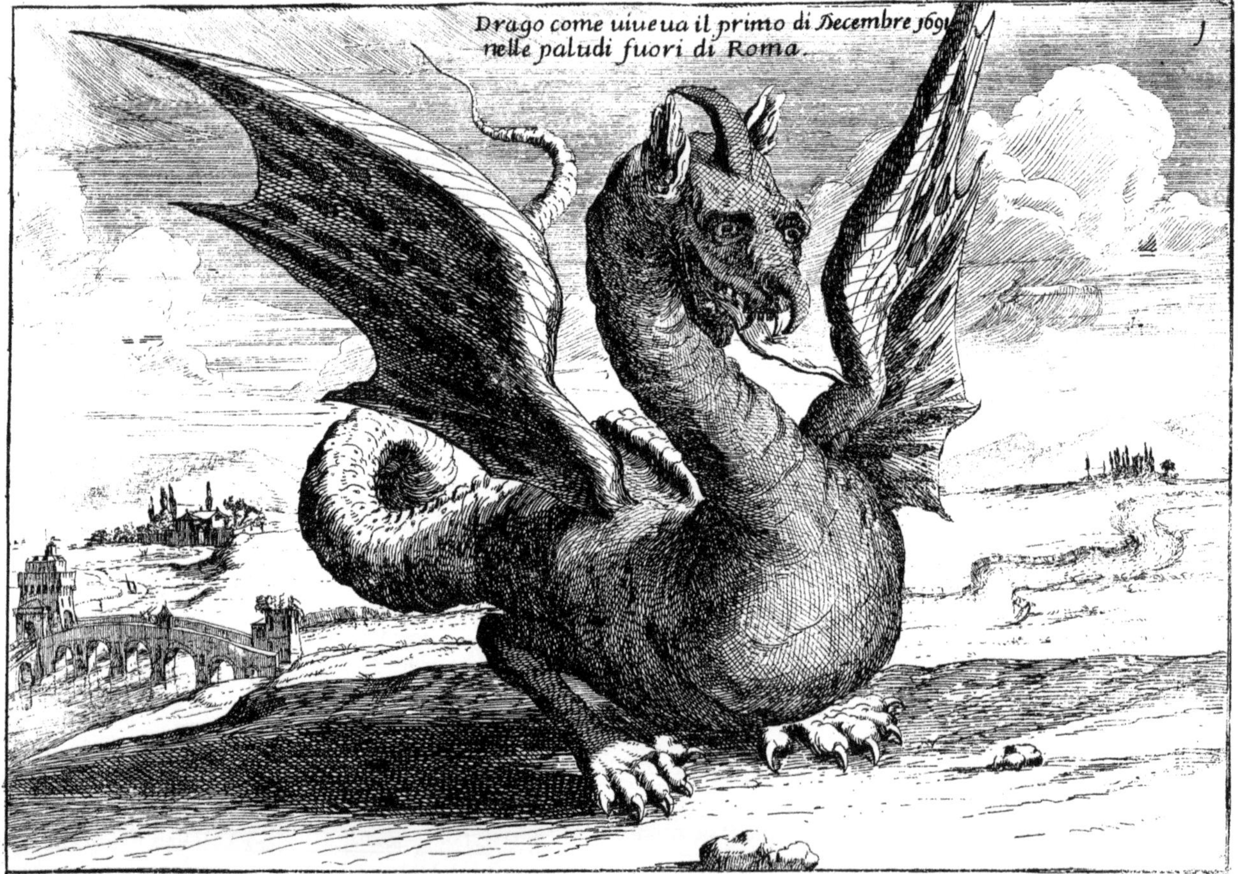

10: A Dragon Chases Animals.

11: Dragon in the Marshes Outside Rome, Cornelis Meijer (attributed to), after Cornelis Meijer, 1696.

12

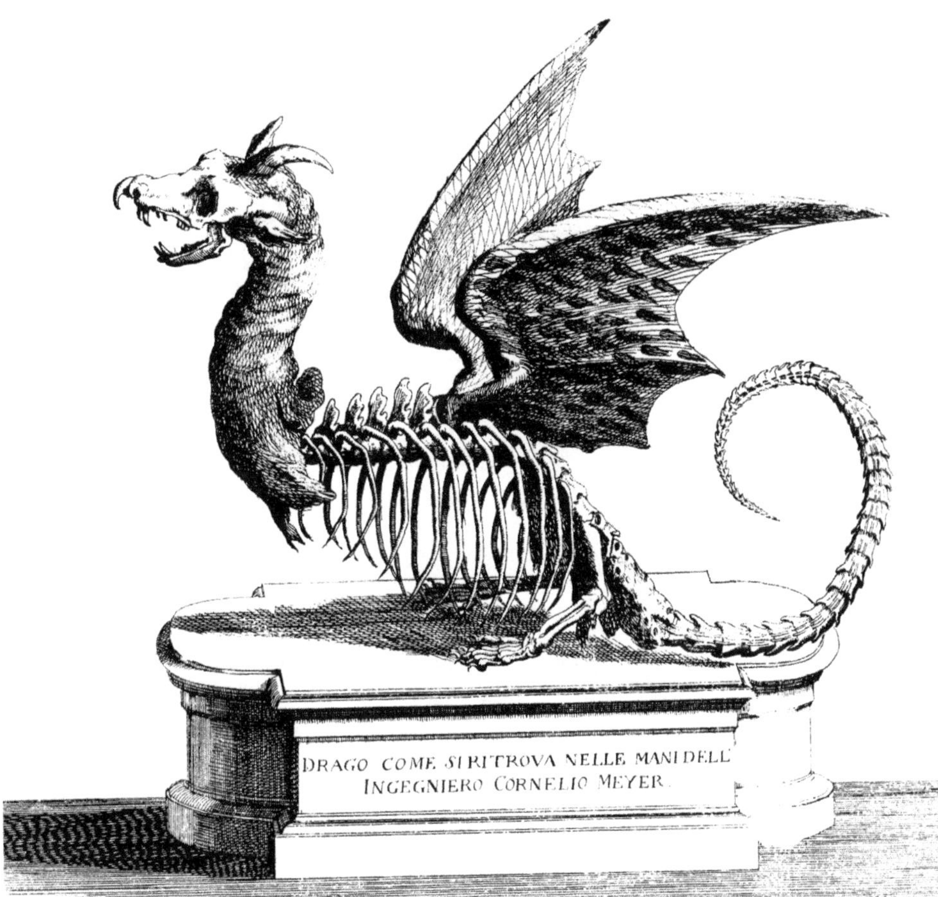

13

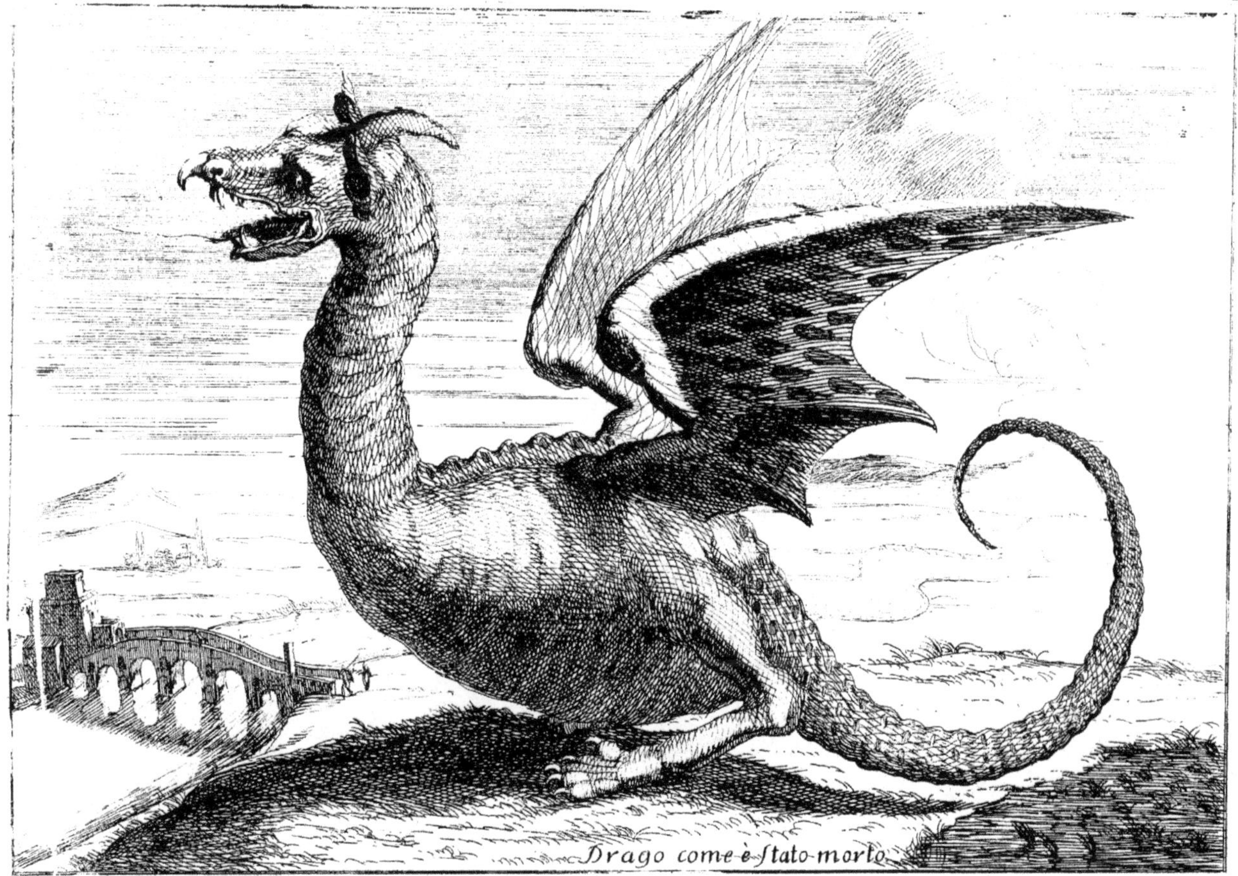

12: Dragon Skeleon,Caspar van Wittel (possibly), after Cornelis Meijer, 1696.

13: Dragon in a Landscape, Cornelis Meijer (attributed to), after Cornelis Meijer, 1696.

14

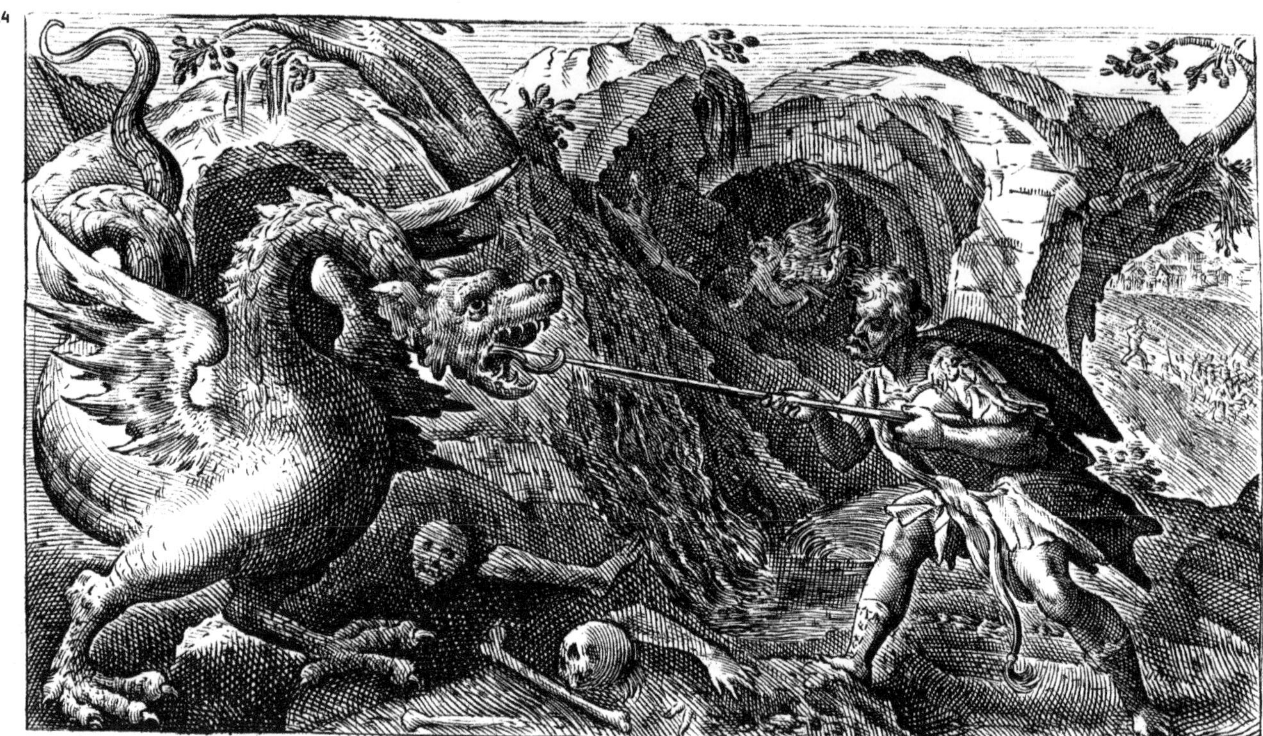

15

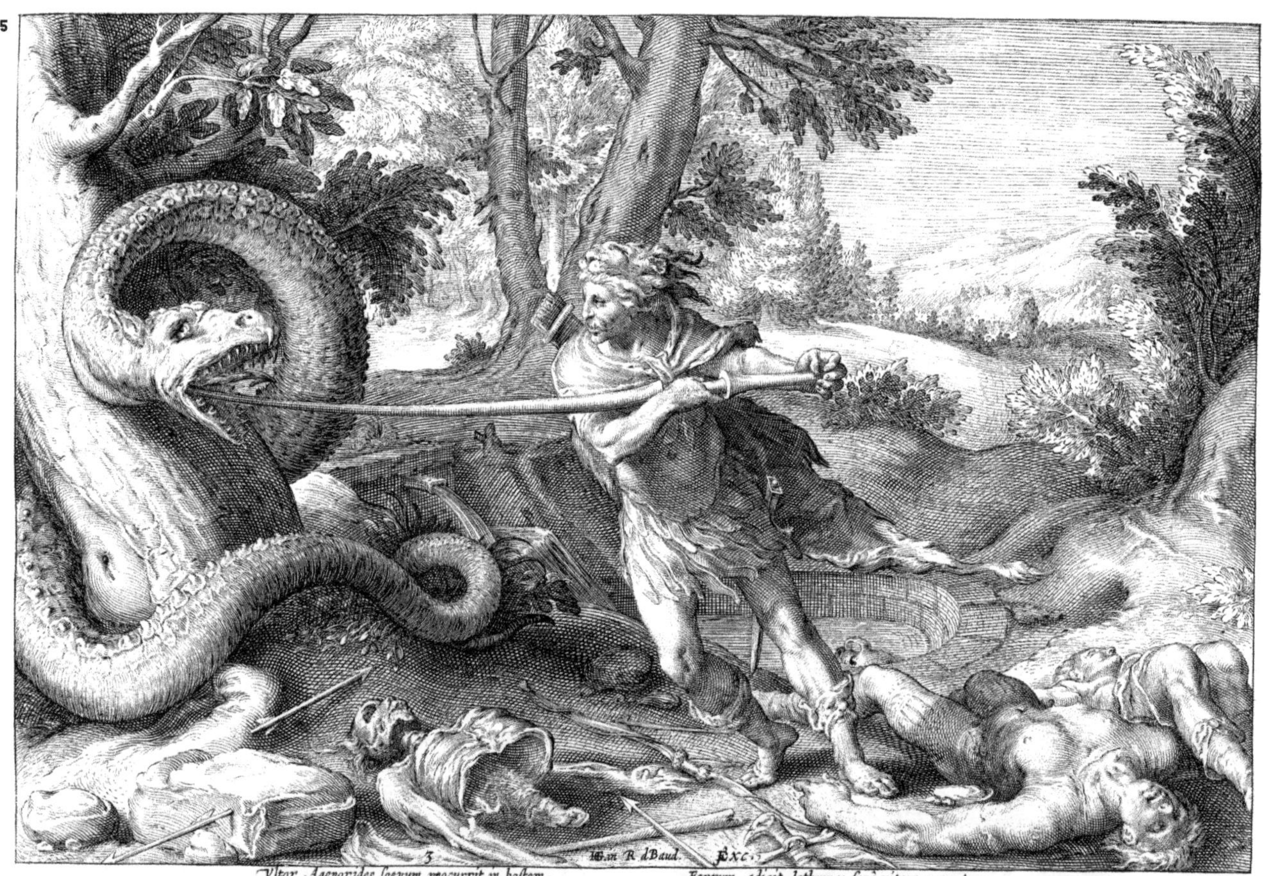

14: Cadmus Slays the Dragon, Crispijn van de Passe (I), 1602 – 1607.

15: Cadmus Slays the Dragon, Hendrick Goltzius (workshop of), after Hendrick Goltzius, 1615.

16

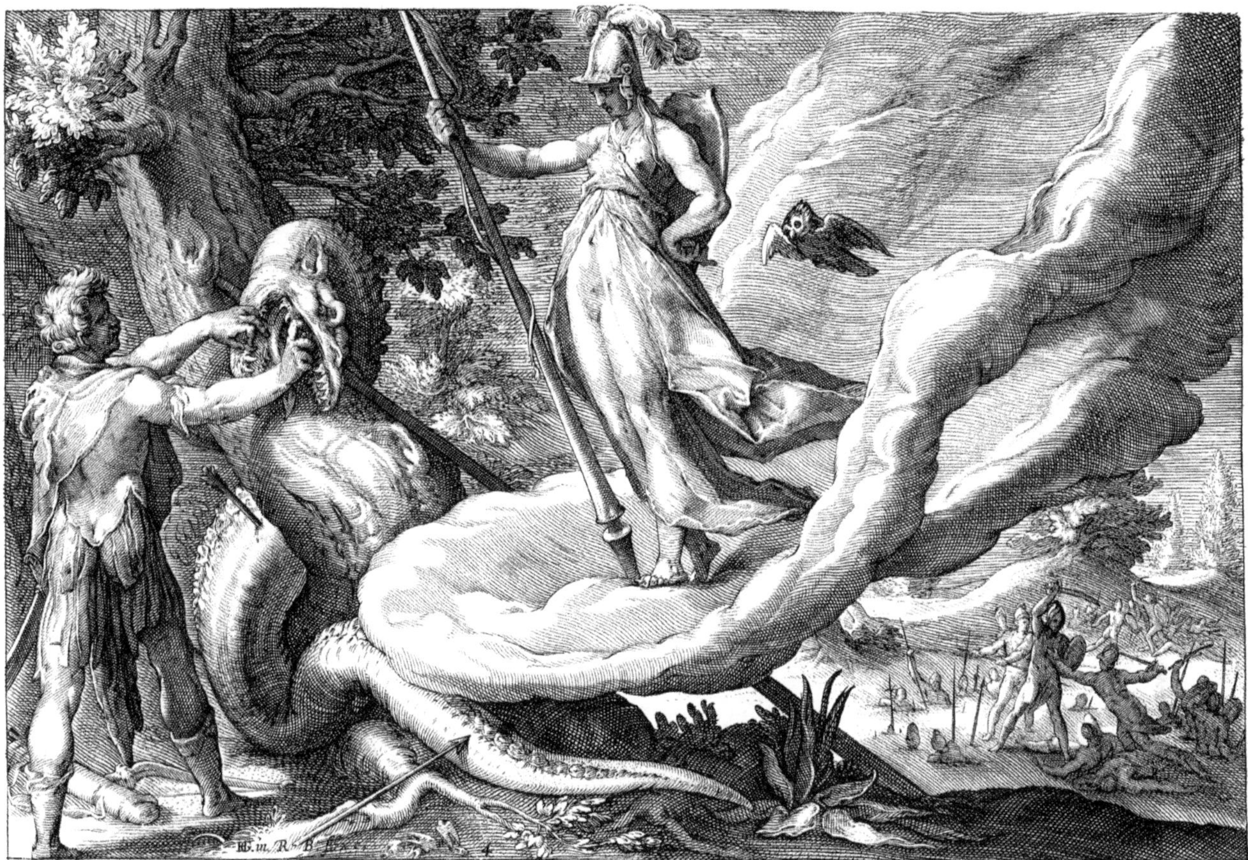

17

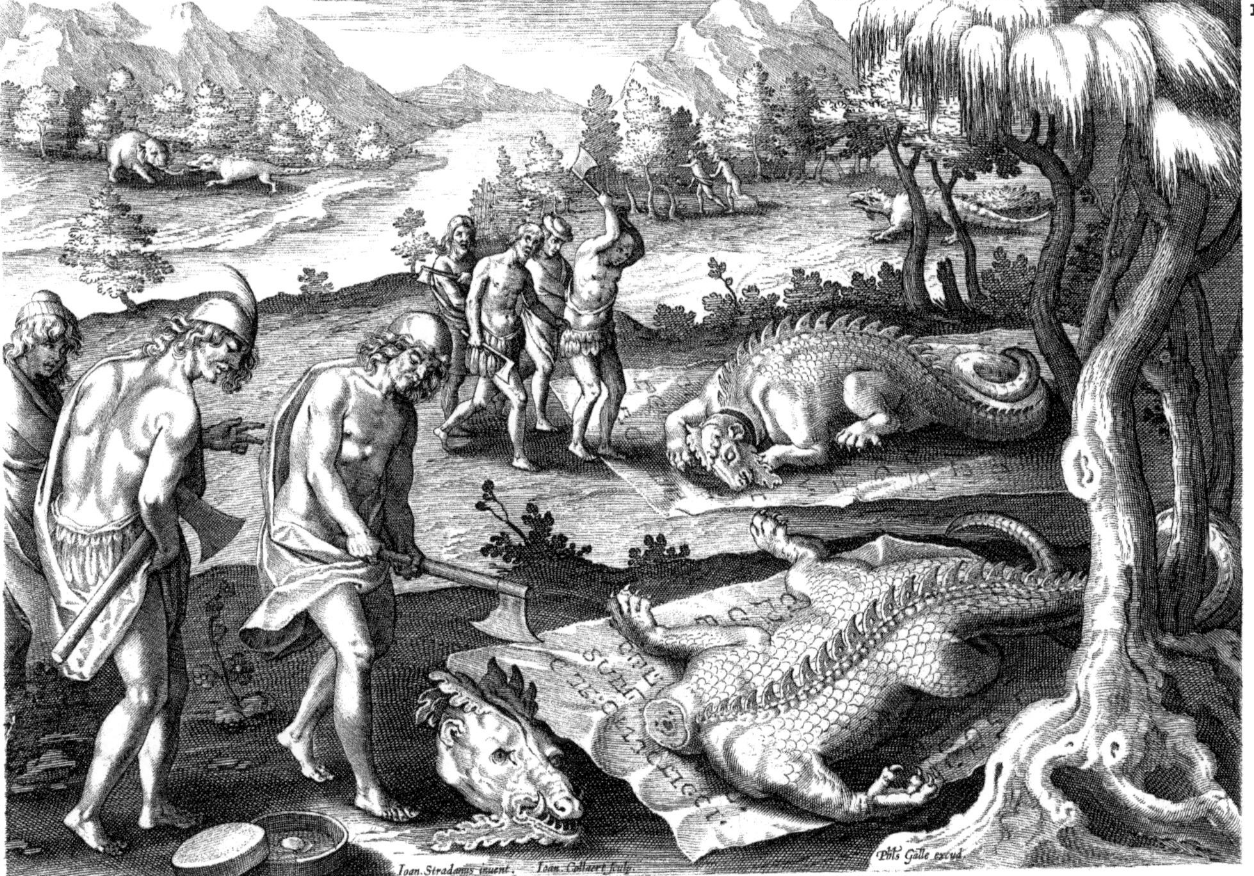

16: Cadmus removing the dragon's teeth.

17: Killing dragons in Egypt.

18

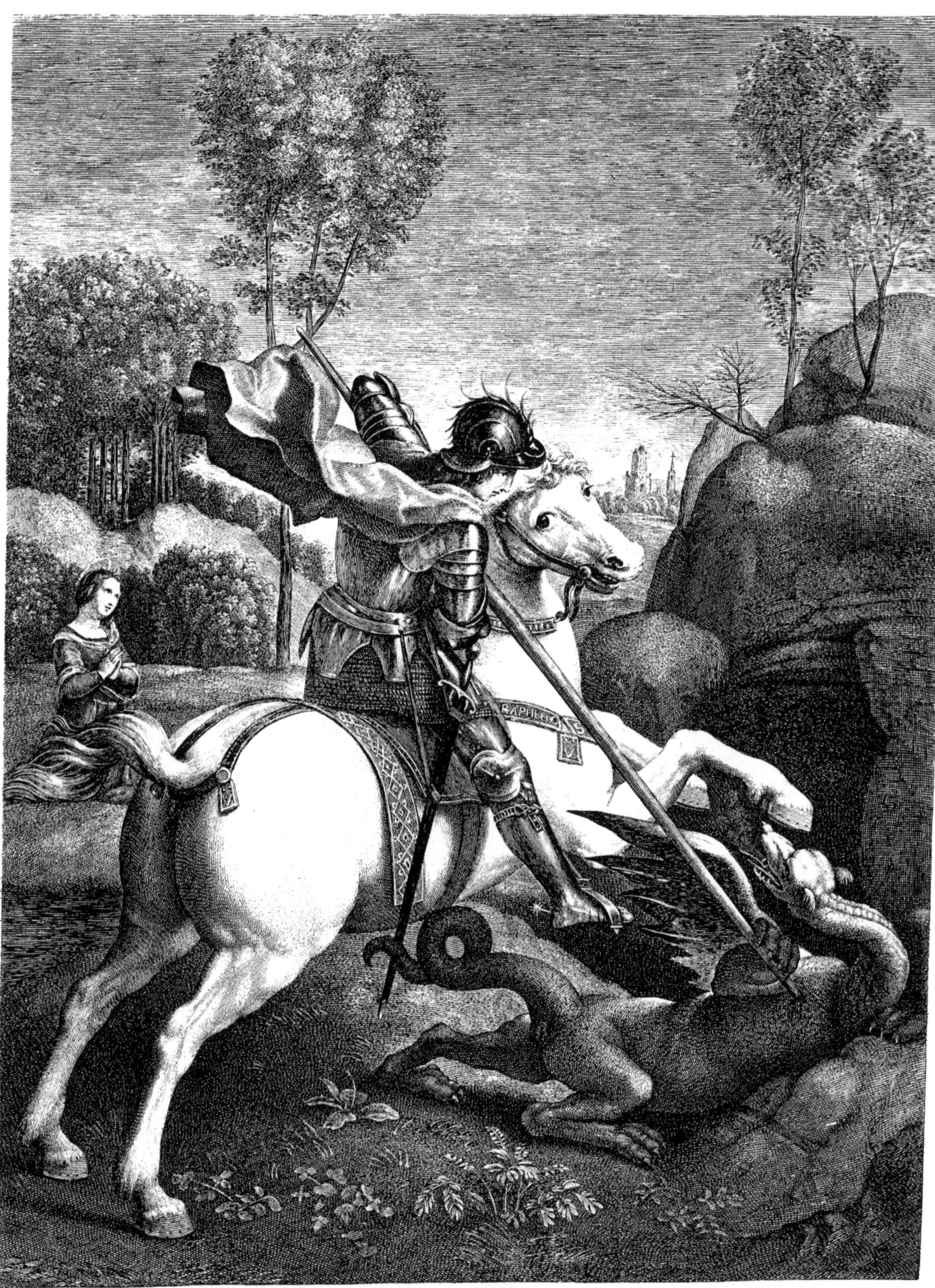

18: H. Joris kills the dragon, Lucas Vorsterman (I), after Rafaël, 1627.

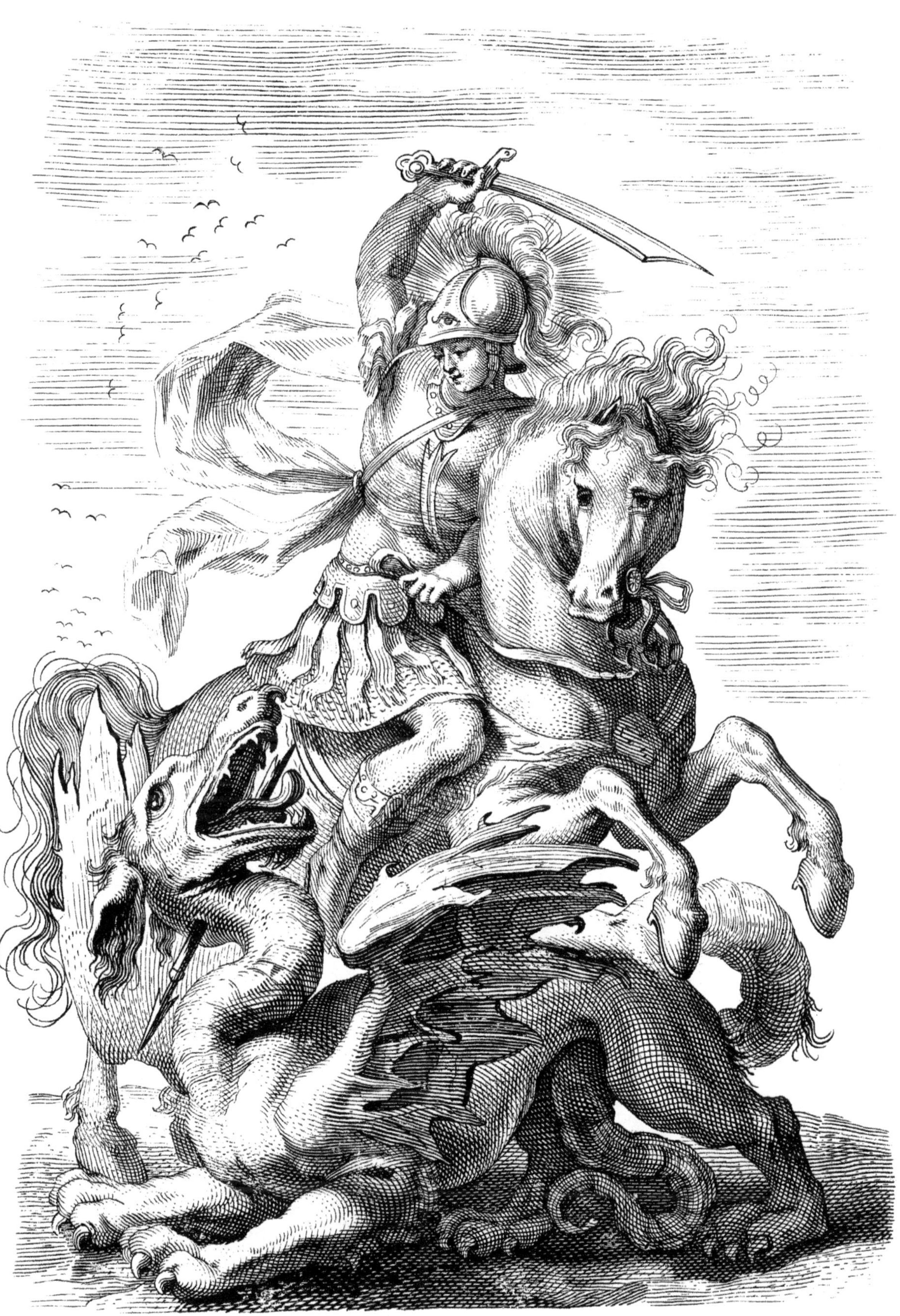

19: H. Joris fighting the dragon, Cornelis Galle (II), 1638 – 1678.

20

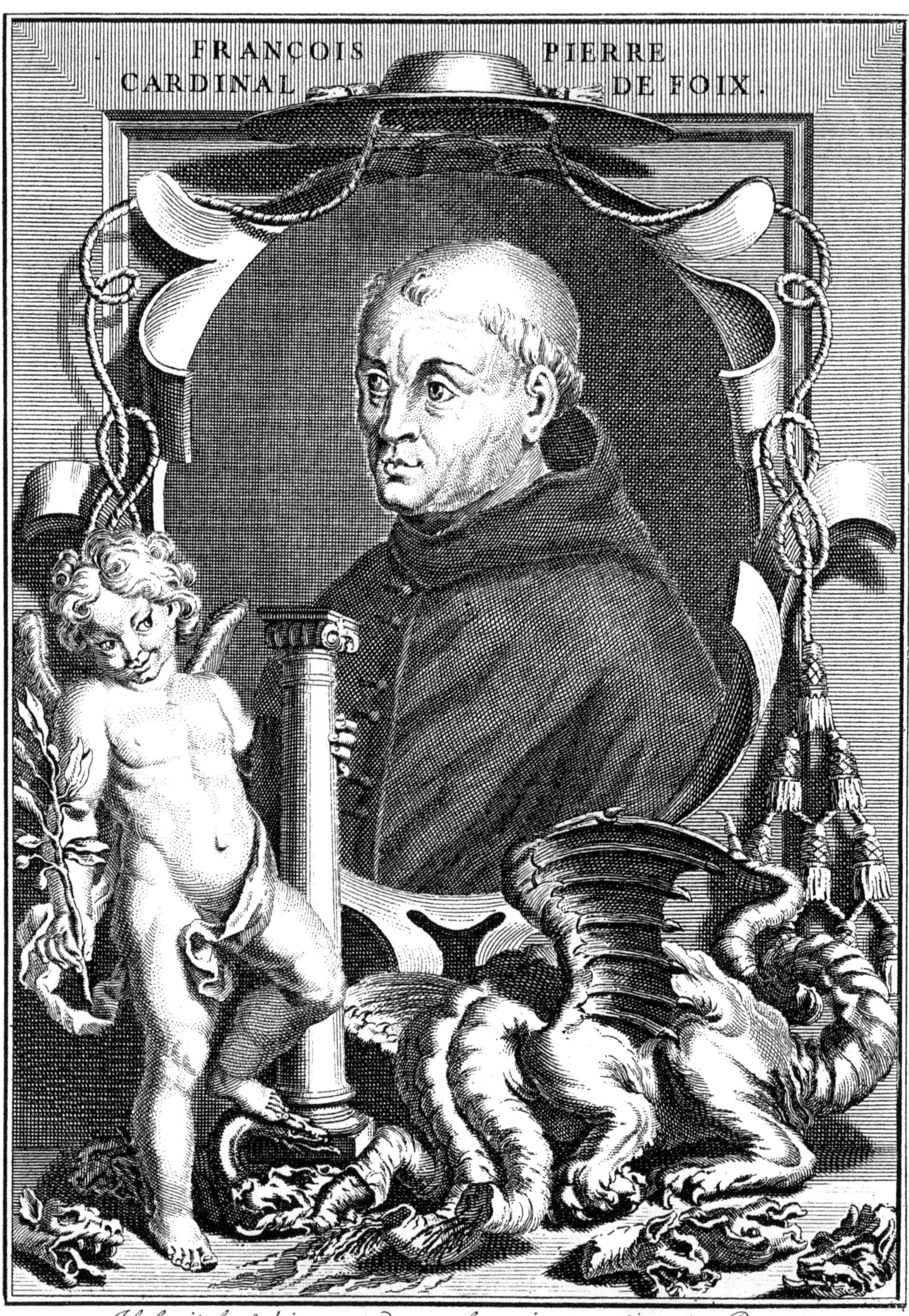

20: Portrait of Pierre de Foix, Bernard Picart, after anonymous, 1713 – 1763.

21

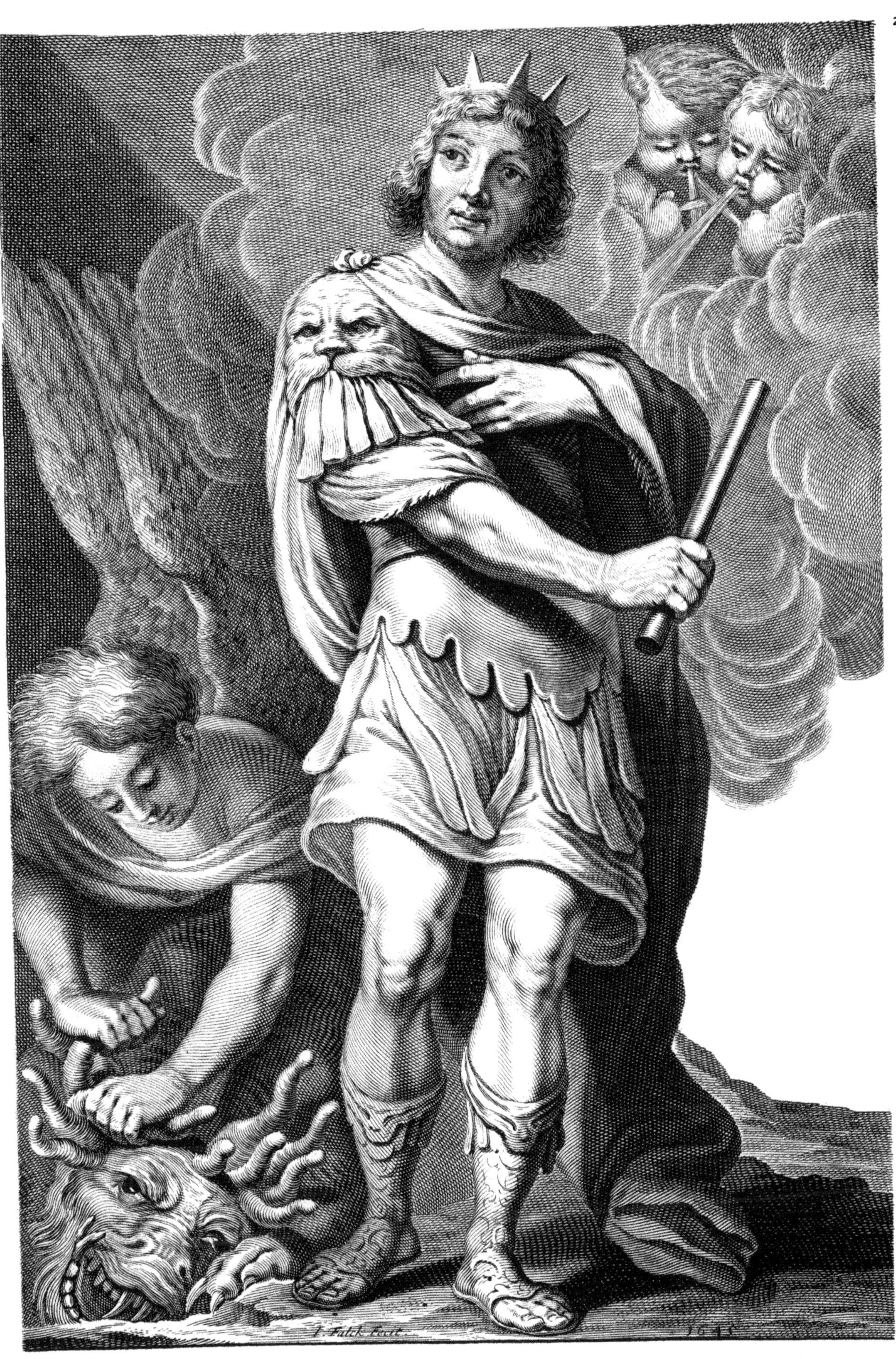

21: Emperor Augustus, Jeremias Falck, after Claude Vignon, 1645.

22

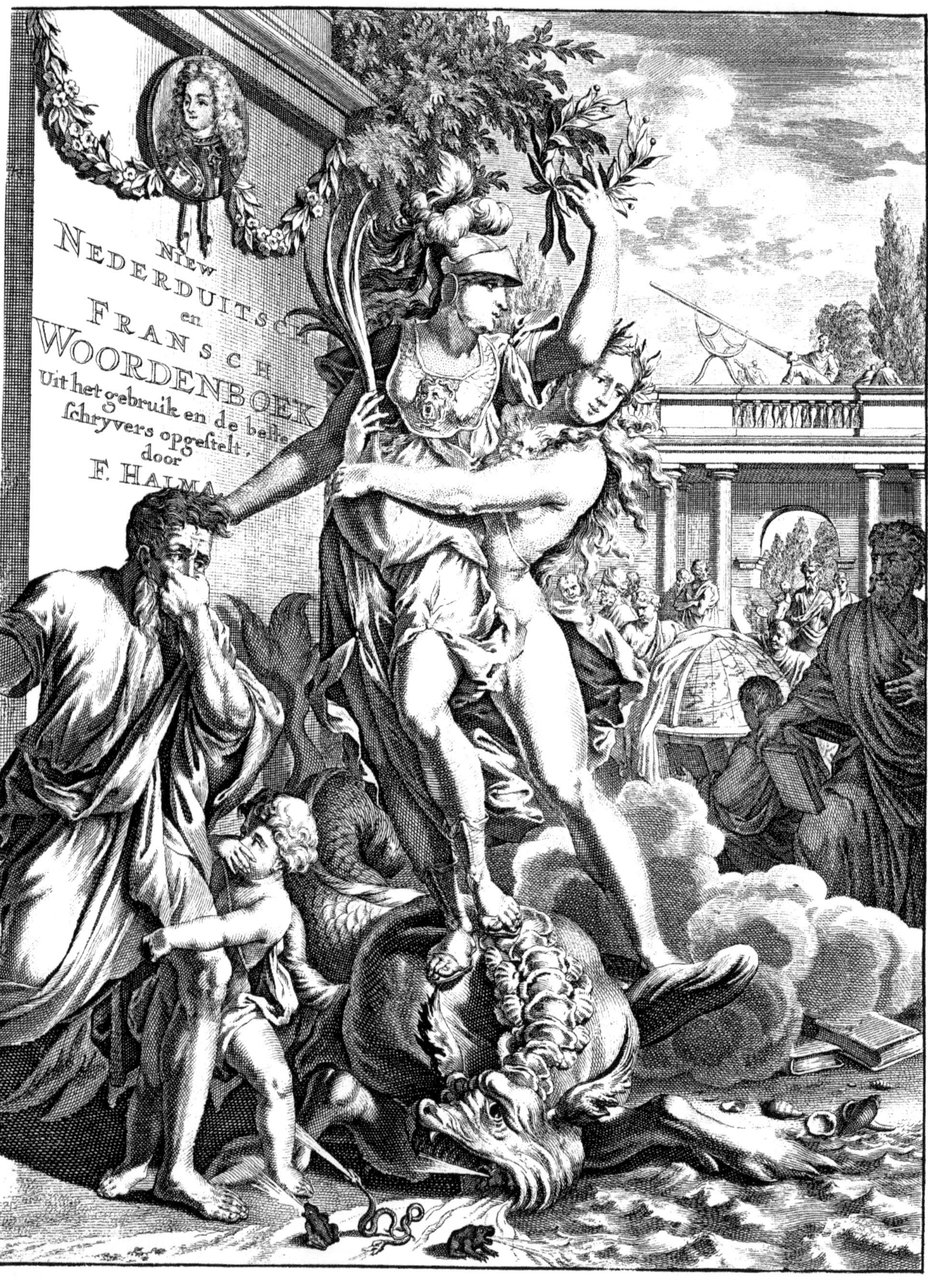

22: Minerva tramples fire–breathing sea monster, anonymous, 1710.

23

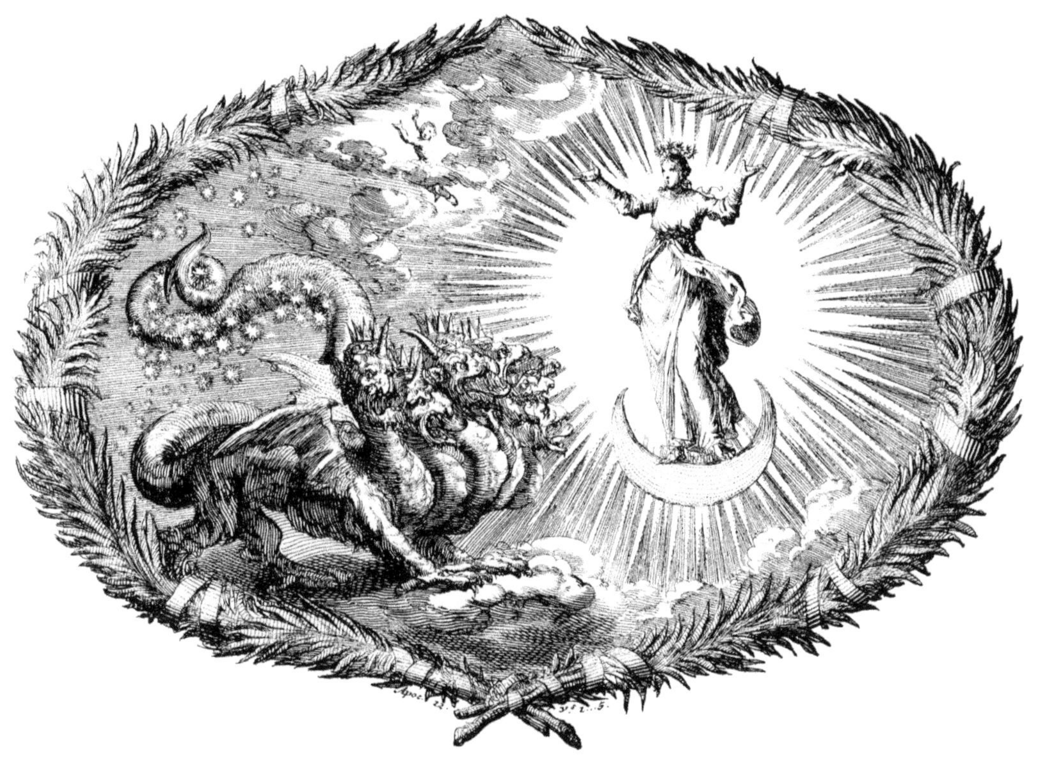

24

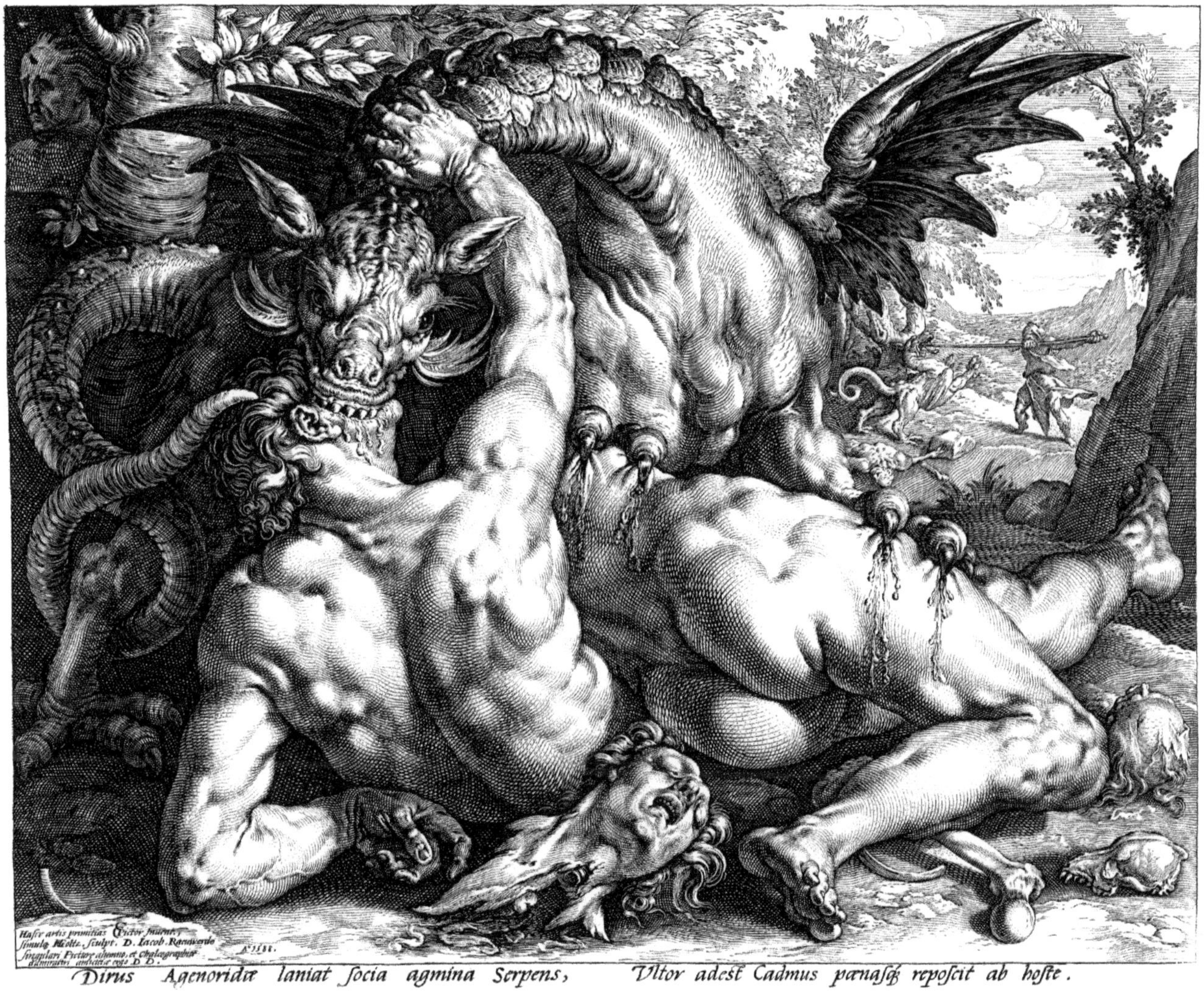

Dirus Agenoridæ laniat ſocia agmina Serpens, Vltor adeſt Cadmus pænaſq; repoſcit ab hoſte.

23: Appearance of the apocalyptic woman and the seven-headed dragon, Jan Luyken, 1700.

24: A dragon devouring the companions of Cadmus, Hendrick Goltzius, after Cornelis Cornelisz. van Haarlem, 1588.

25

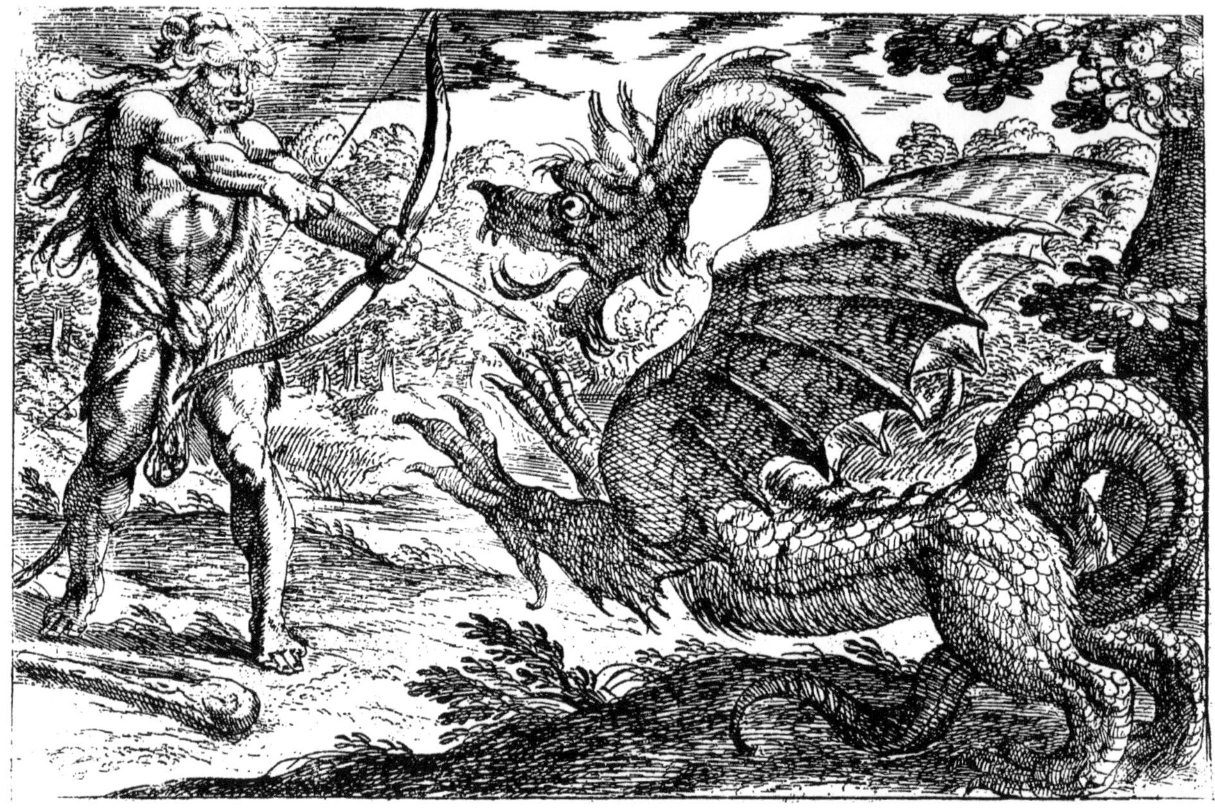

26

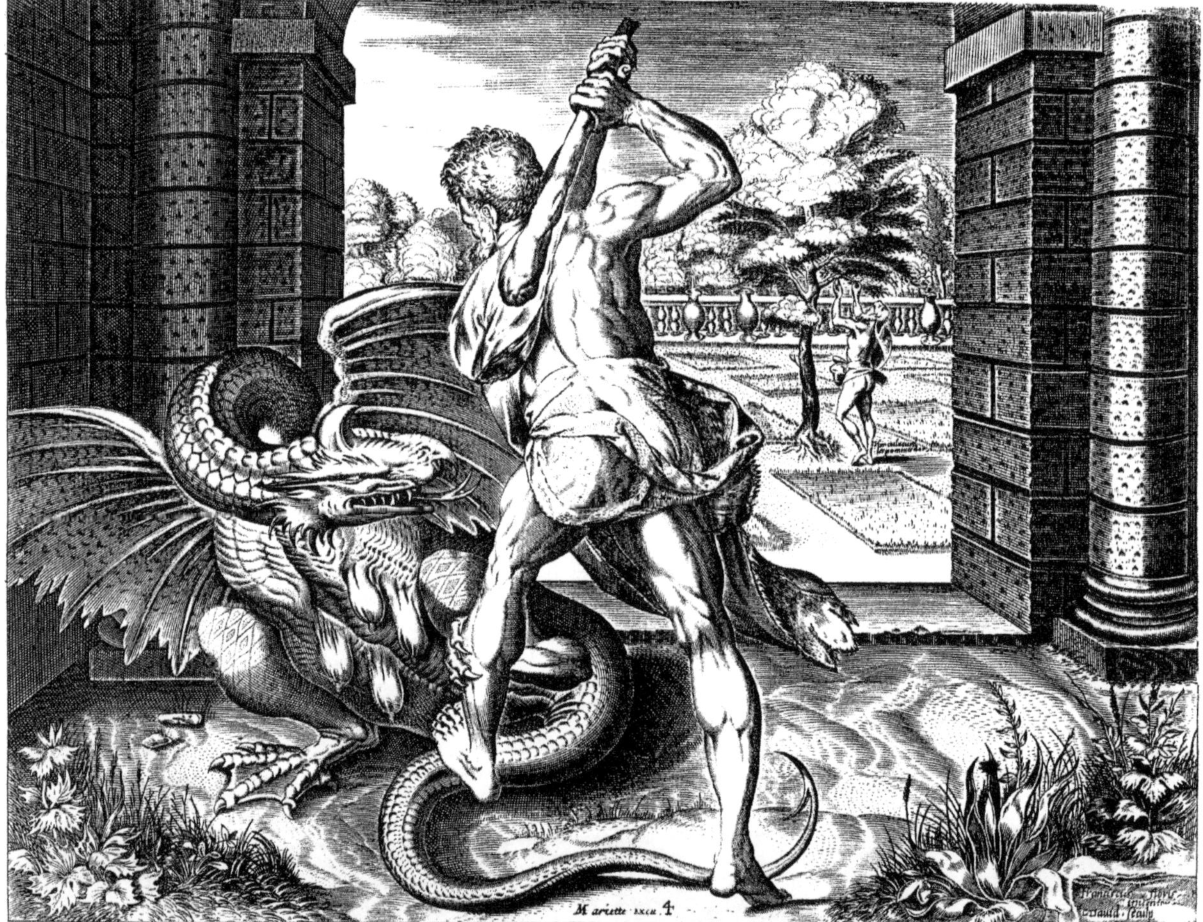

25: Hercules and the Dragon Ladon, Antonio Tempesta, 1608.

26: Hercules kills Ladon and picks the golden apples of the Hesperides, Charles David, after Frans Floris.

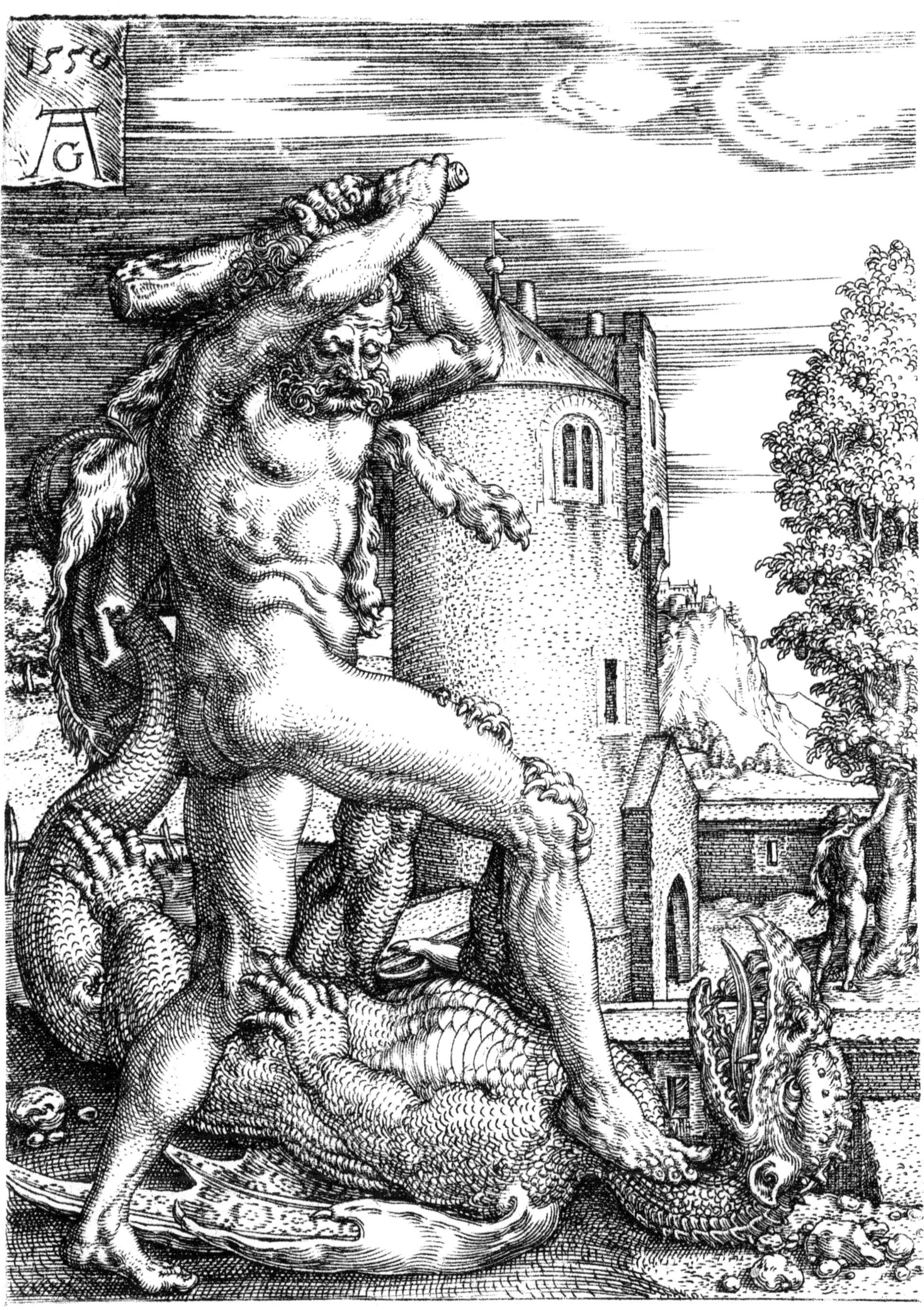

27: Hercules Slays the Dragon Ladon, Heinrich
Aldegrever, after anonymous, 1550.

28

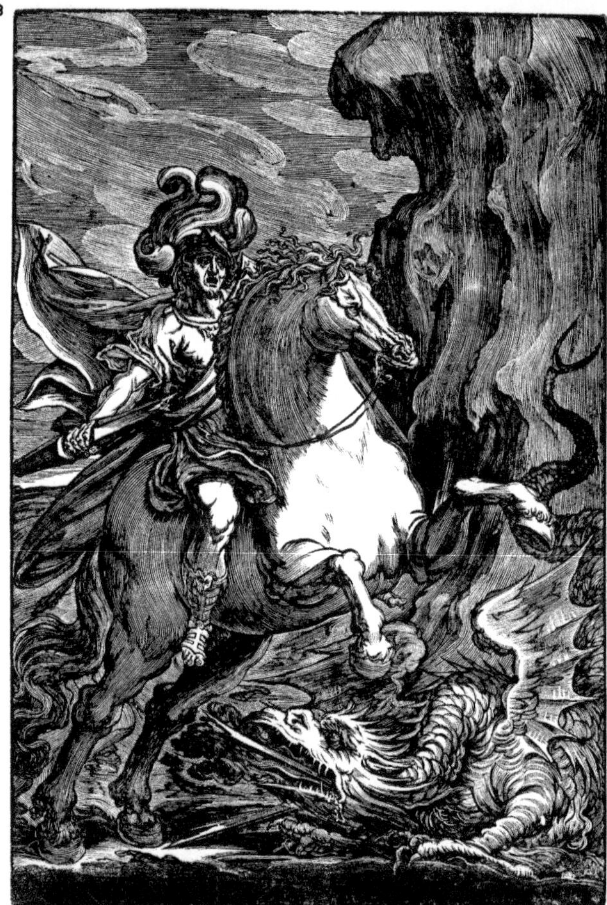

29

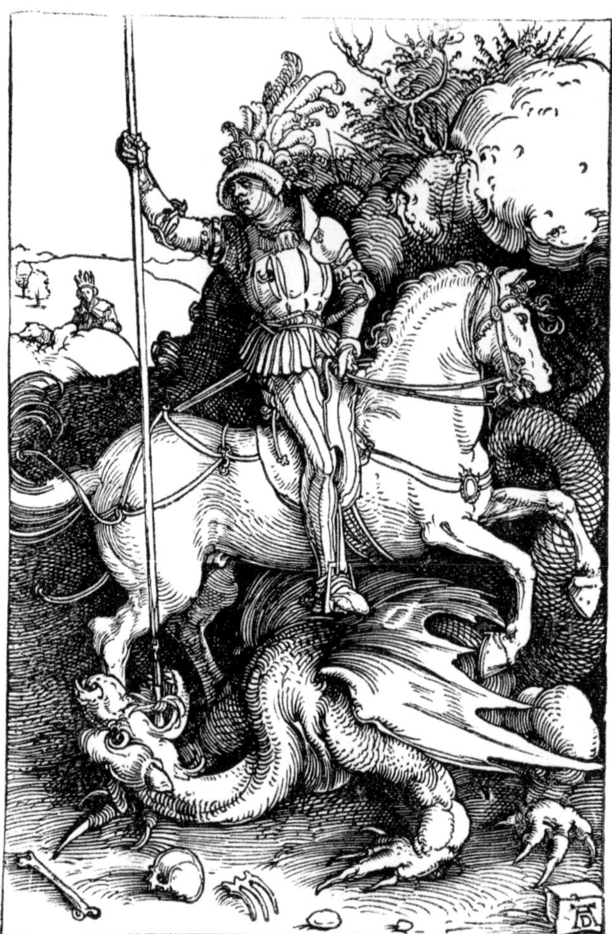

30

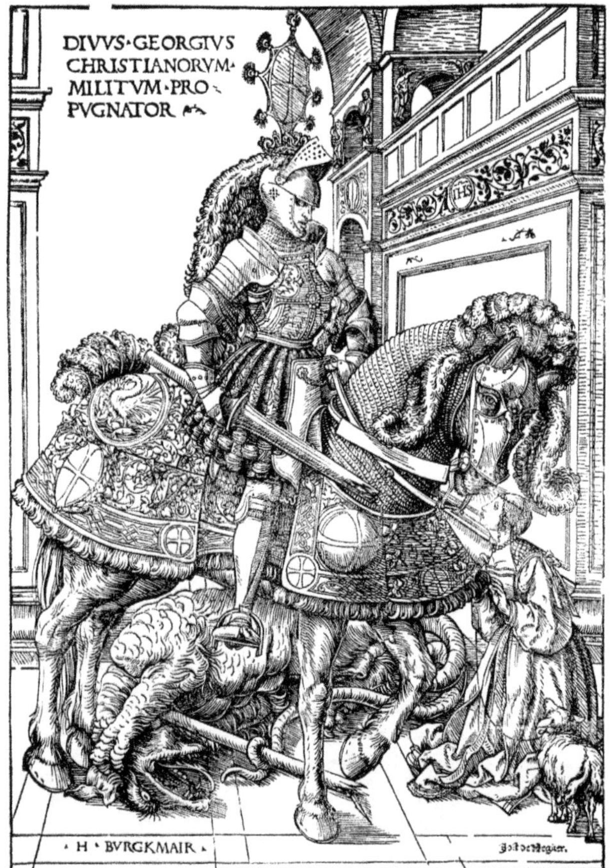

31

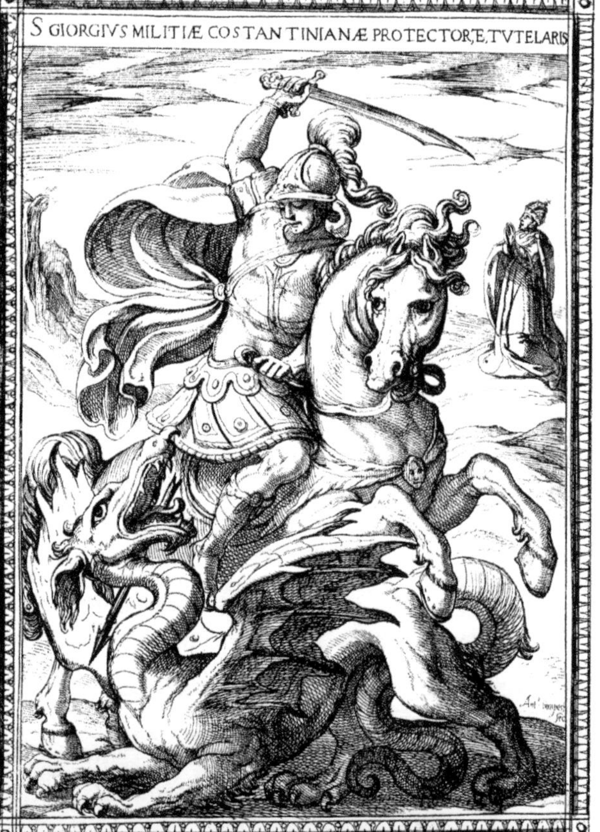

28: Saint George and the Dragon, Giuseppe Scolari, 1550 – 1600.

29: Saint George Slaying the Dragon, Albrecht Dürer, 1504 – 1505.

30: Saint George with the Princess and the Slain Dragon, Hans Burgkmair (I), 1508.

31: Saint George Killing the Dragon, Antonio Tempesta, 1565 – 1630.

32

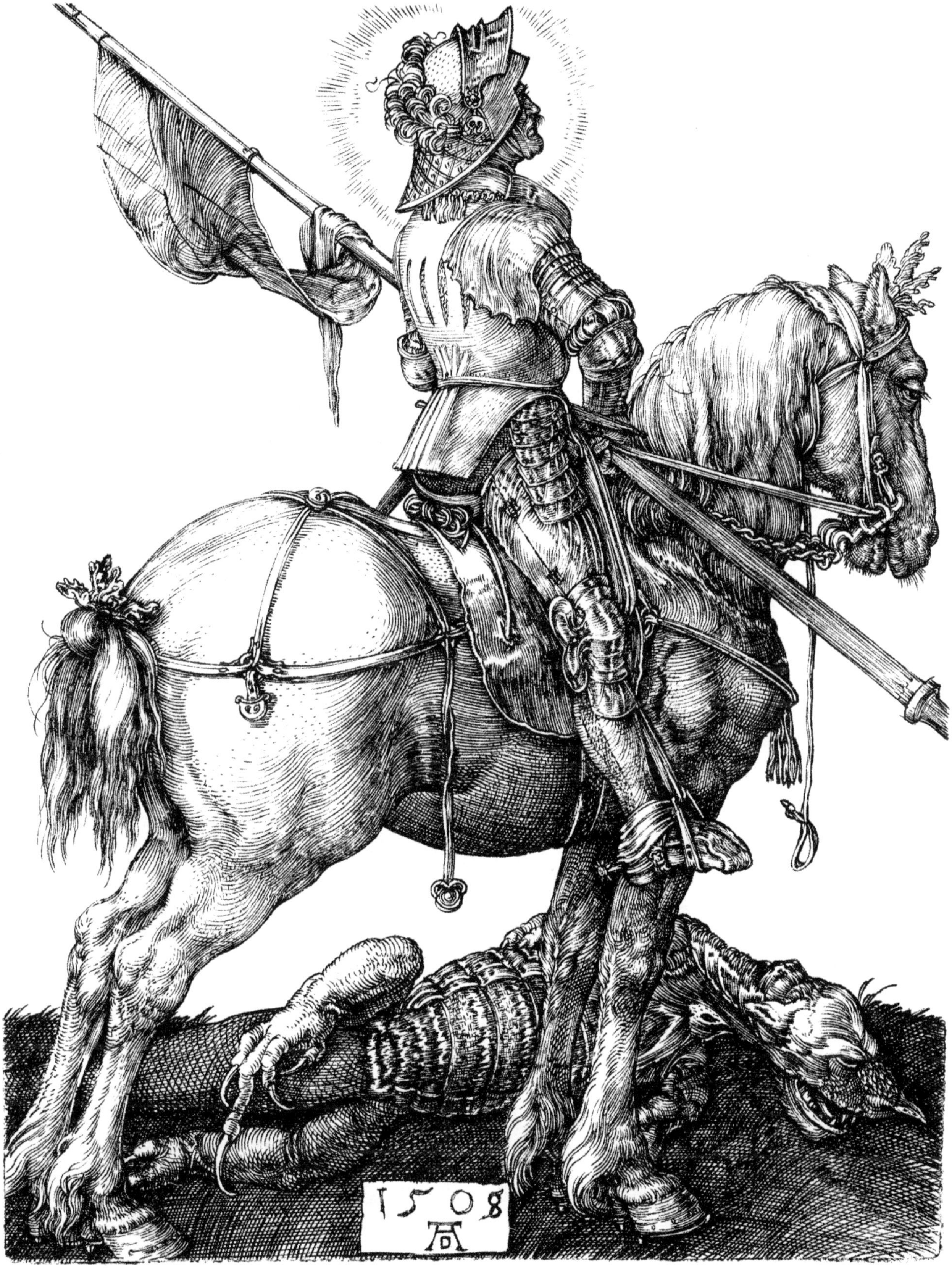

32: Saint George on horseback next to the slain dragon, Albrecht Dürer, 1508.

33

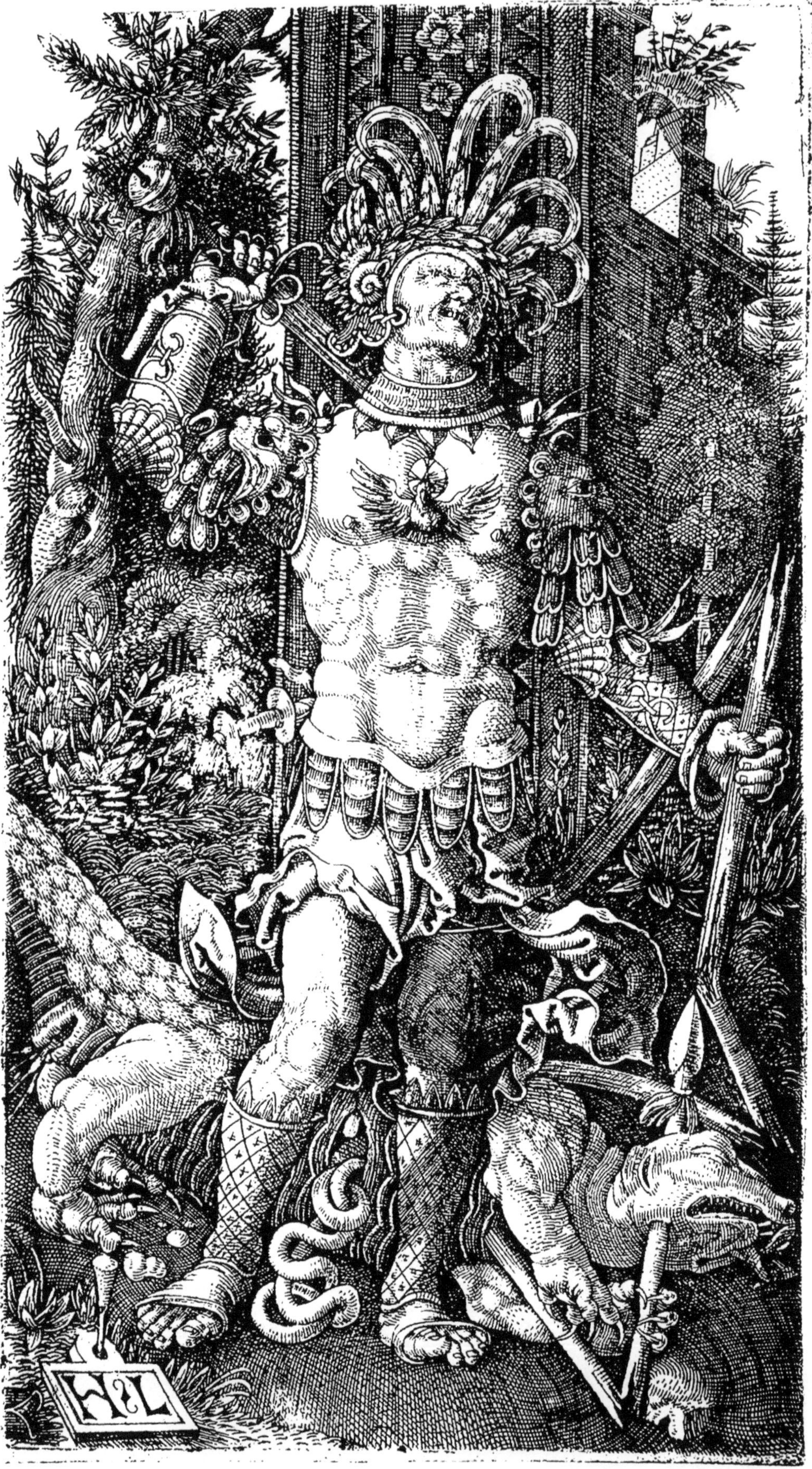

33: St. George and the Dragon.

34

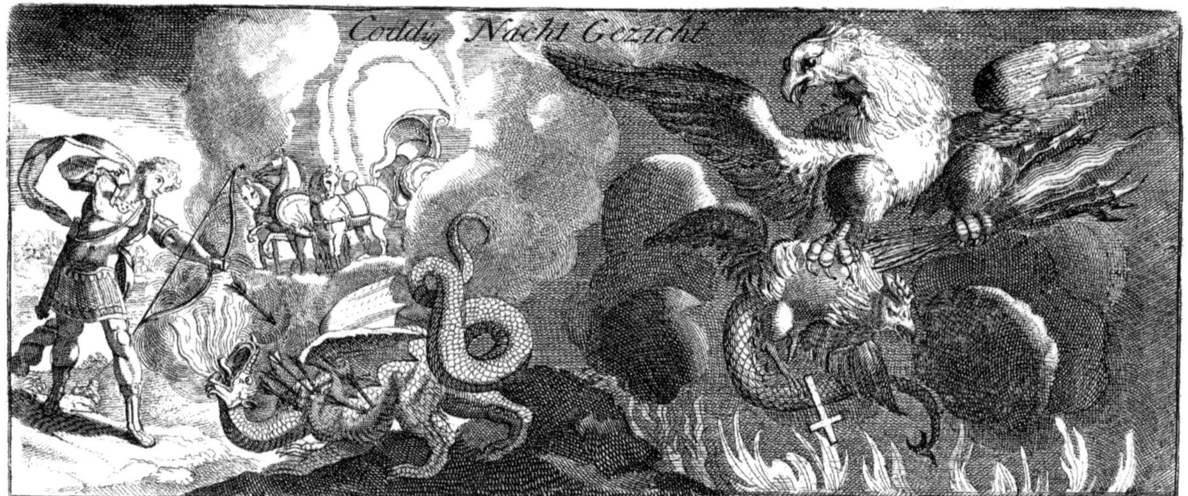

35

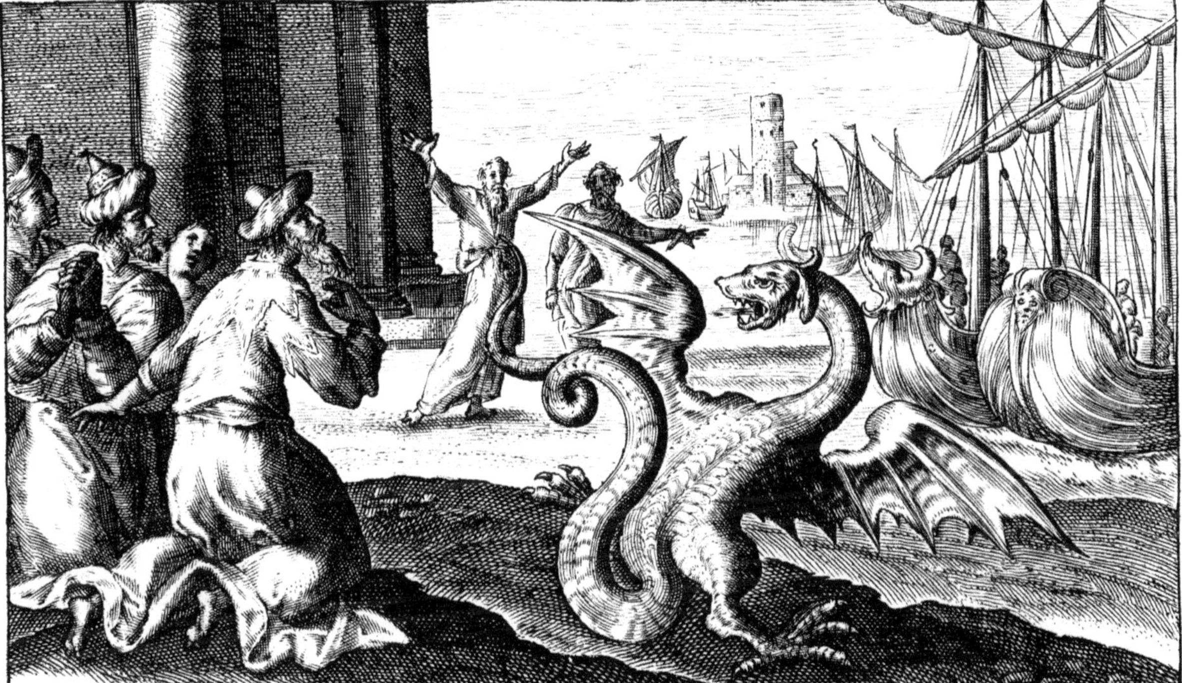

36

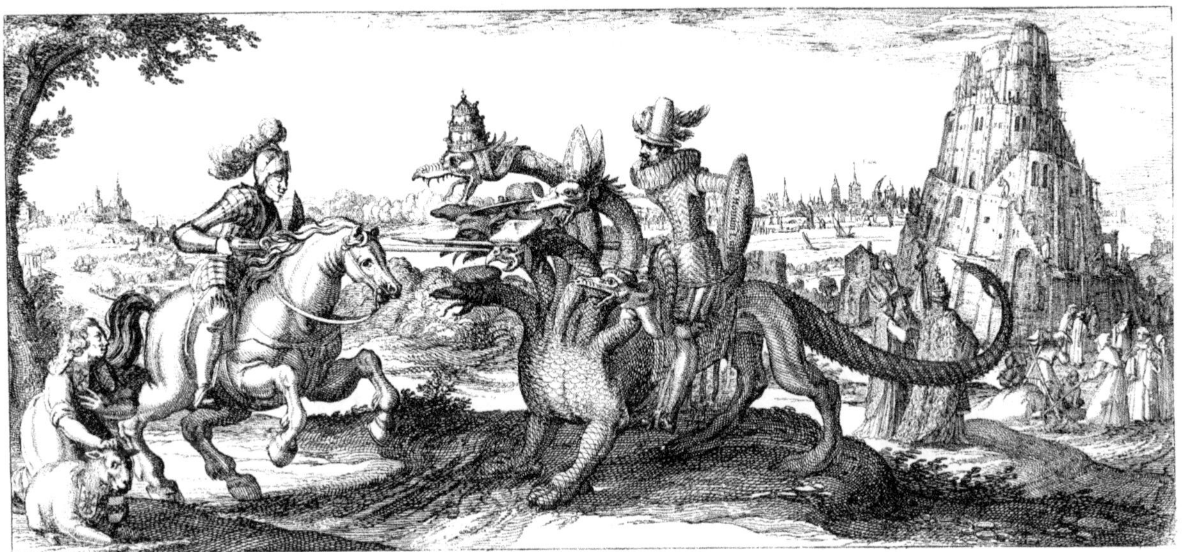

34: Coddig Nacht View, 1705, Carel Allard (attributed to), 1706 – 1707.

35: Aesculapius travels to Rome, Crispijn van de Passe (I), 1602 – 1607.

36: The Cleves Saint George, 1615, Claes Jansz, 1615.

37

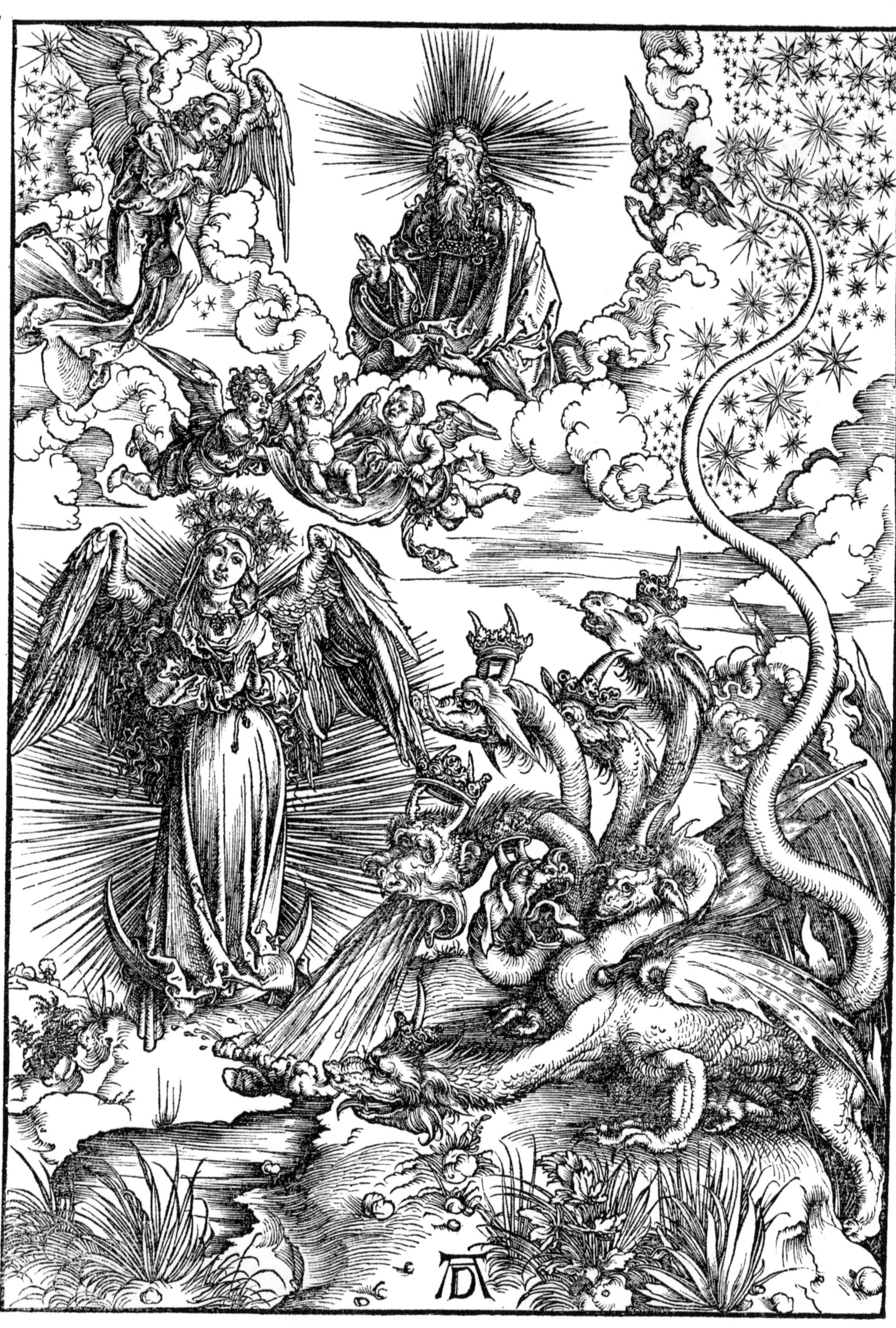

37: The Apocalyptic Woman and the Seven-Headed Dragon, Albrecht Dürer, 1511.

38

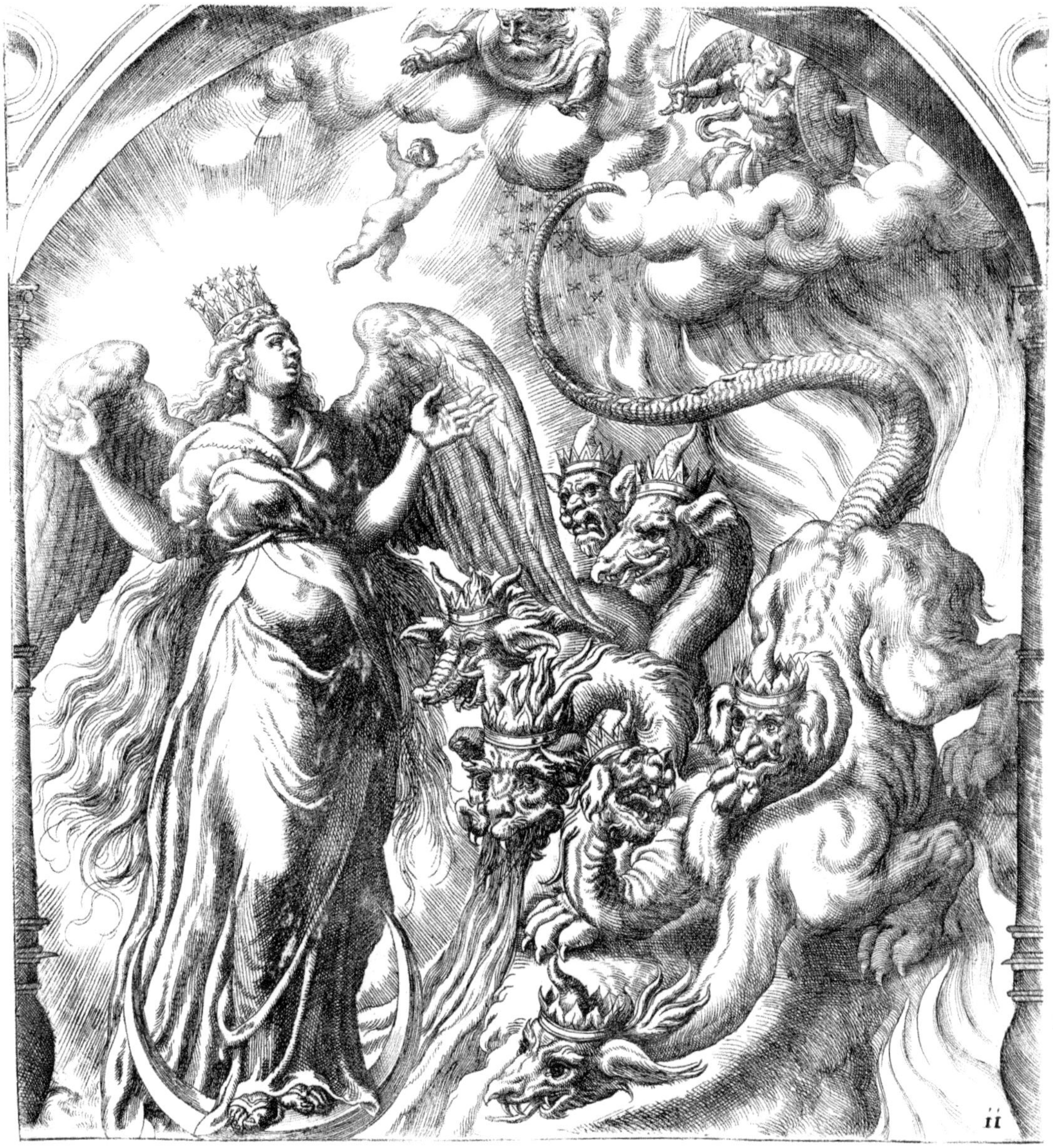

39

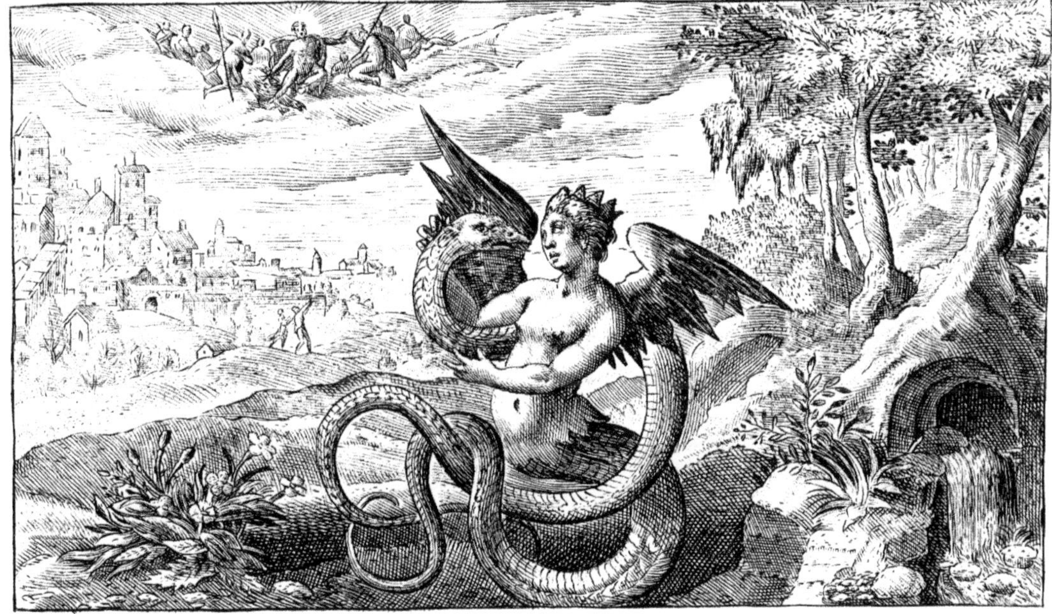

38: Apparition of the Apocalyptic Woman and the Seven-Headed Dragon, Gerard van Groeningen, 1563 – 1574.

39: Harmonia and Cadmus, Crispijn van de Passe (I), 1602 – 1607.

40

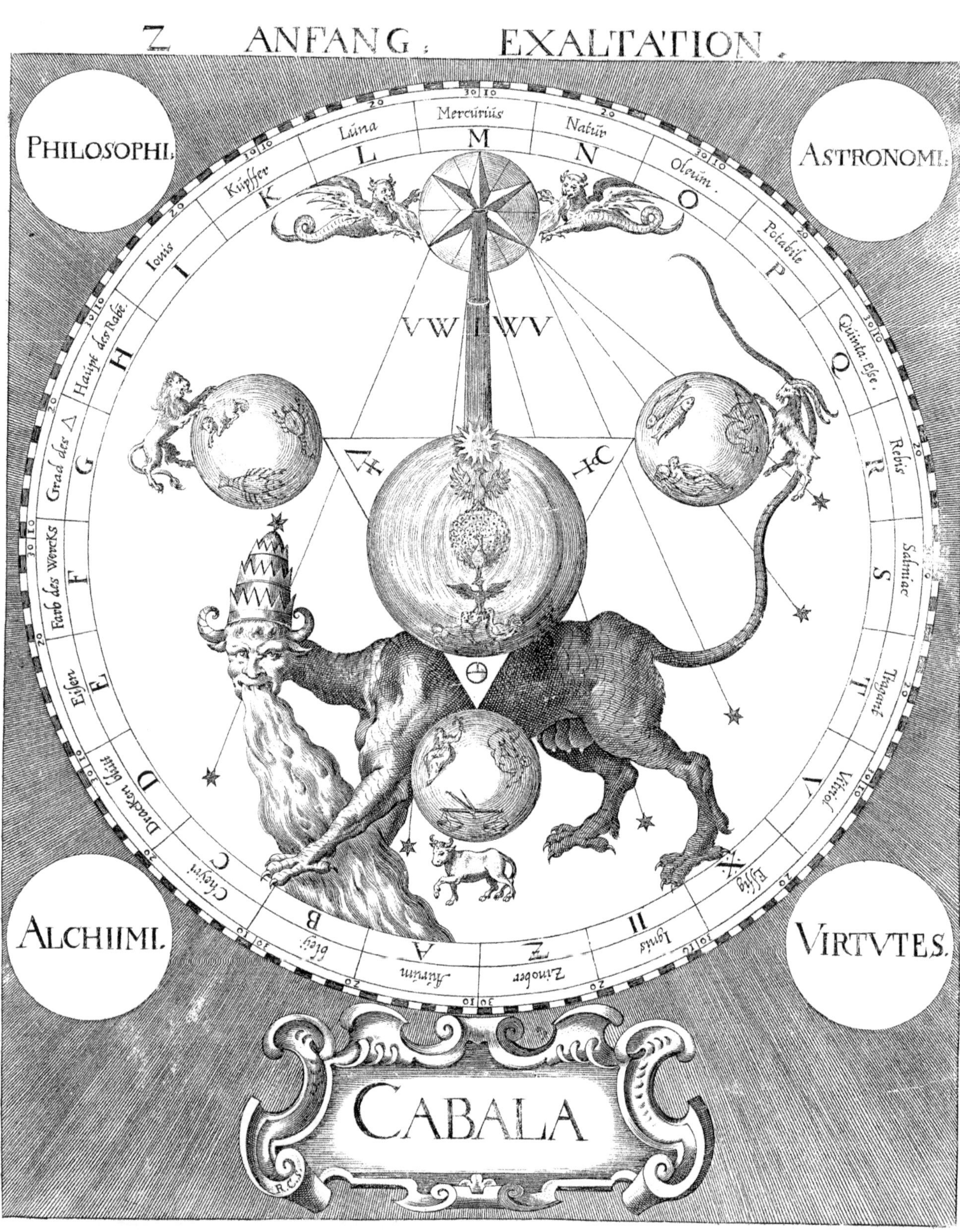

40: Beginning of the Ascension, Raphael Custos, 1615.

41

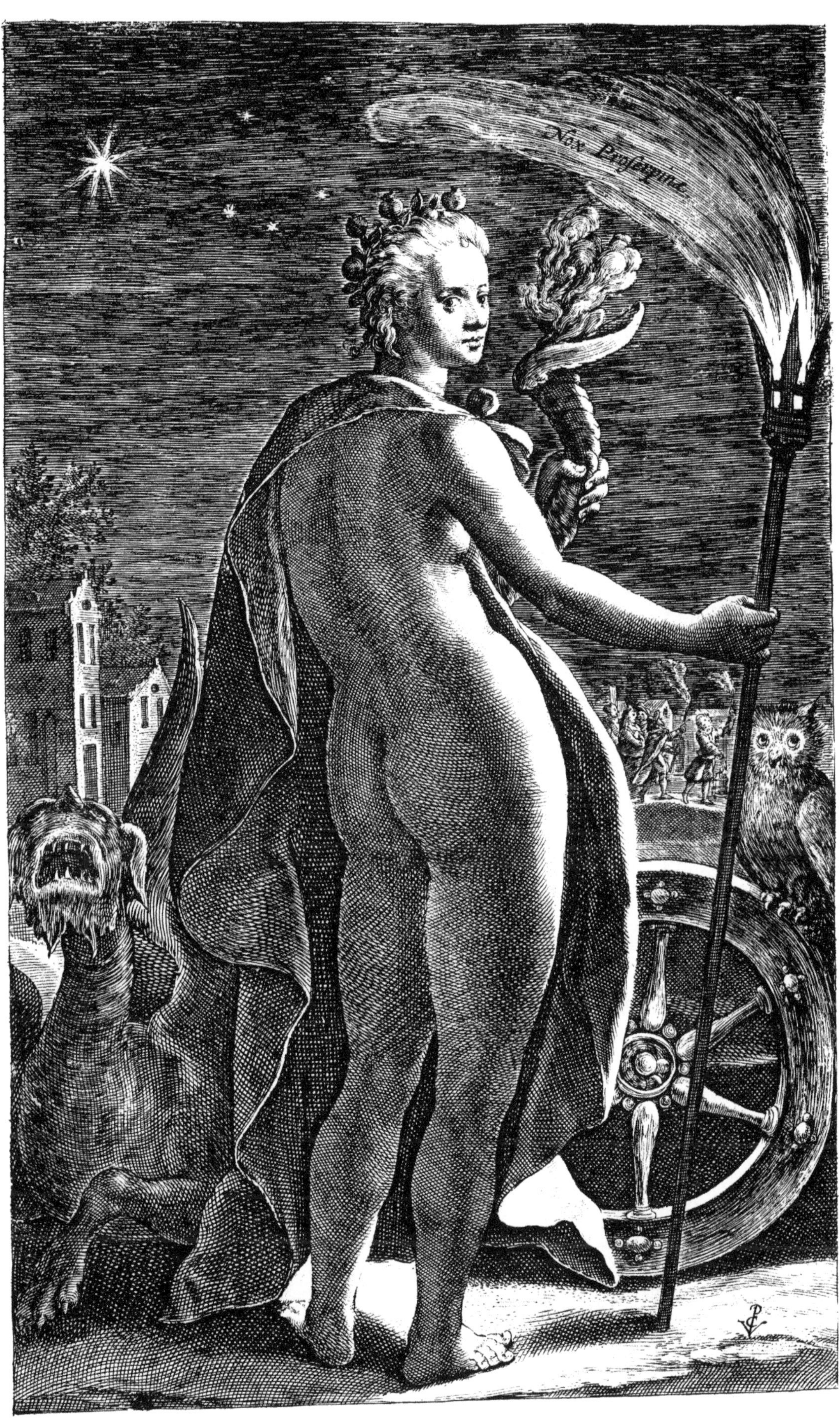

41: Night, Crispijn van de Passe (I), 1611 – 1637.

42

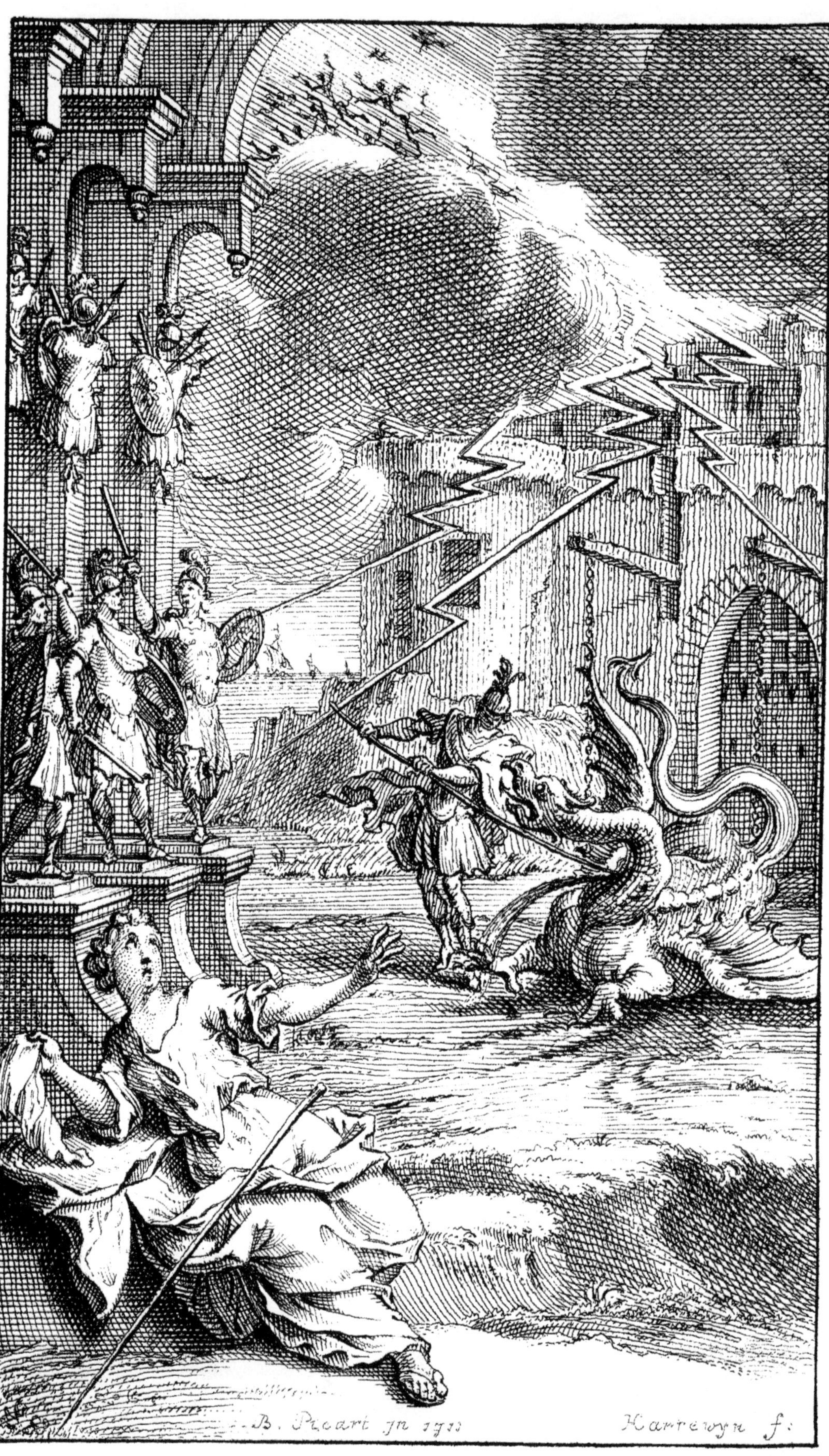

42: H. Joris and the dragon, Jacobus Harrewijn, after Bernard Picart, 1711.

43

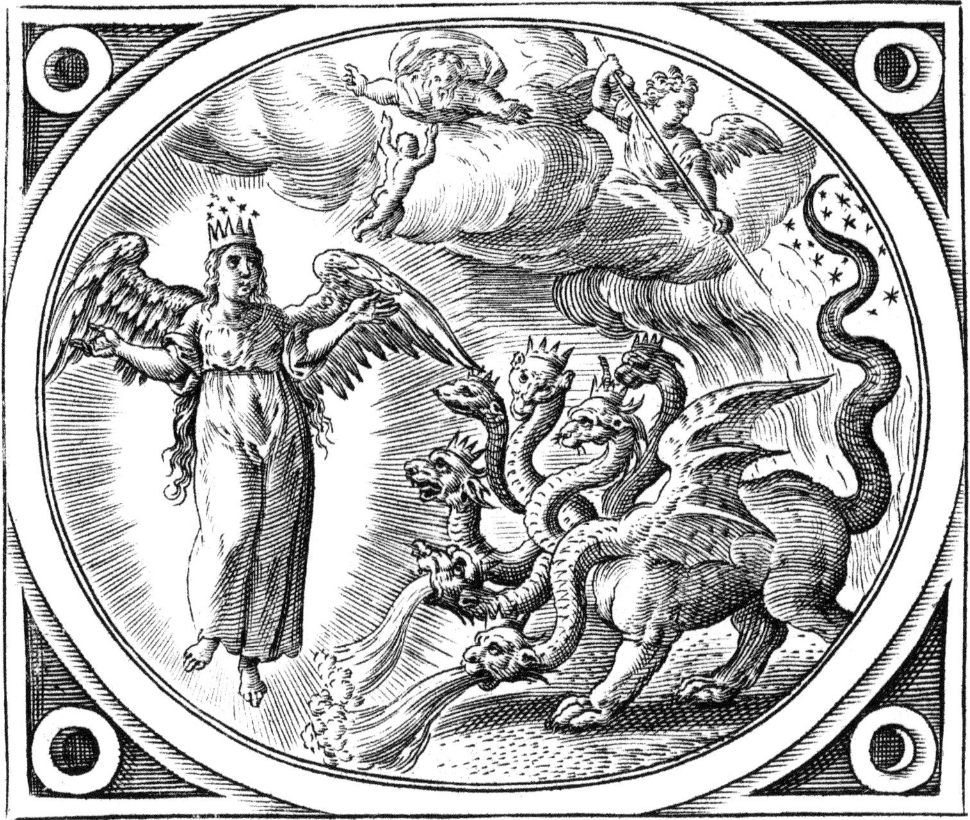

44

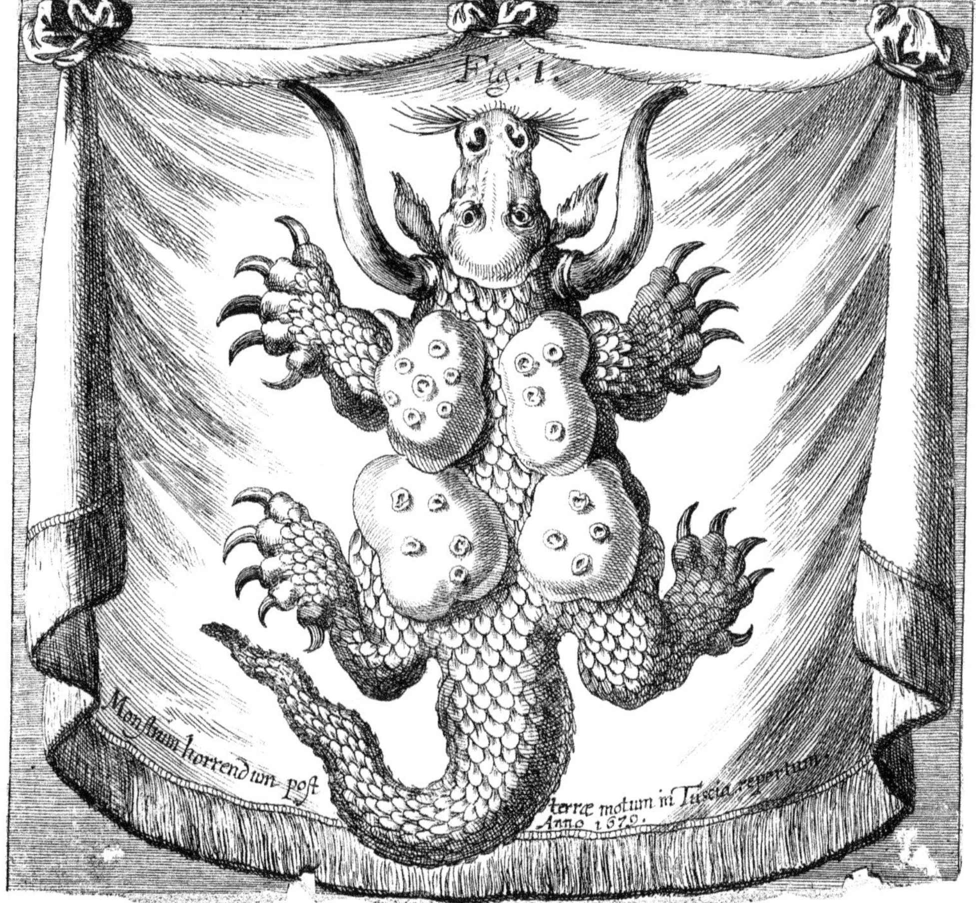

43: Woman in labor and seven-headed dragon, adriaen collaert (attributed to), after jan snellinck (I), 1585.

44: Monster, anonymous, 1679 – 1685.

45

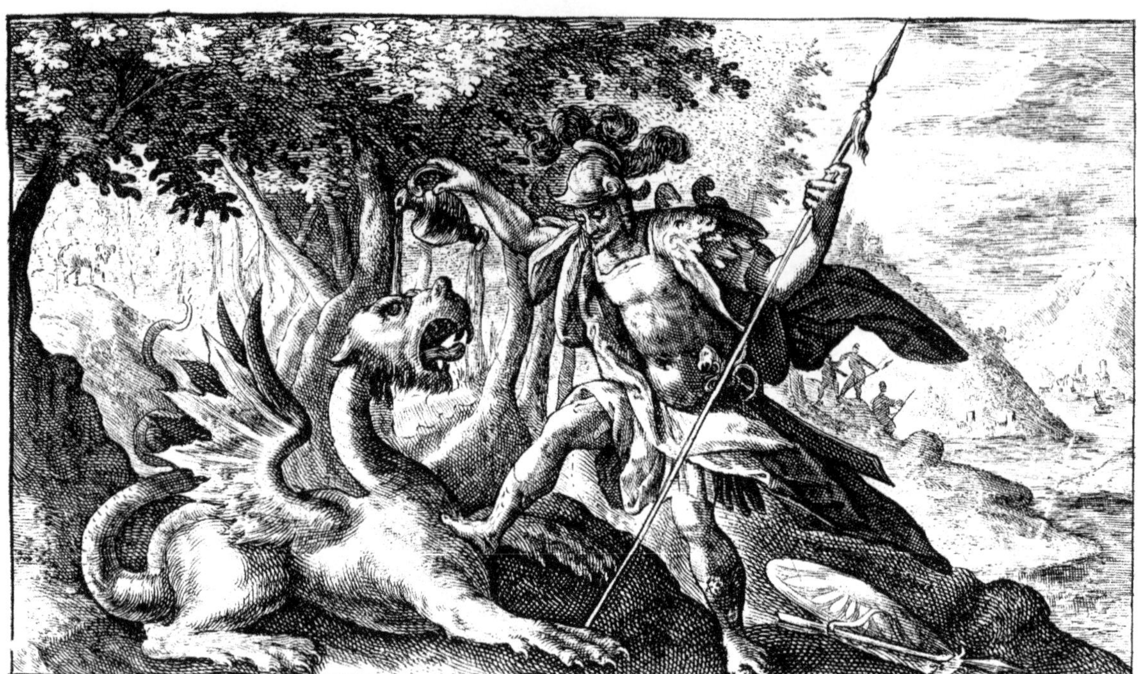

Æsonides herbis sopit catuq; Draconem,
Arboris auricomæ qui vigil acer erat.

Post modo felici securus obambulat horto,
Aurea cumq; sua vellere mala rapit.

46

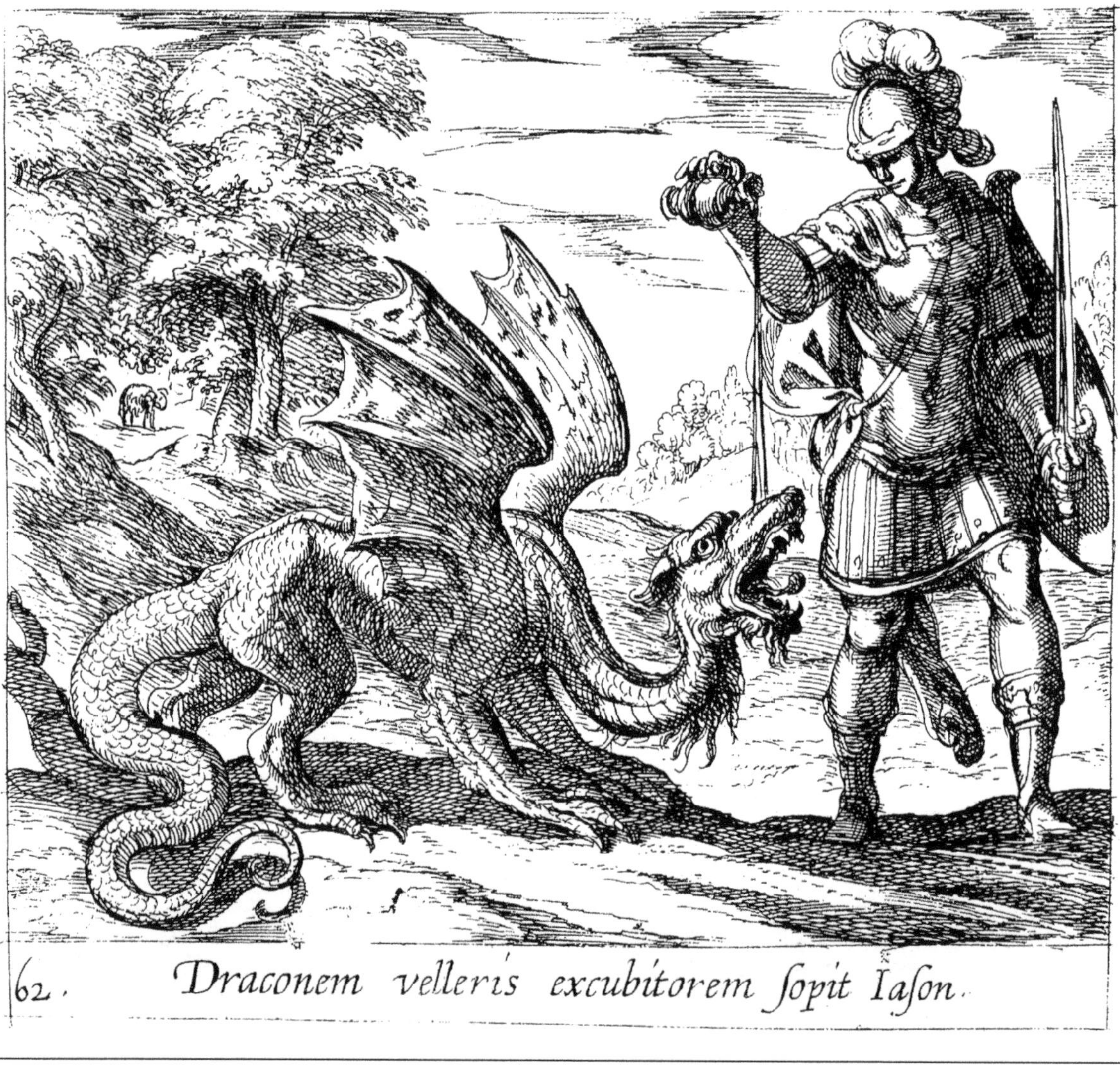

62. Draconem velleris excubitorem sopit Iason.

45: Jason obtains the Golden Fleece, Crispijn van de Passe (I), 1602 – 1607.

46: Jason Put the Dragon to Sleep, Antonio Tempesta, 1606.

47

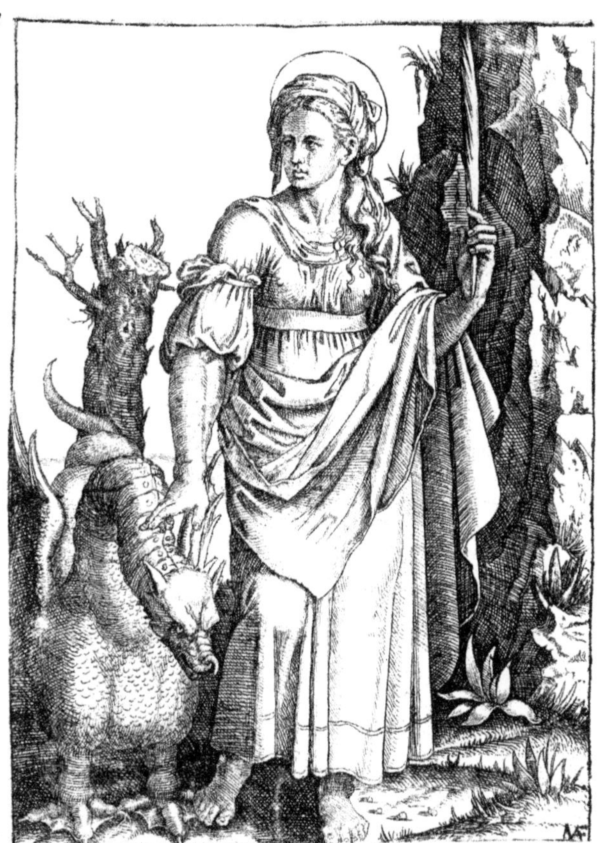

48

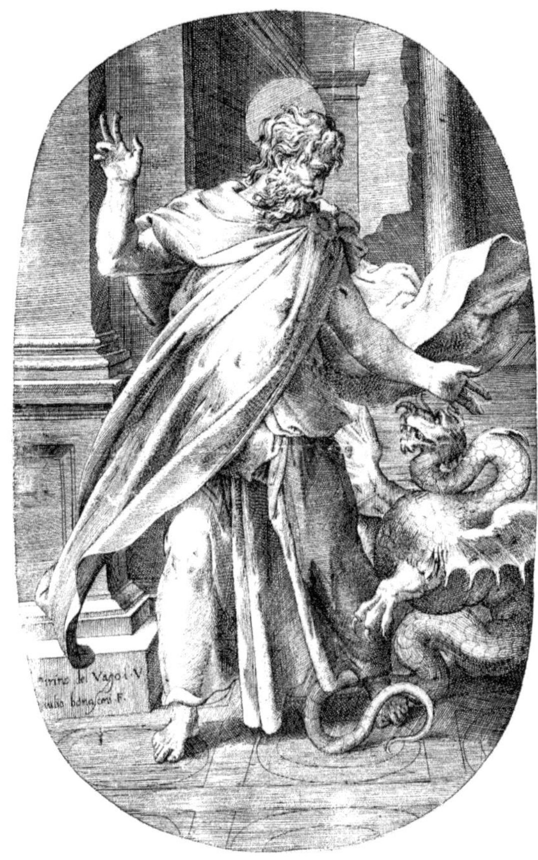

49

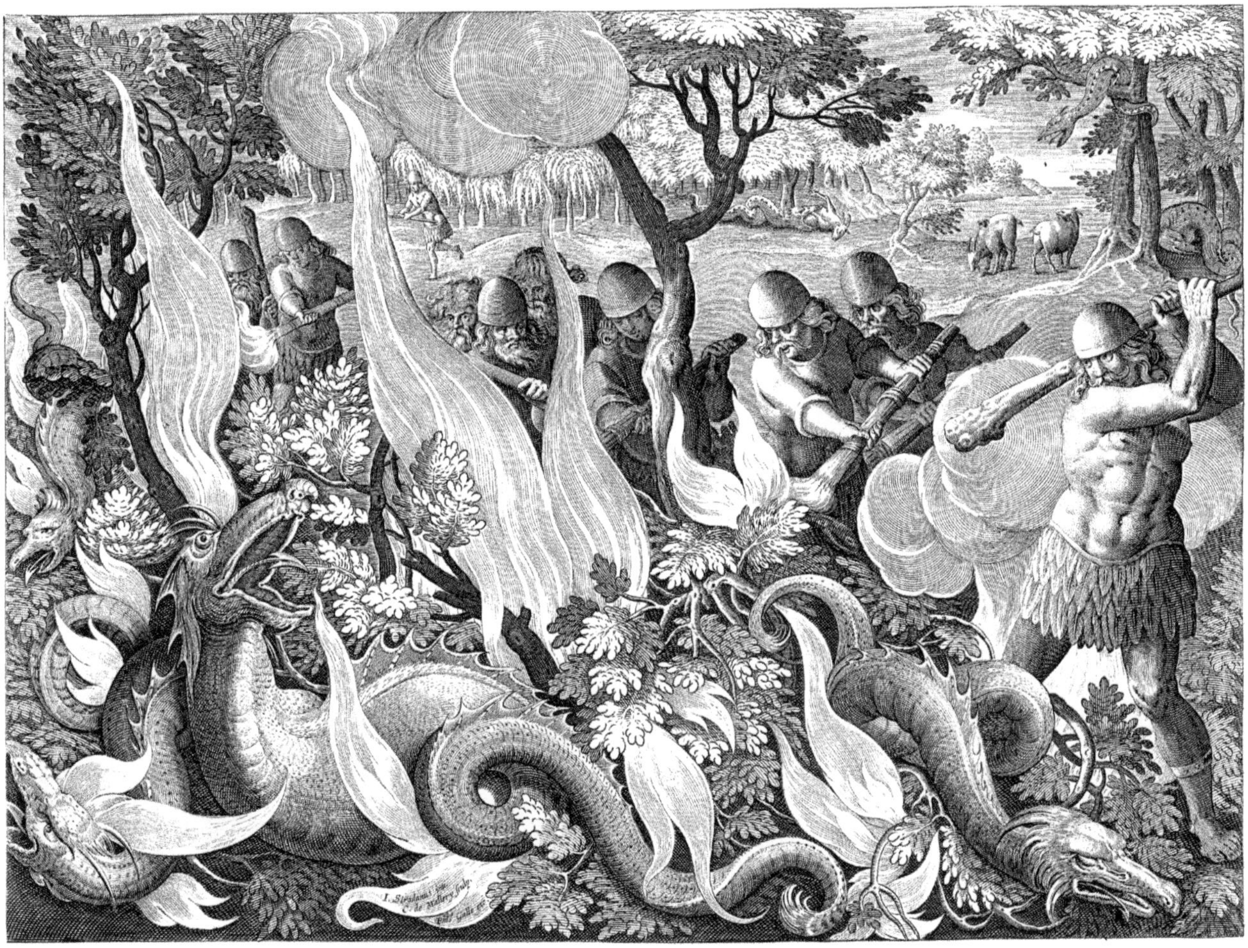

47: Saint Margaret of Antioch with dragon, Marcantonio Raimondi, after Francesco di Francia, 1500 – 1510.

48: Man with Dragon, Giulio Bonasone, 1501.

49: Water Snake Hunting in India, Karel van Mallery, after Jan van der Straet, 1594 – 1598.

50

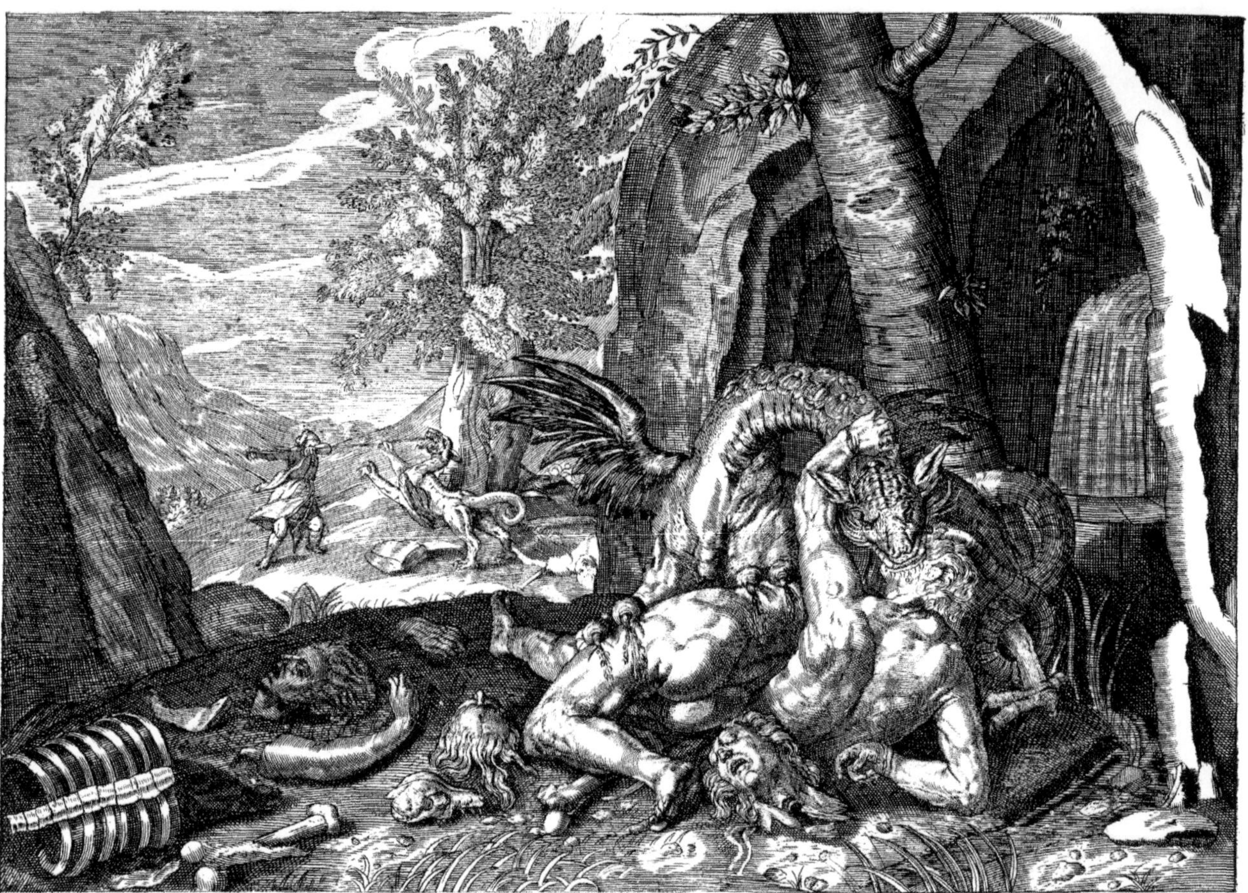

51

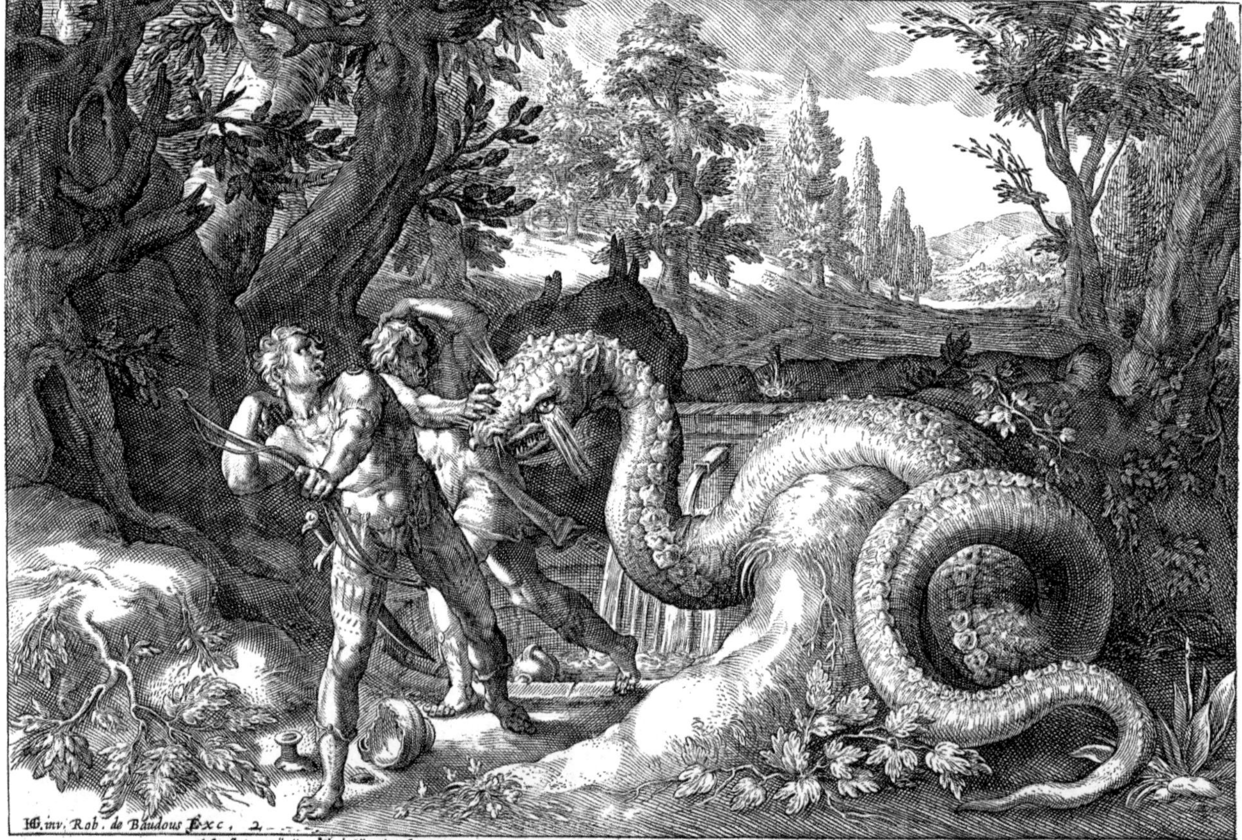

50: Companions of Cadmus Devoured by a Dragon, anonymous, c. 1636–1670.

51: Companions of Cadmus Devoured by a Dragon, Hendrick Goltzius (workshop of), after Hendrick Goltzius, 1615.

52

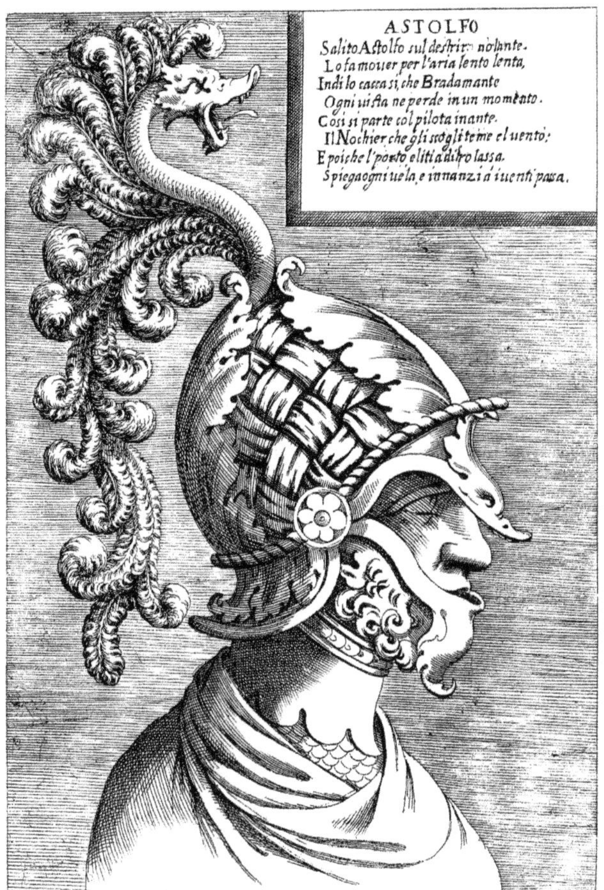

53

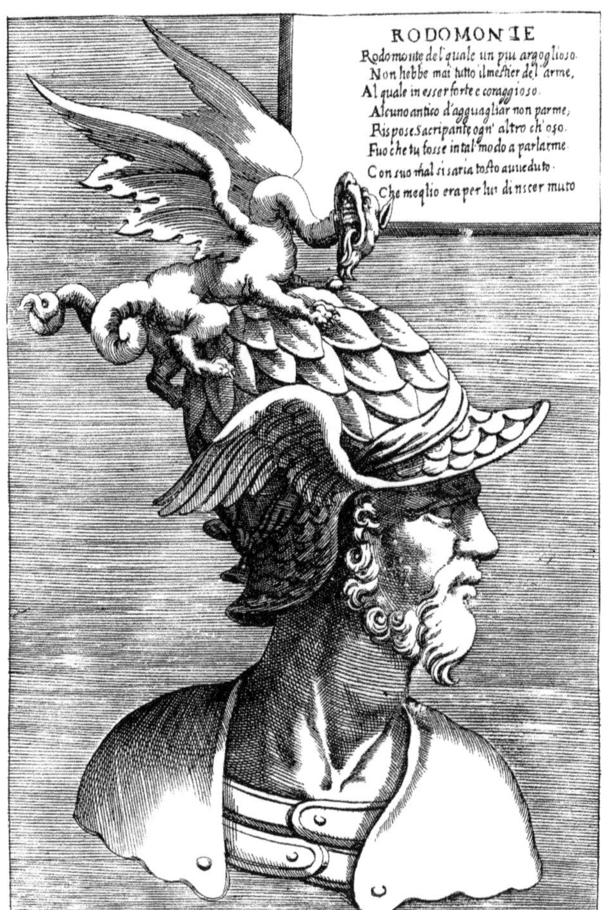

54

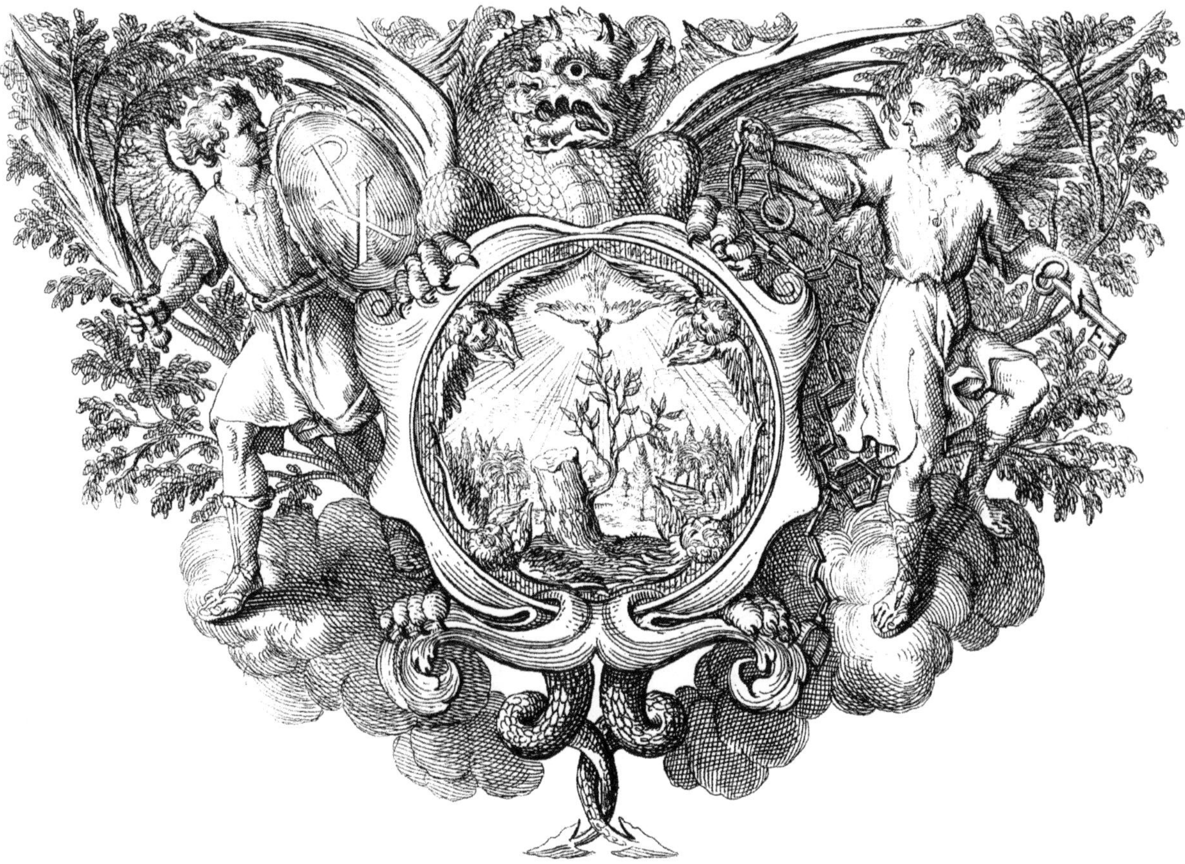

52: Bust of Astolfo, anonymous 1550.

53: Bust van Rodomonte, anonymous, 1550 – 1599.

54: Tree stump with new shoot above which the dove of the Holy Spirit, Caspar Luyken, 1705.

55

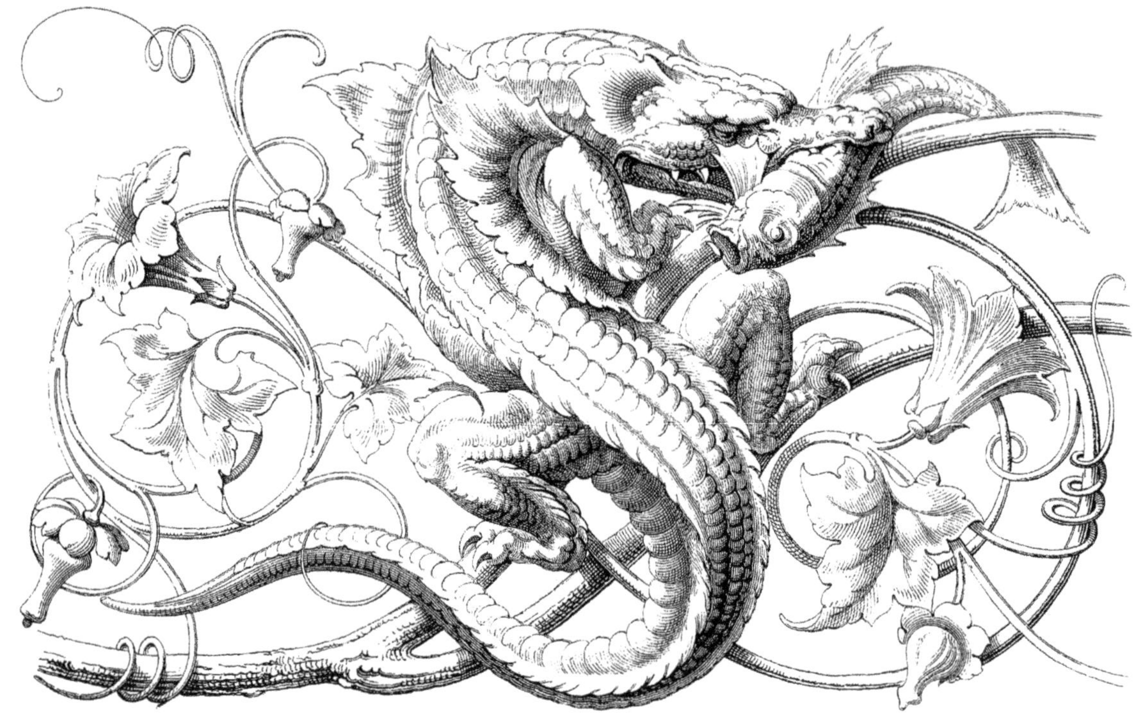

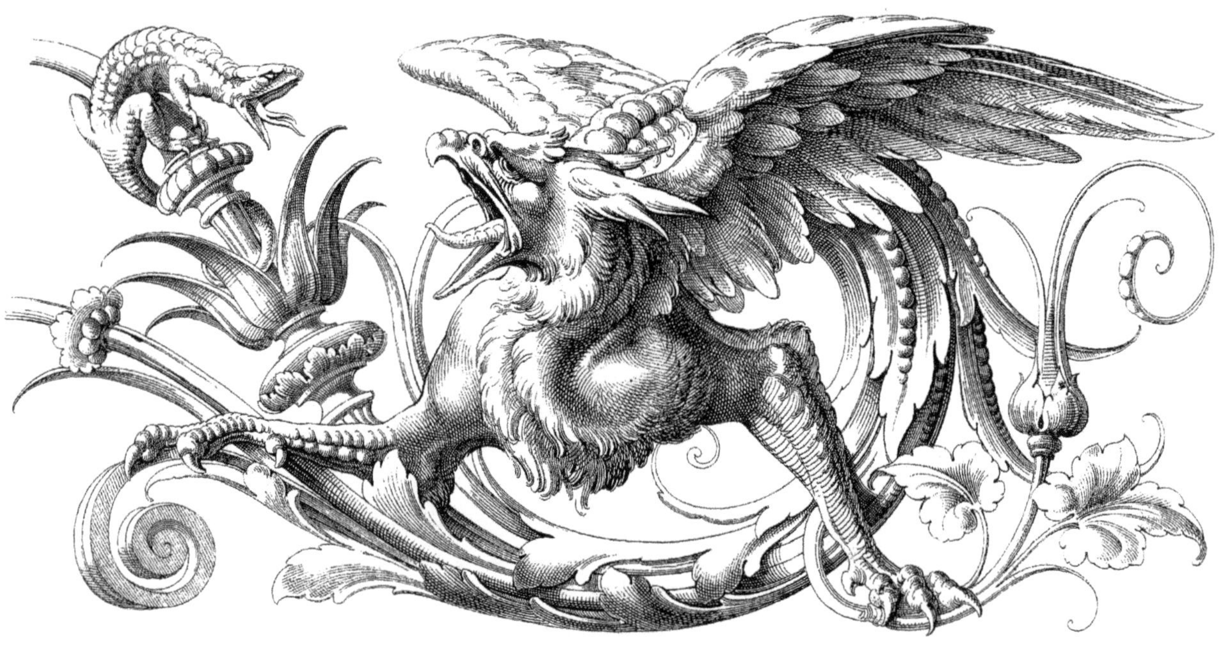

55: Dragon and griffin on a tendril, Michel Liénard, 1866.

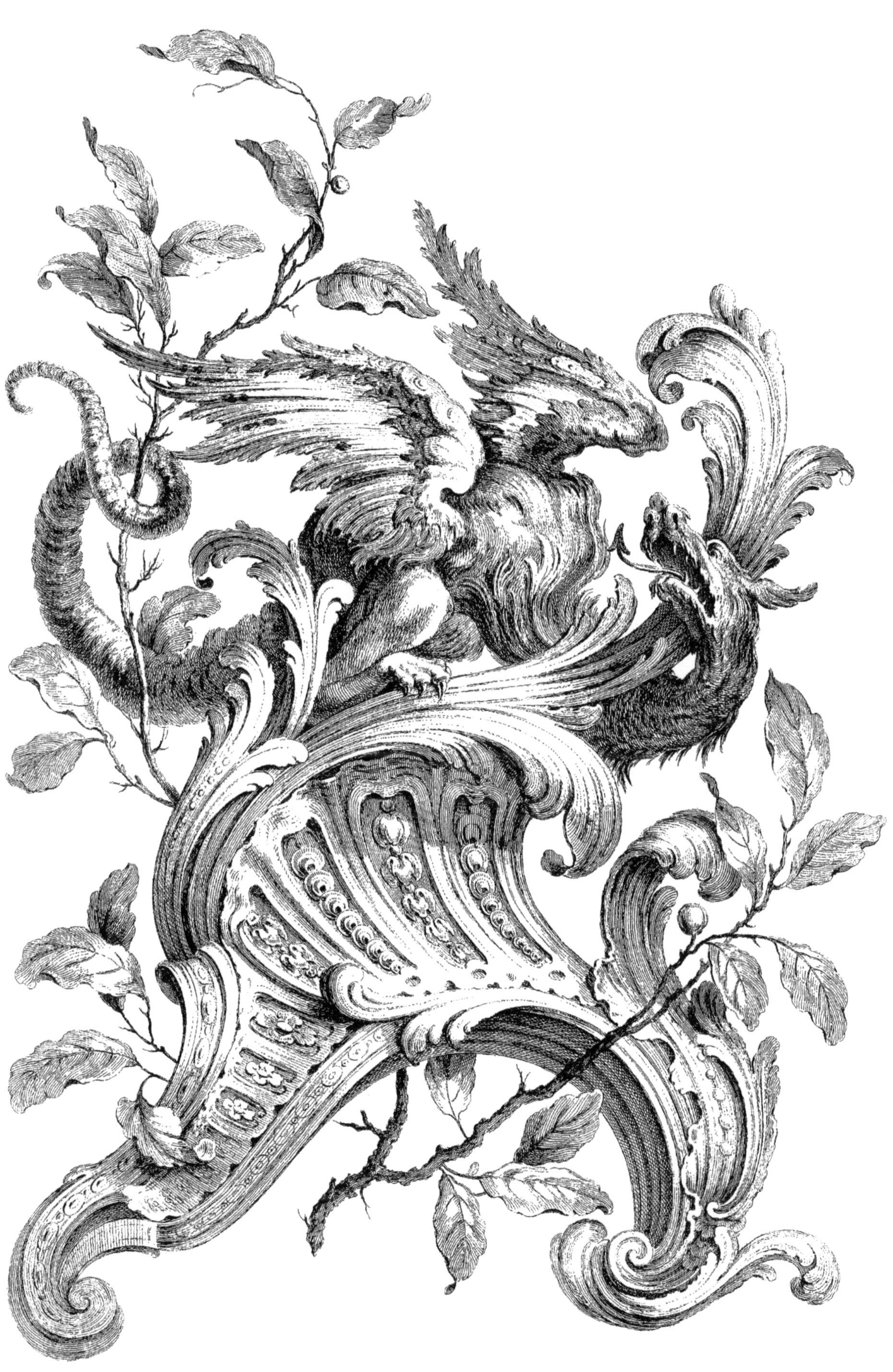

56: Ornament with dragon.

57

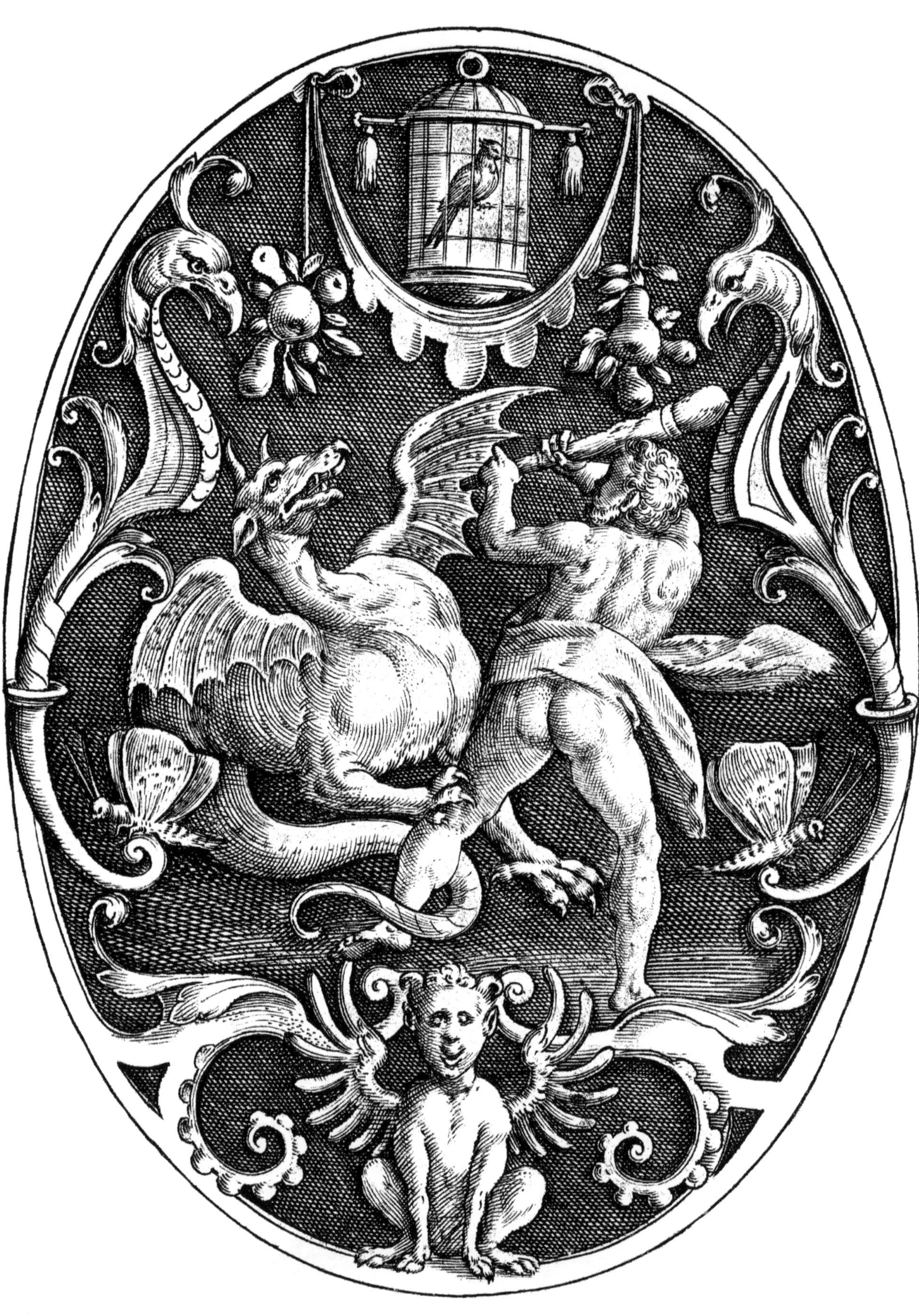

57: Hercules slays the dragon Ladon, Gerard de Jode, after Marcus Geeraerts, 1519 – 1591.

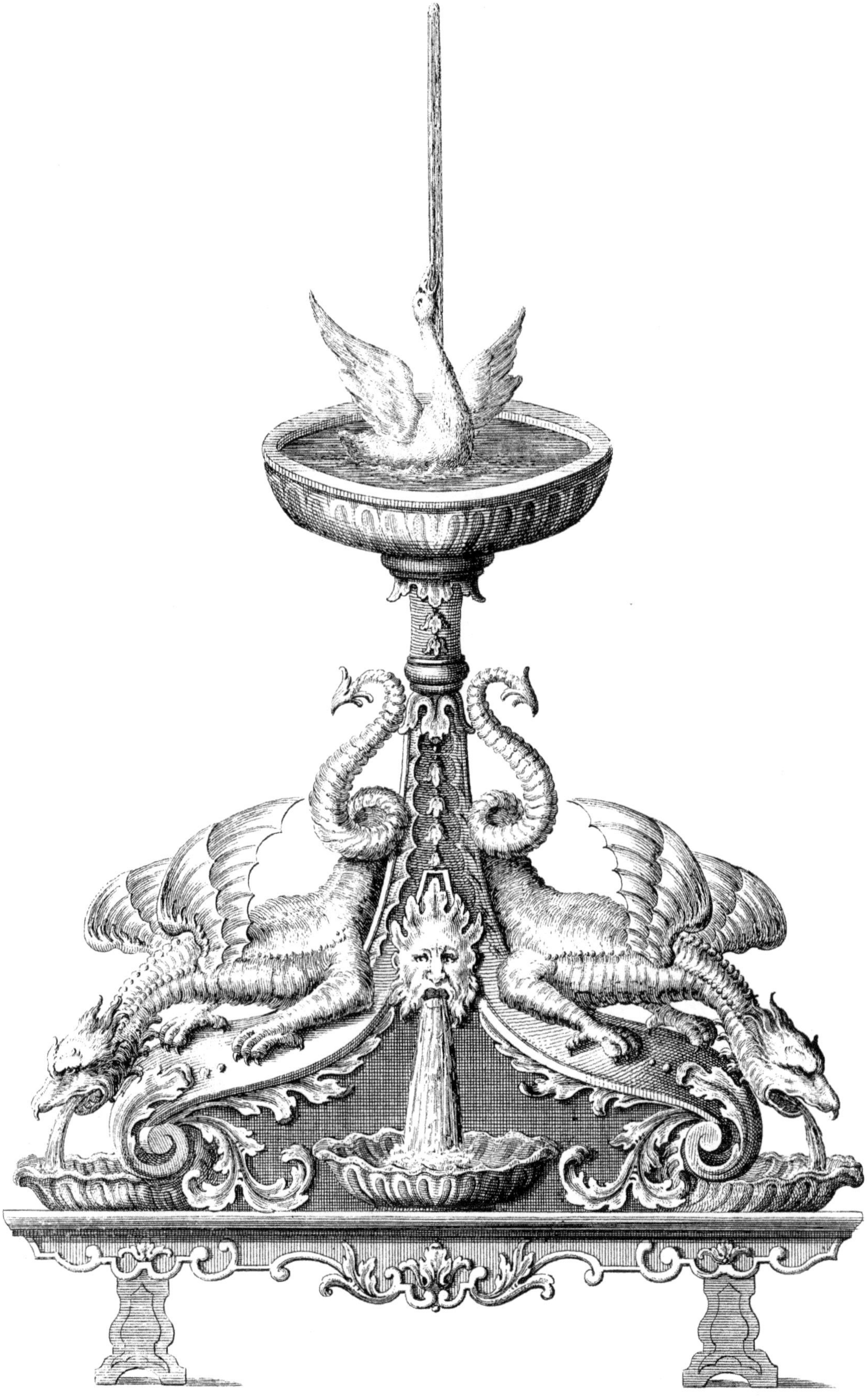

58: Design for a fountain, anonymous, Gerrit de Grendel, 1708 – 1756.

59

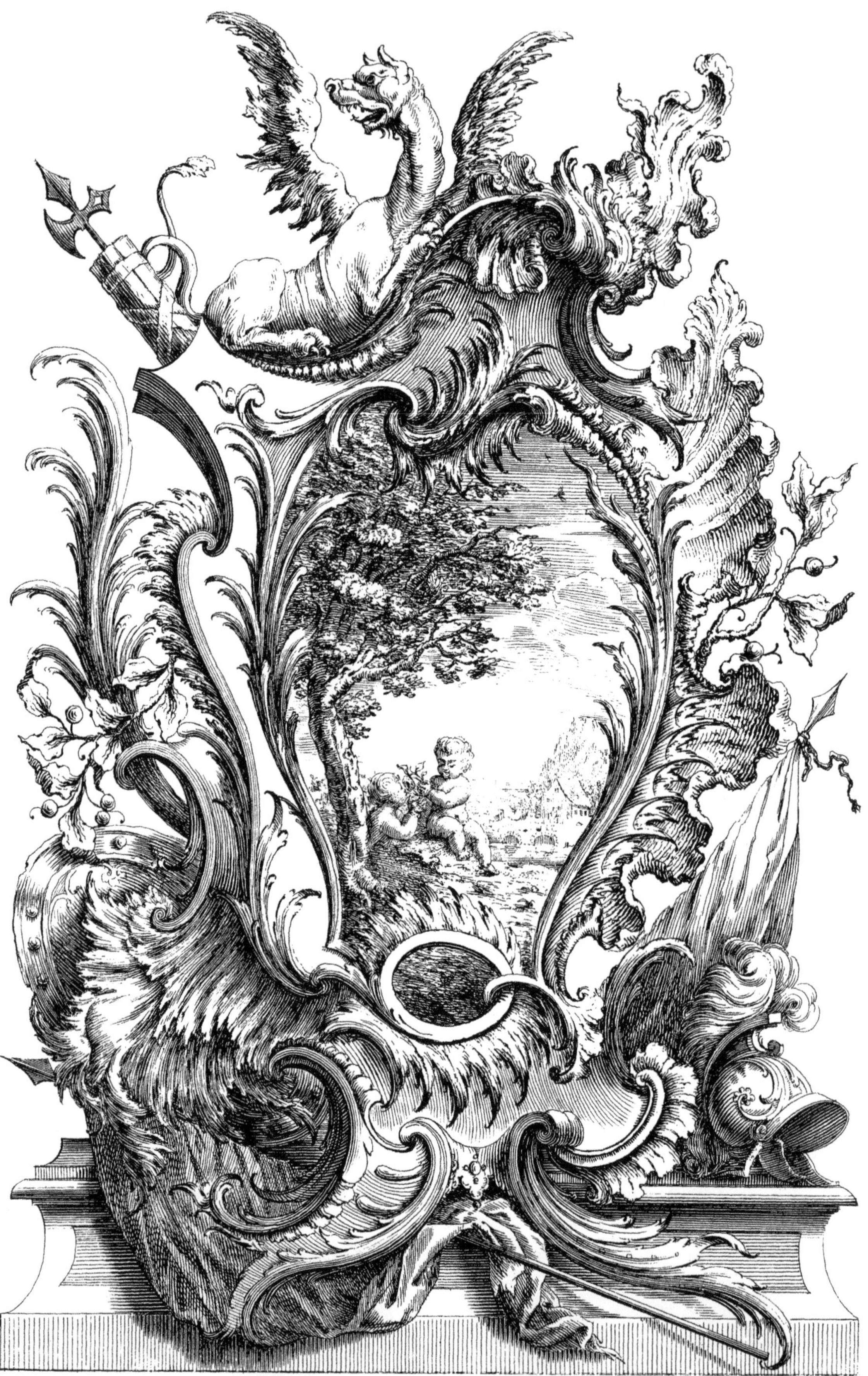

59: Cartouche with a dragon, 1738.

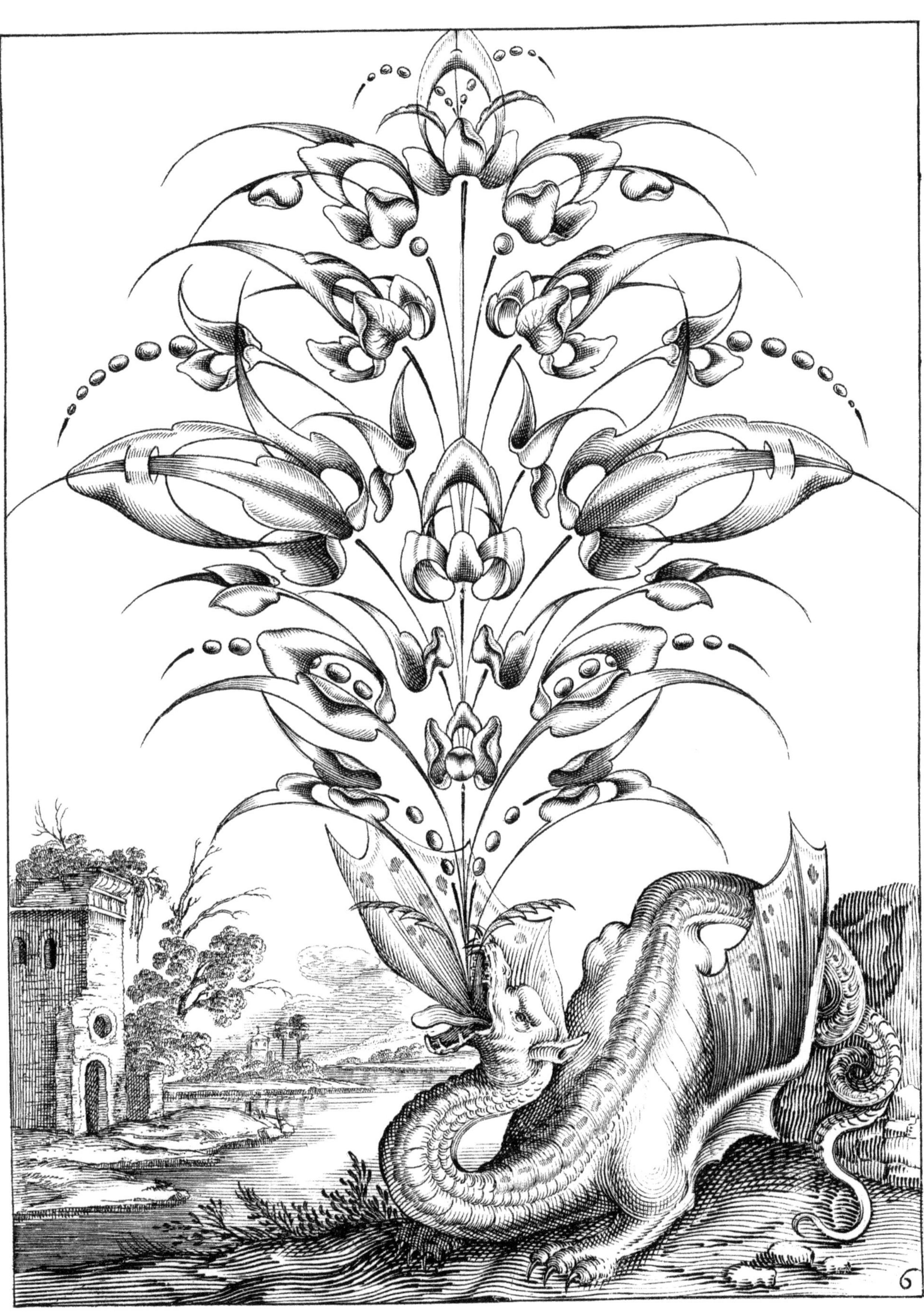

60: Goldsmith's bouquet sprouting from dragon's mouth, Balthazar Moncornet, after Balthasar Le Mersier, 1626.

61

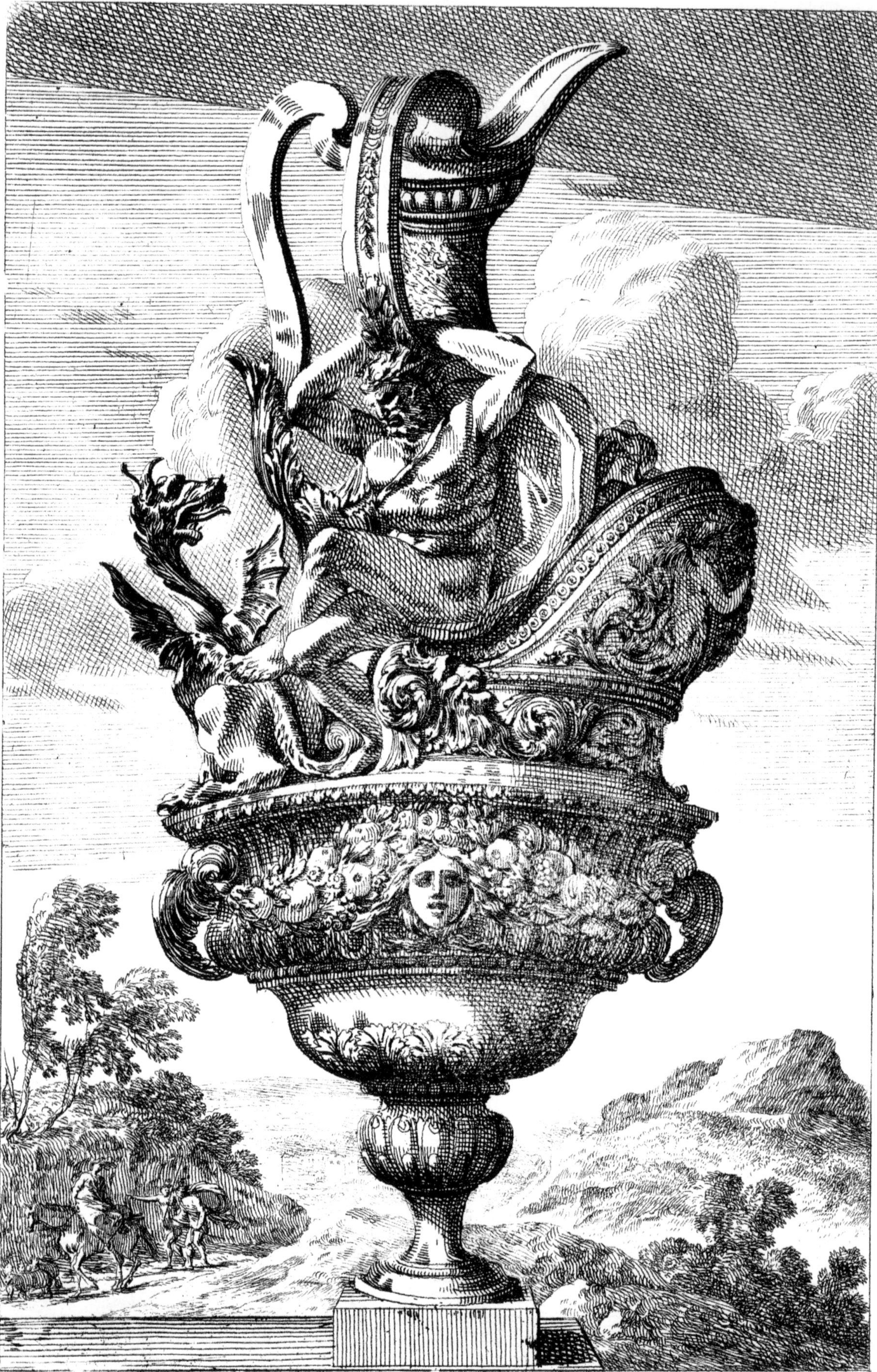

61: Pitcher with a naked man and dragon, Jean Lepautre, 1628–1732.

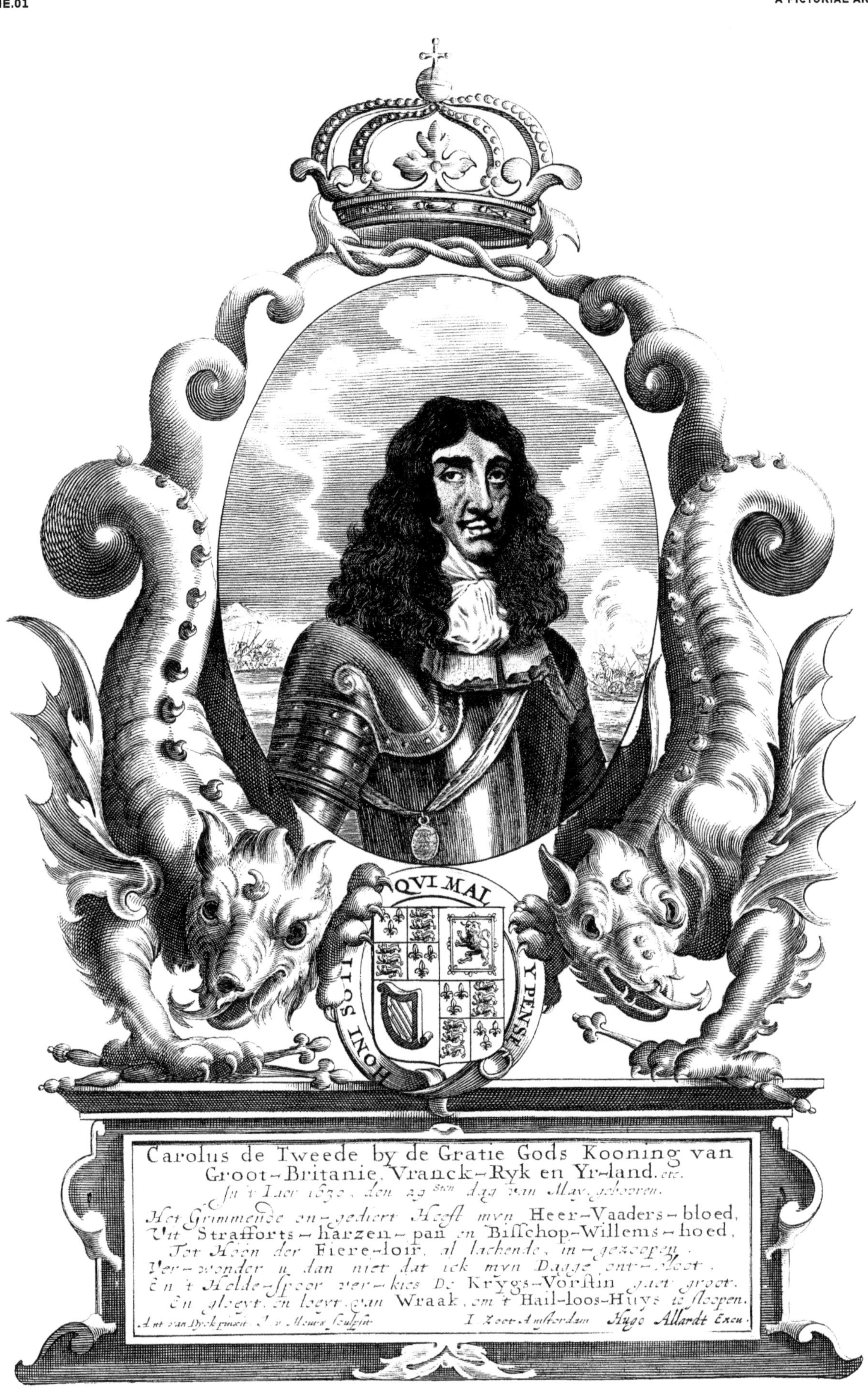

62: Portrait of King Charles II of England, Jacob van Meurs, after Anthony van Dyck, 1649 – 1680.

63

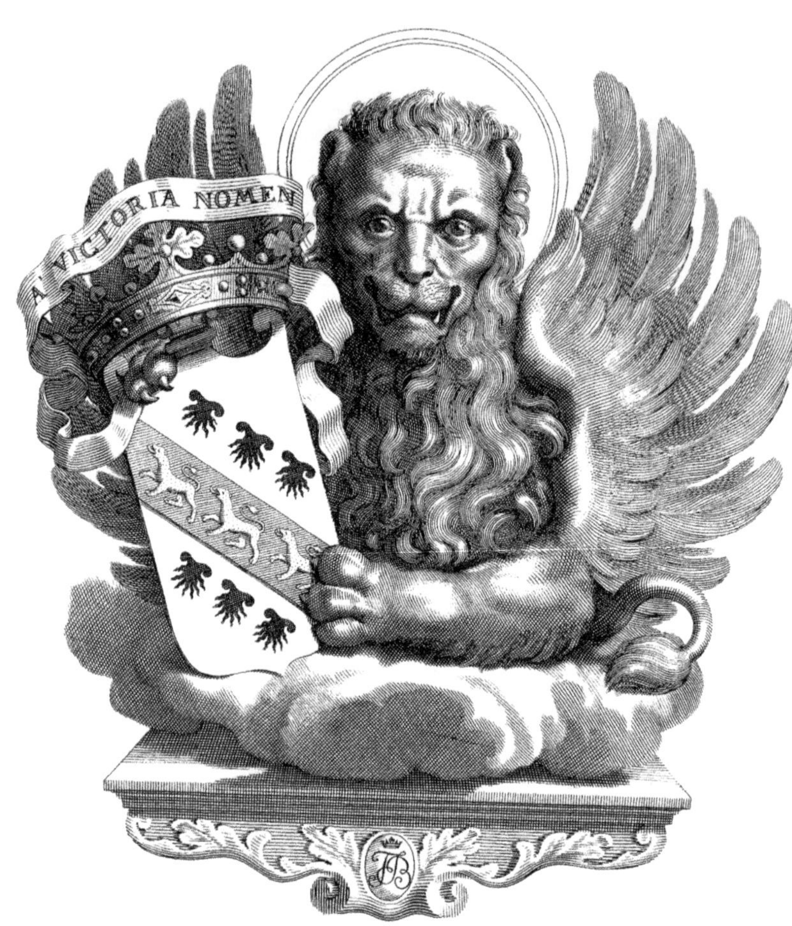

64

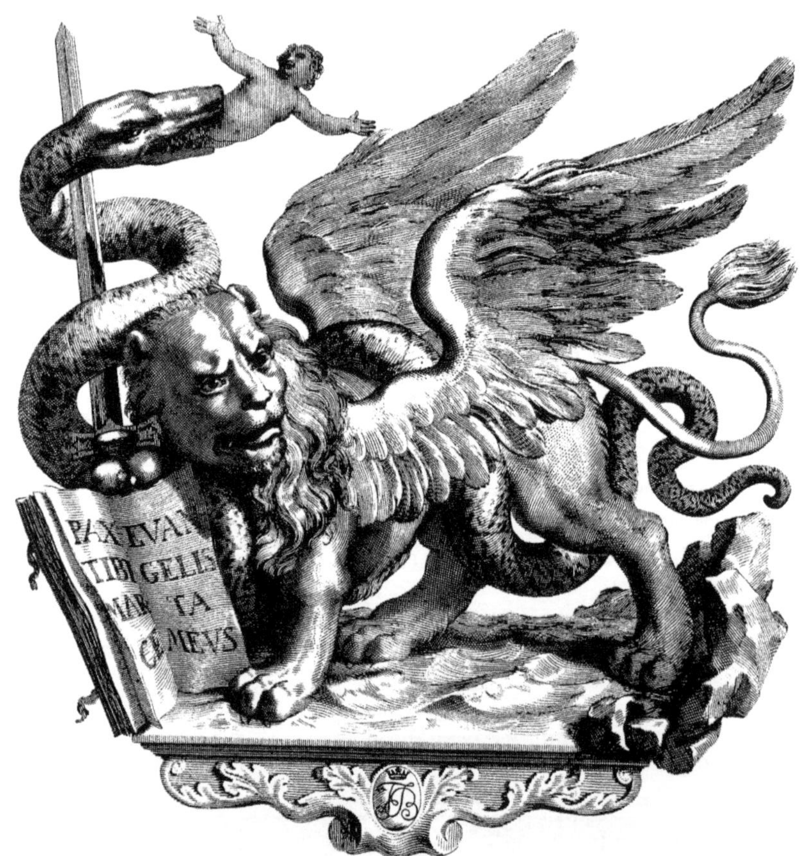

63: Crowned coat of arms with the lion of Saint Mark, Robert van Audenaerd, 1673 – 1743.

64: Allegory of the Battle between Venice and Milan, Robert van Audenaerd, 1673–1743.

65

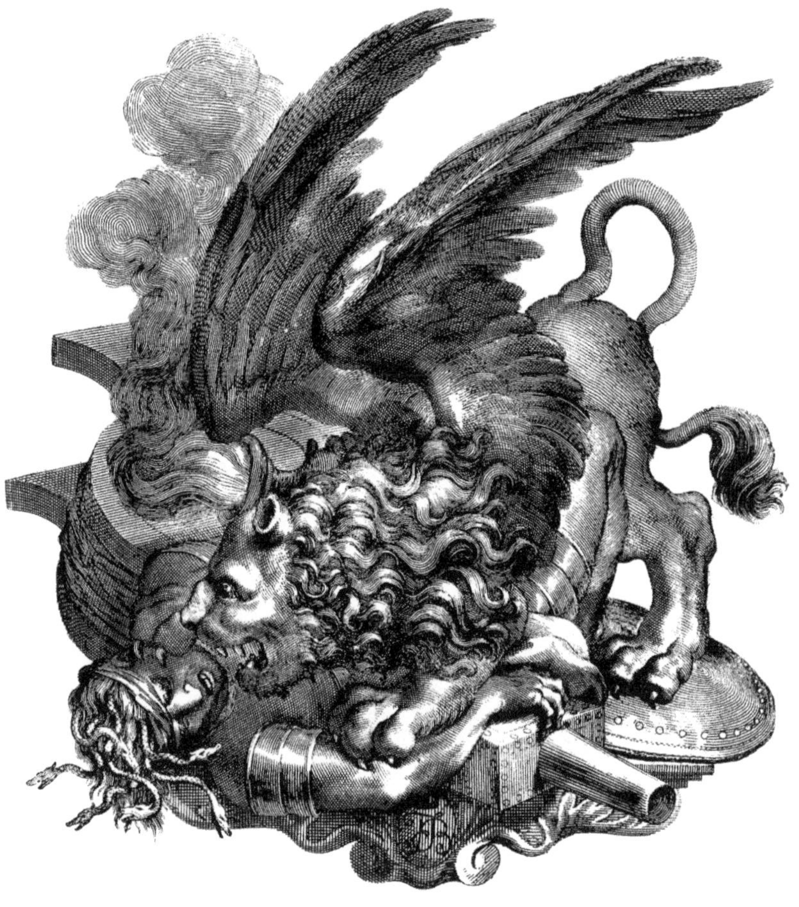

66

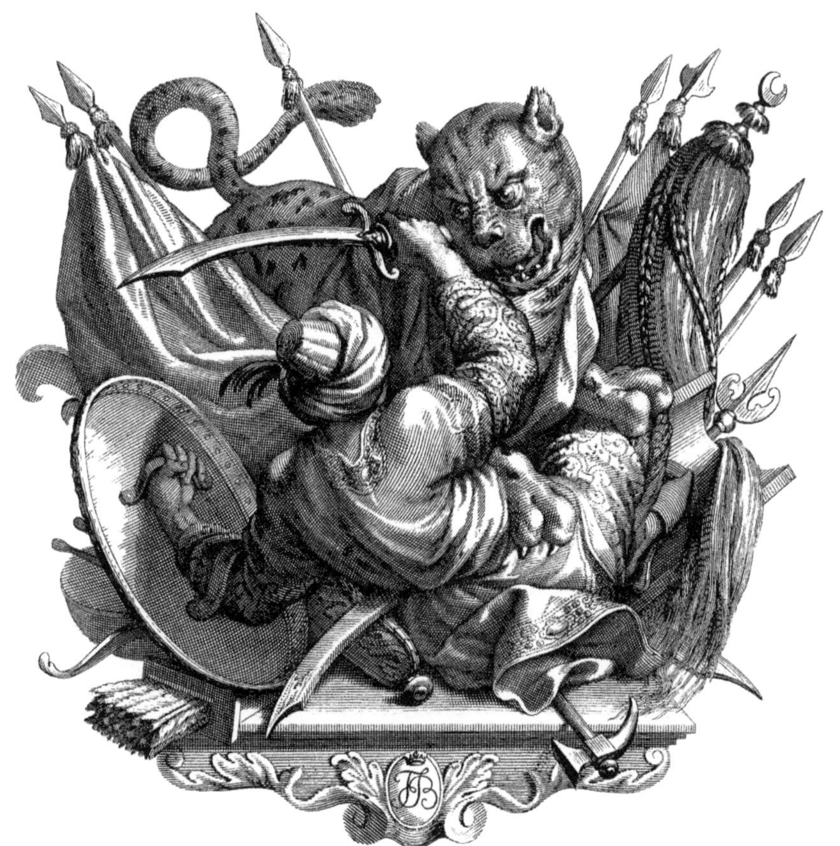

65: Medusa crushed by the lion of Saint Mark, Robert van Audenaerd, 1673 – 1743.

66: Ottoman man attacked by a lioness, Robert van Audenaerd, 1673 – 1743.

67

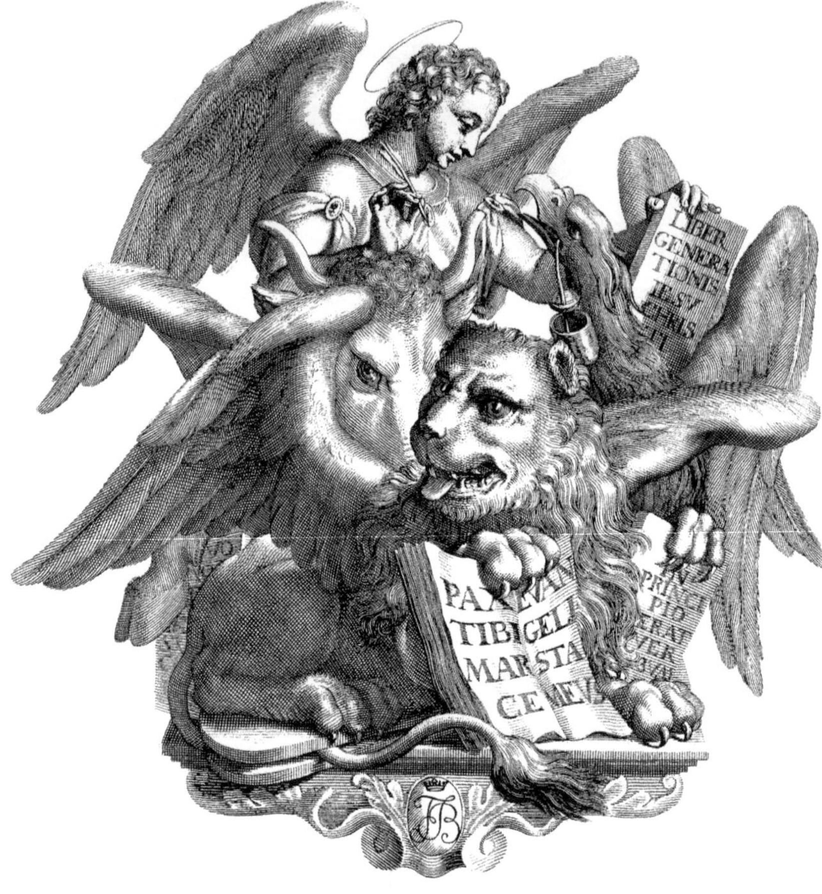

68

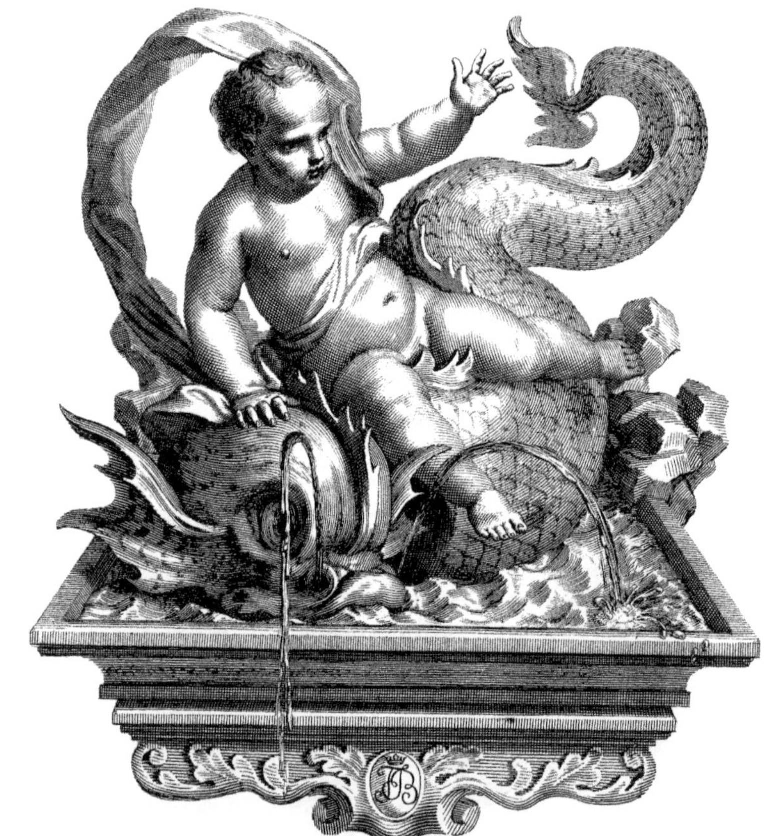

67: Symbols of the Four Evangelists, Robert van Audenaerd, 1673–1743.

68: Personification of the Friendly Mind, Robert van Audenaerd, 1673 – 1743.

69

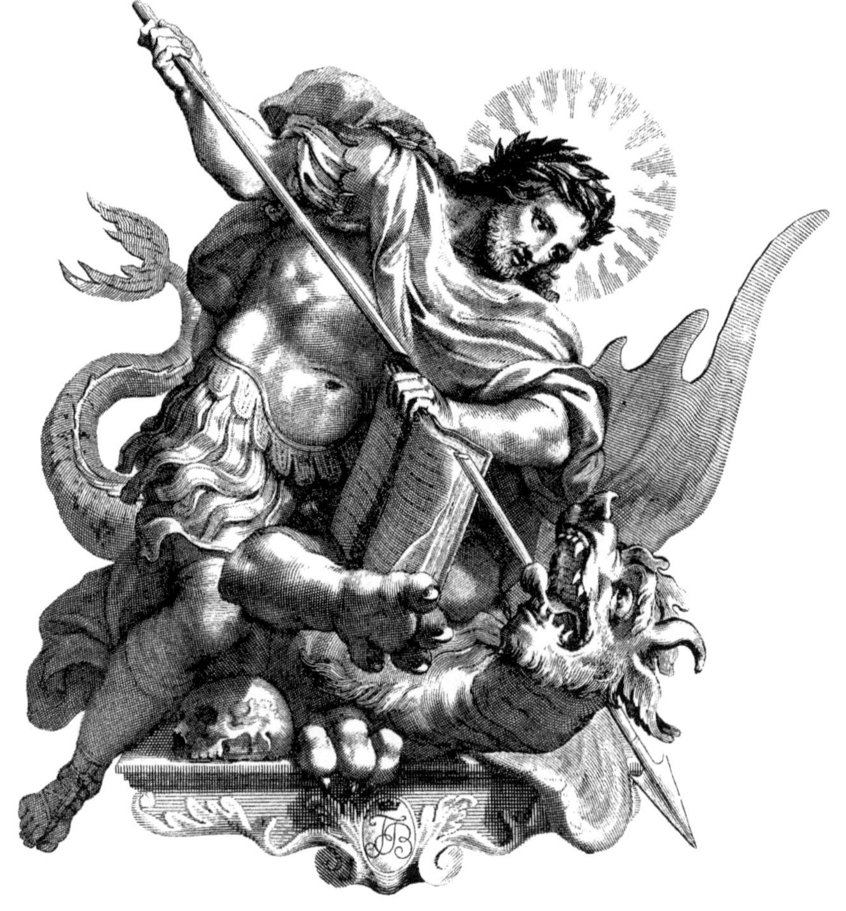

70

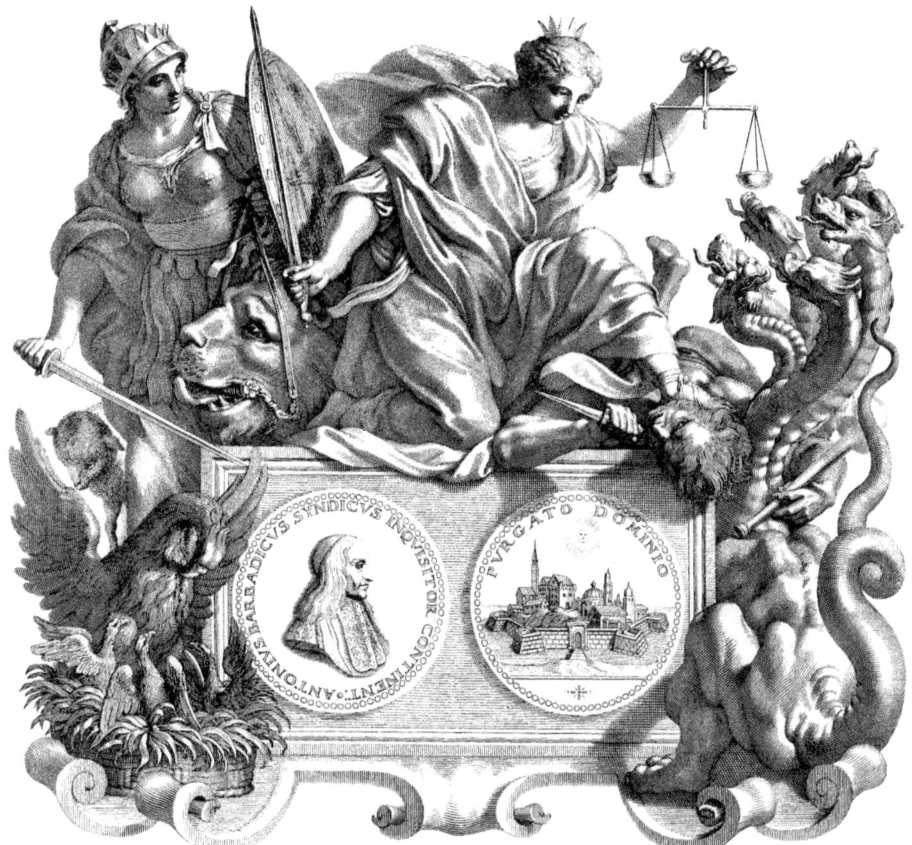

69: Personifications of Good Existence.

70: Portrait of Antonio Barbarigo and the Personifications of Power, Justice and Wrath, Robert van Audenaerd, 1673 – 1743.

71

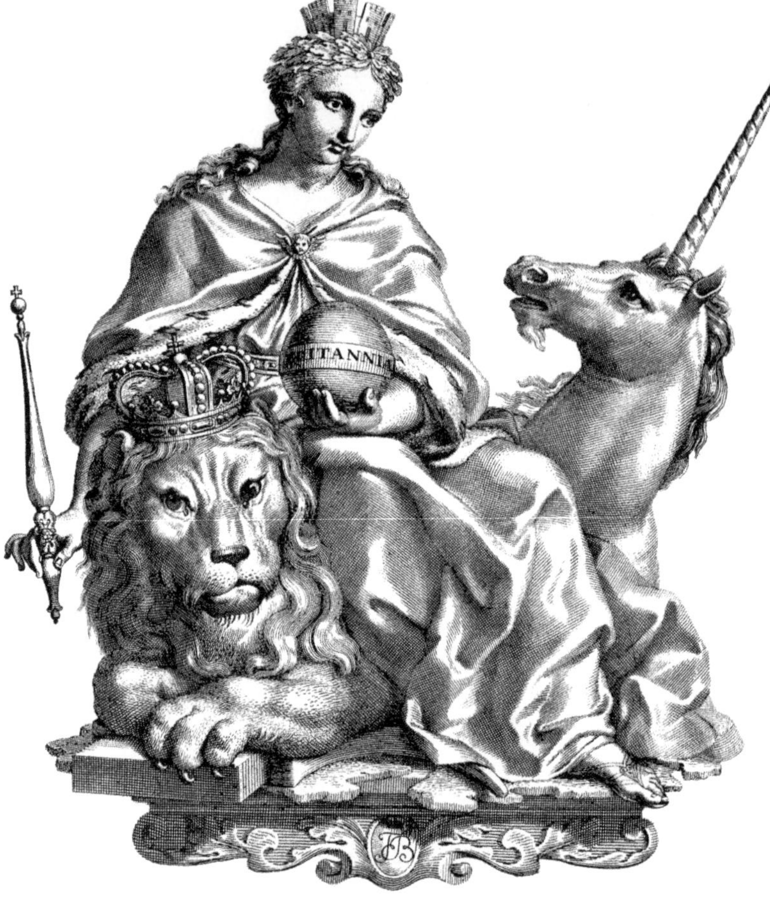

72

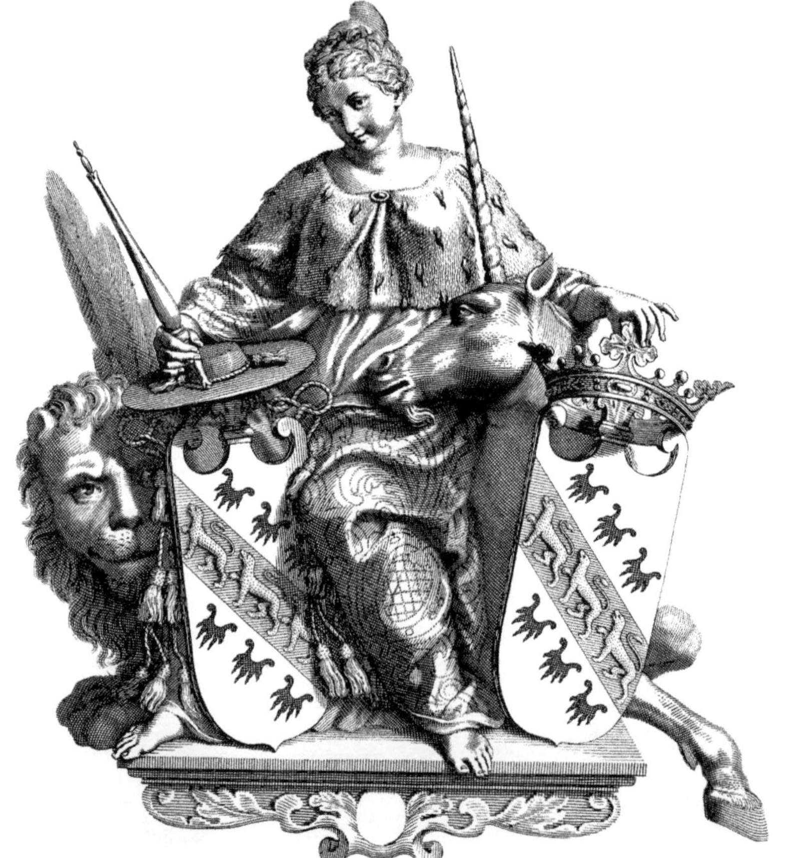

71: Personification of Britannia, Robert van Audenaerd, 1673–1743.

72: Personification of Venice, Robert van Audenaerd, 1673–1743.

73

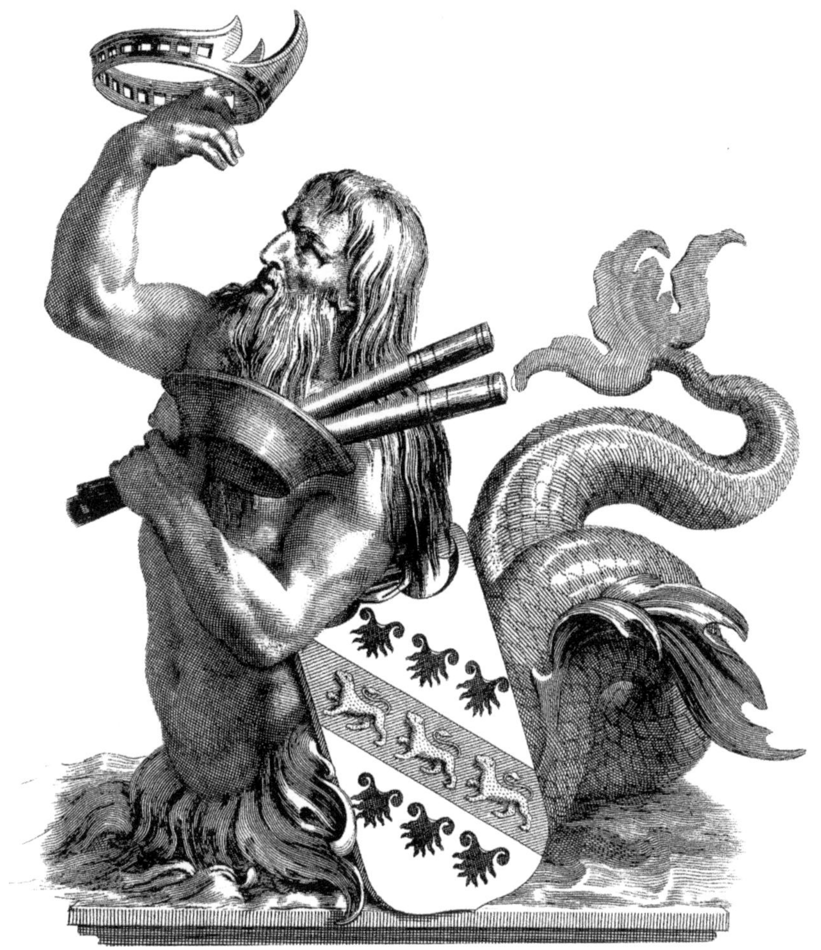

74

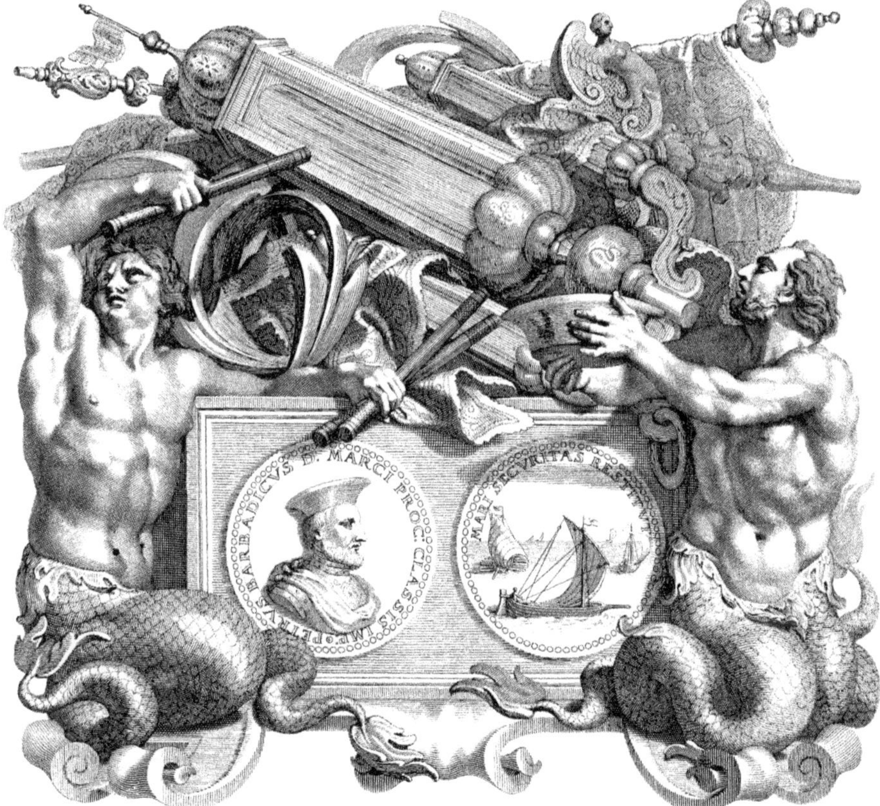

73: Merman with the coat of arms of Barbarigo, Robert van Audenaerd, 1673 – 1743.

74: Portrait of Pietro Barbarigo with mermaids, Robert van Audenaerd, 1673 – 1743.

75

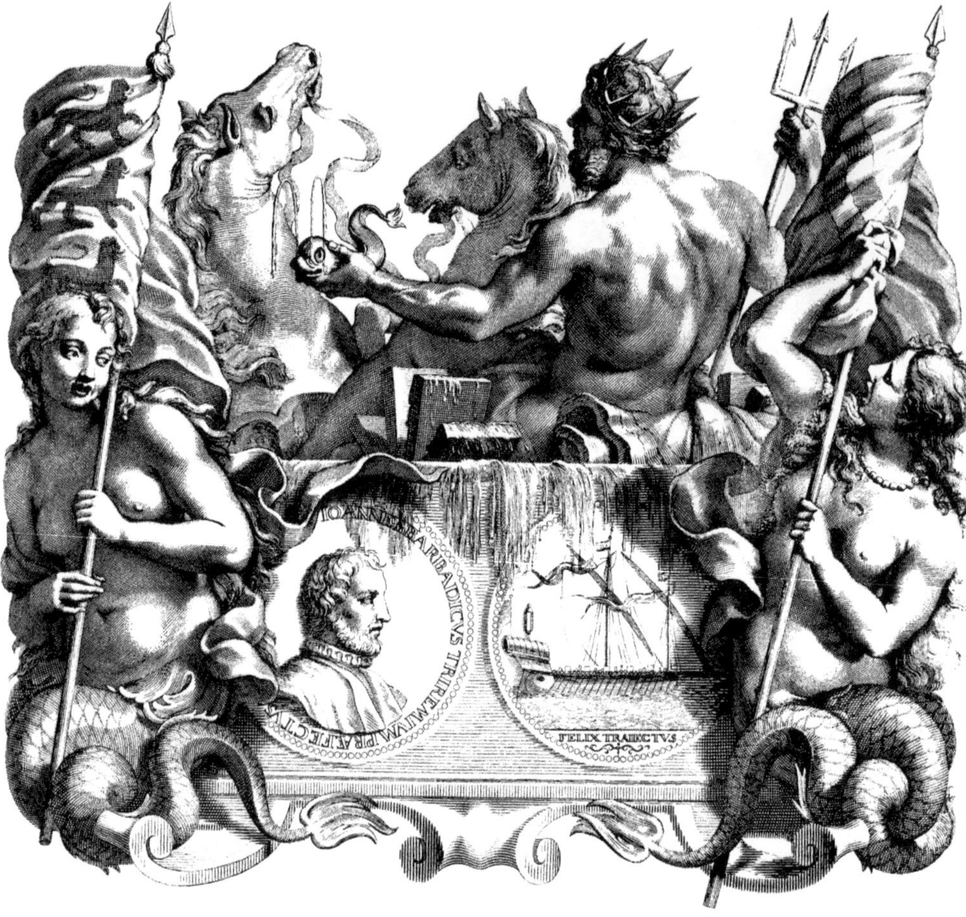

76

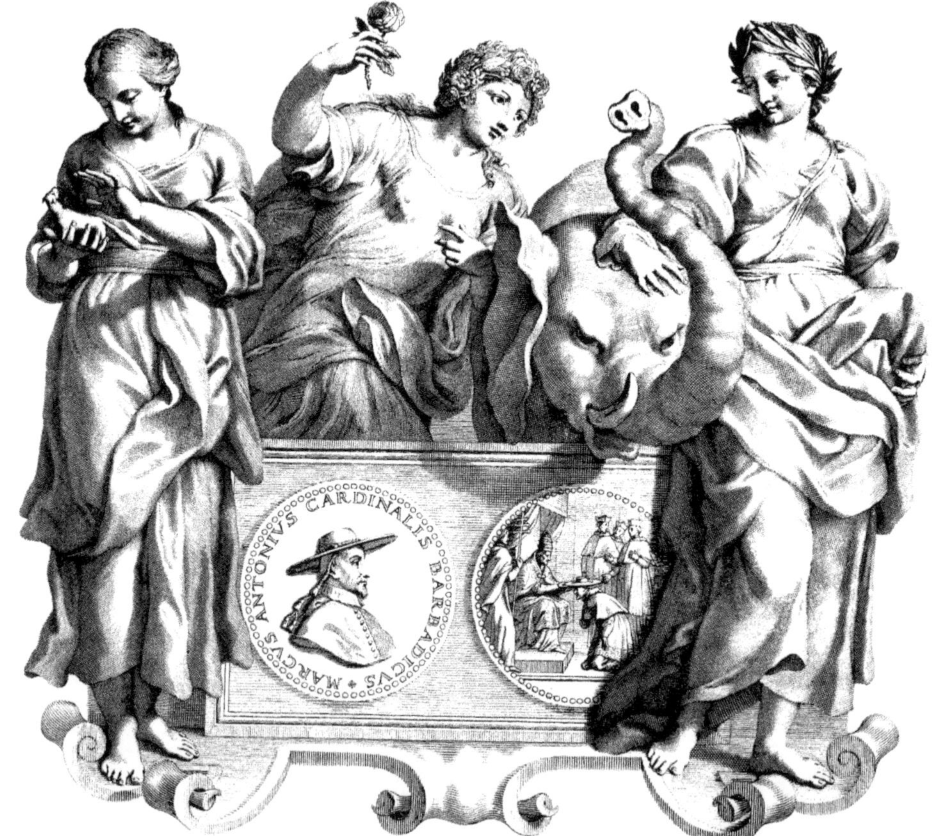

75: Portrait of Giovanni Barbarigo, Neptune and Two Mermaids, Robert van Audenaerd, 1673 – 1743.

76: Portrait of Marcantonio Barbarigo and the Personifications of Politeness, Kindness and Meekness, Robert van Audenaerd, 1673 – 1743.

77

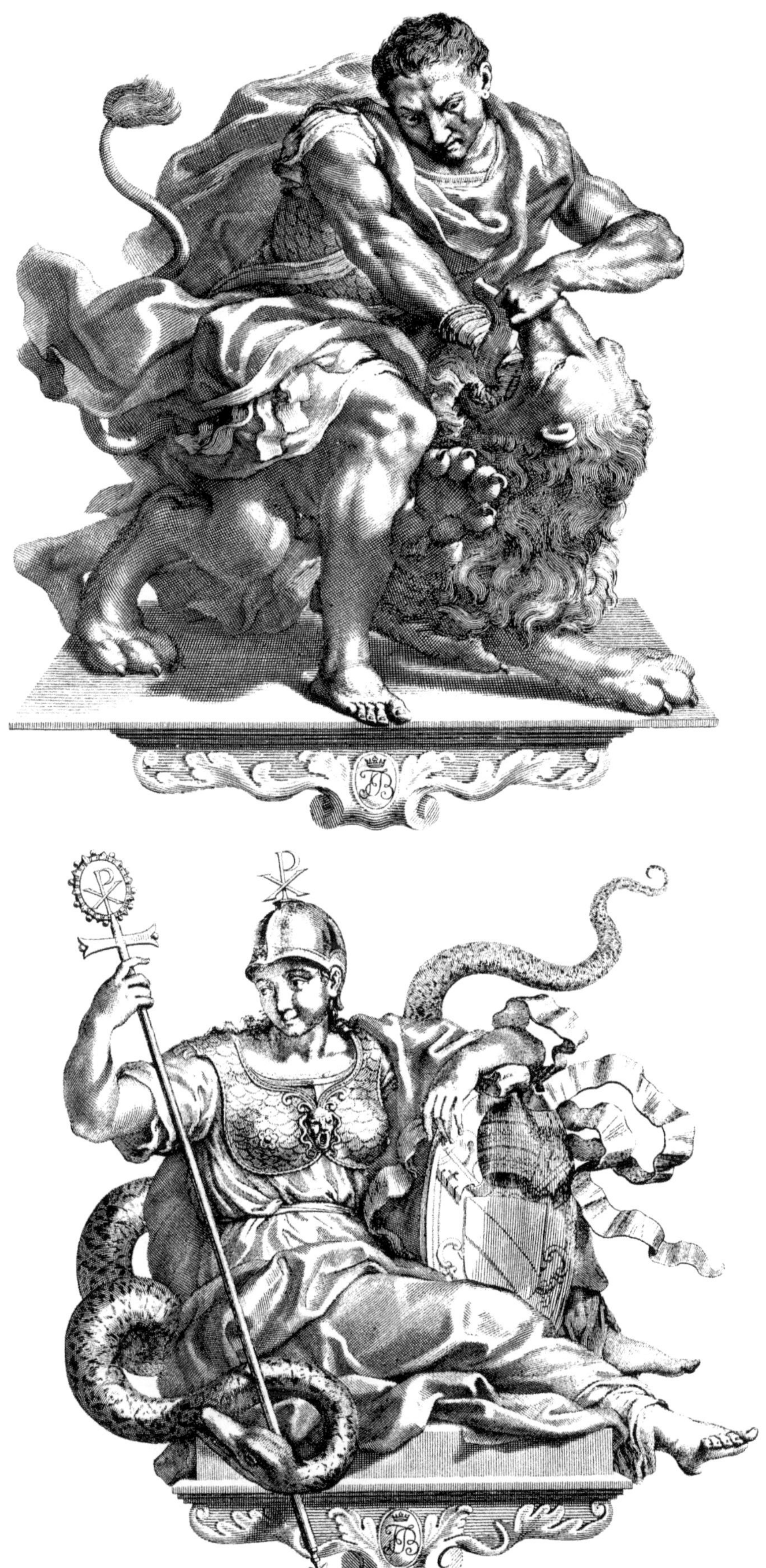

78

77: Personification of Courage, Robert van Audenaerd, 1673–1743.

78: Personification of Holy Rome with the coat of arms of Pope Eugene IV, Robert van Audenaerd, 1673 – 1743.

79

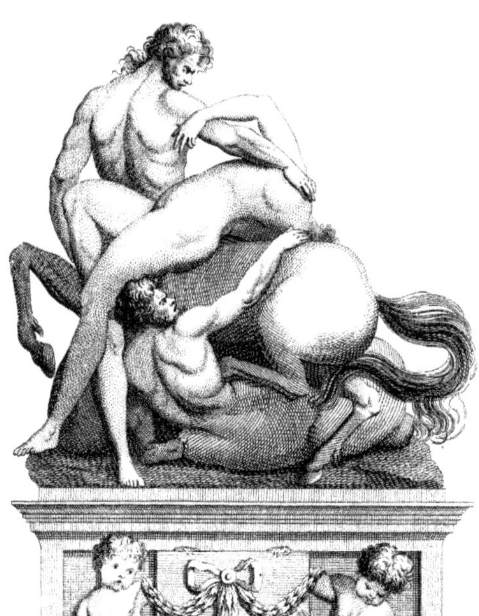

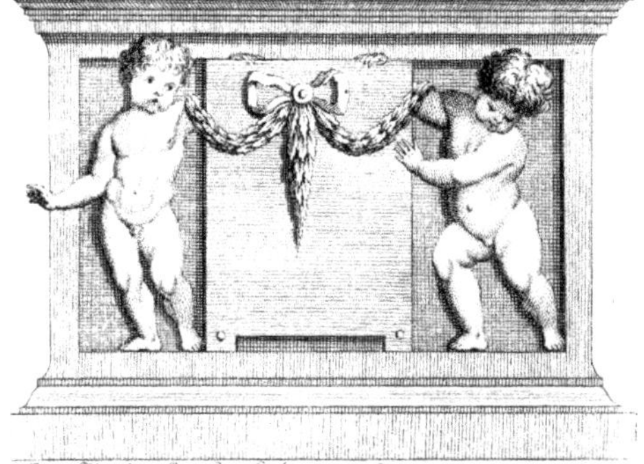

80

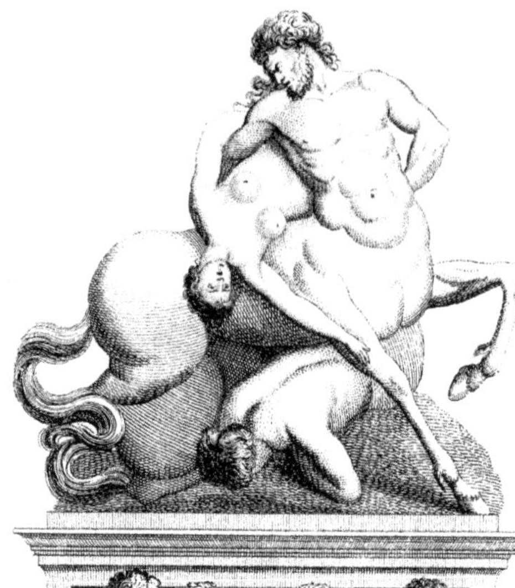

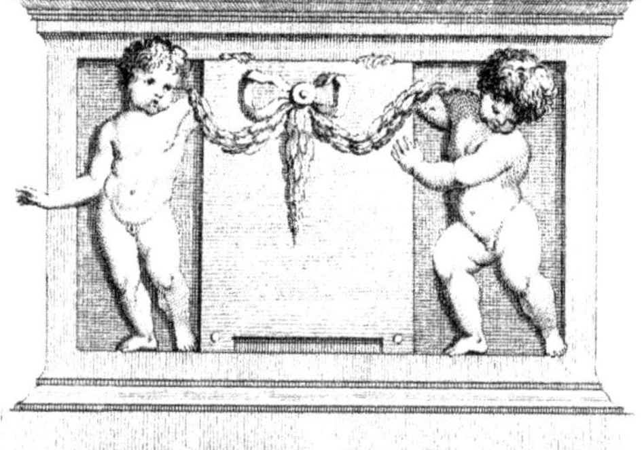

81

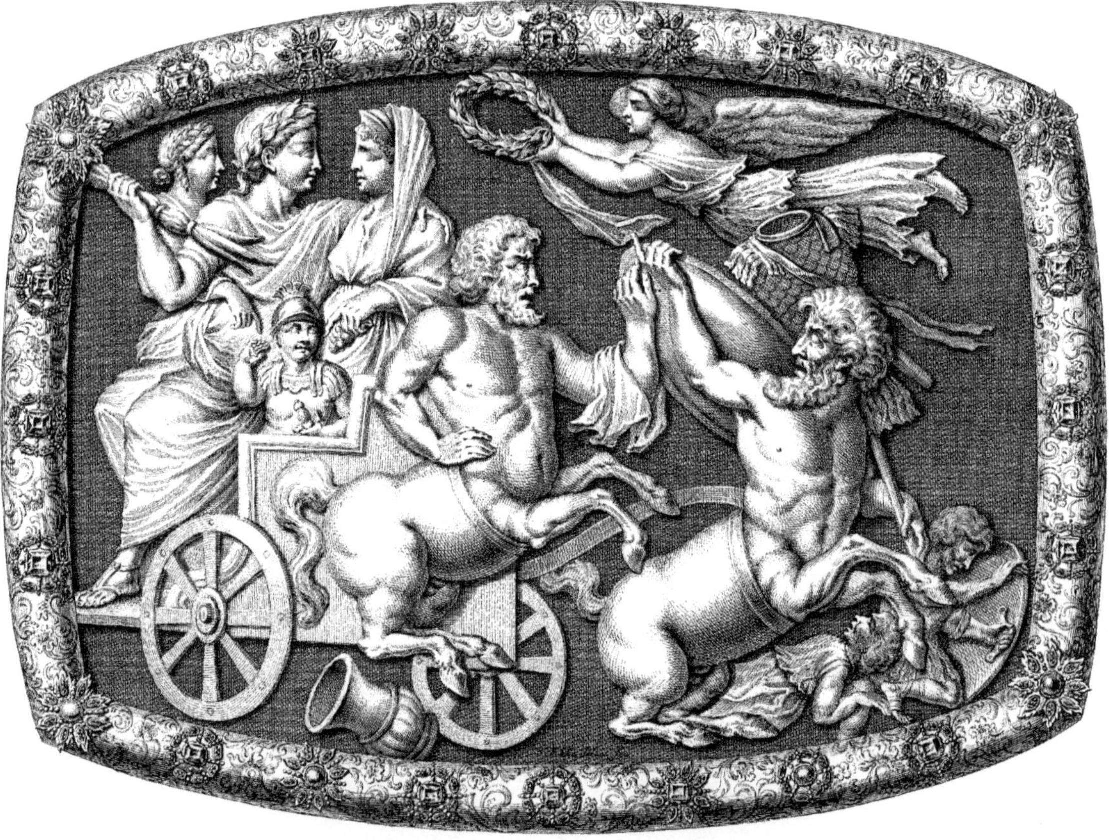

79: Battle of Centaurs, Antoine Alexandre Joseph Cardon–1772.

80: Battle of Centaurs, Antoine Alexandre Joseph Cardon, after Guiliam van den Kleboom, 1772 – 1773.

81: Onyx with a Roman float and two centaurs, Simon Fokke, 1765 – 1767.

82

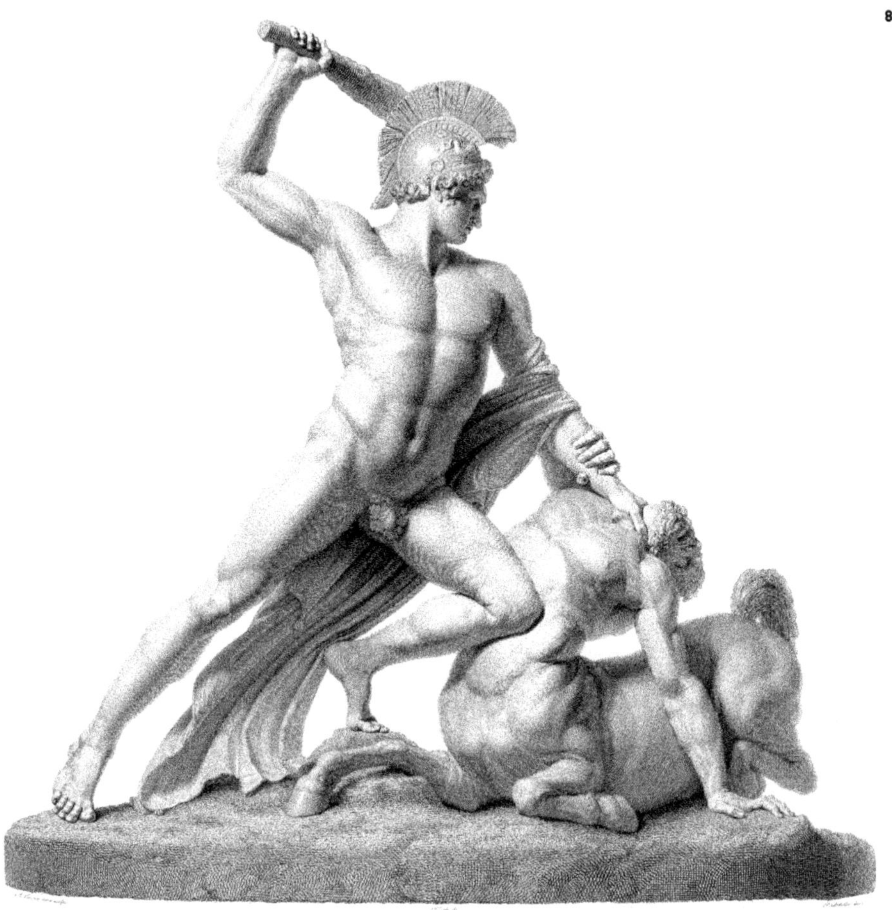

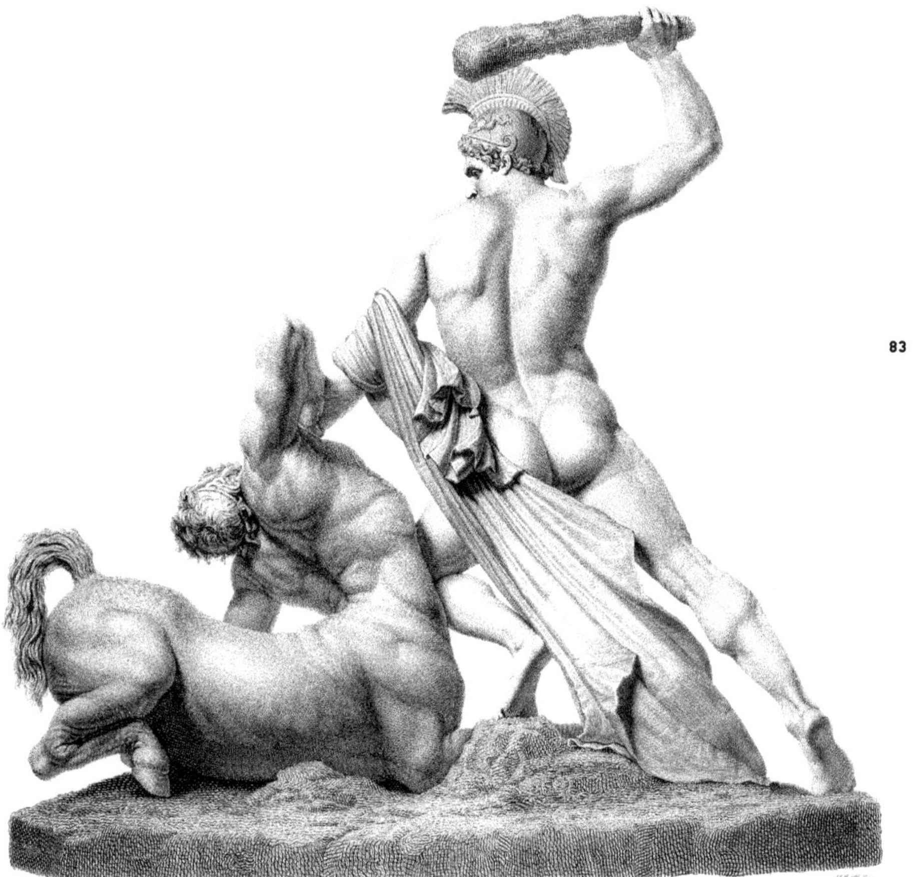

83

82: Theseus conquers the centaur, Pietro Bonato, after Giovanni Tognolli, after Antonio Canova, 1775 – 1827.

83: Theseus conquers the centaur, Pietro Bonato, after Giovanni Tognolli, after Antonio Canova, 1775 – 1827.

84

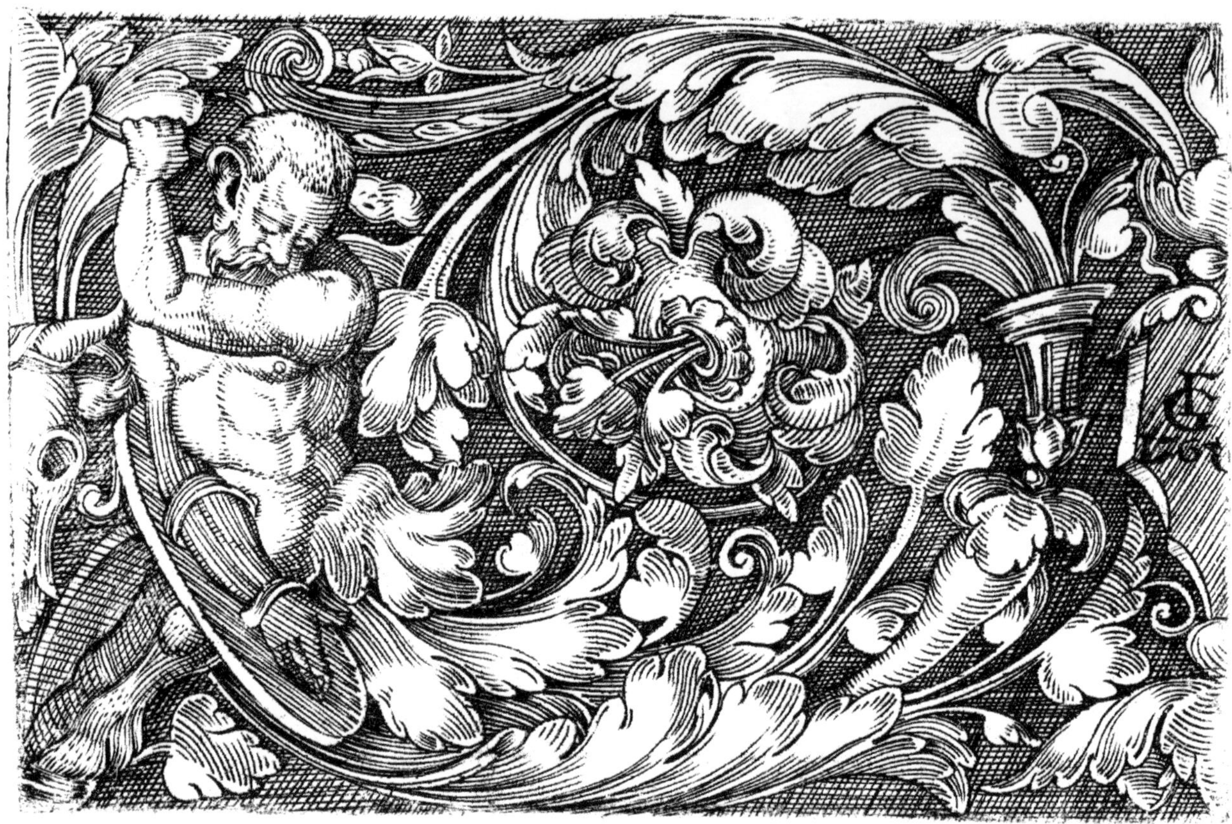

85

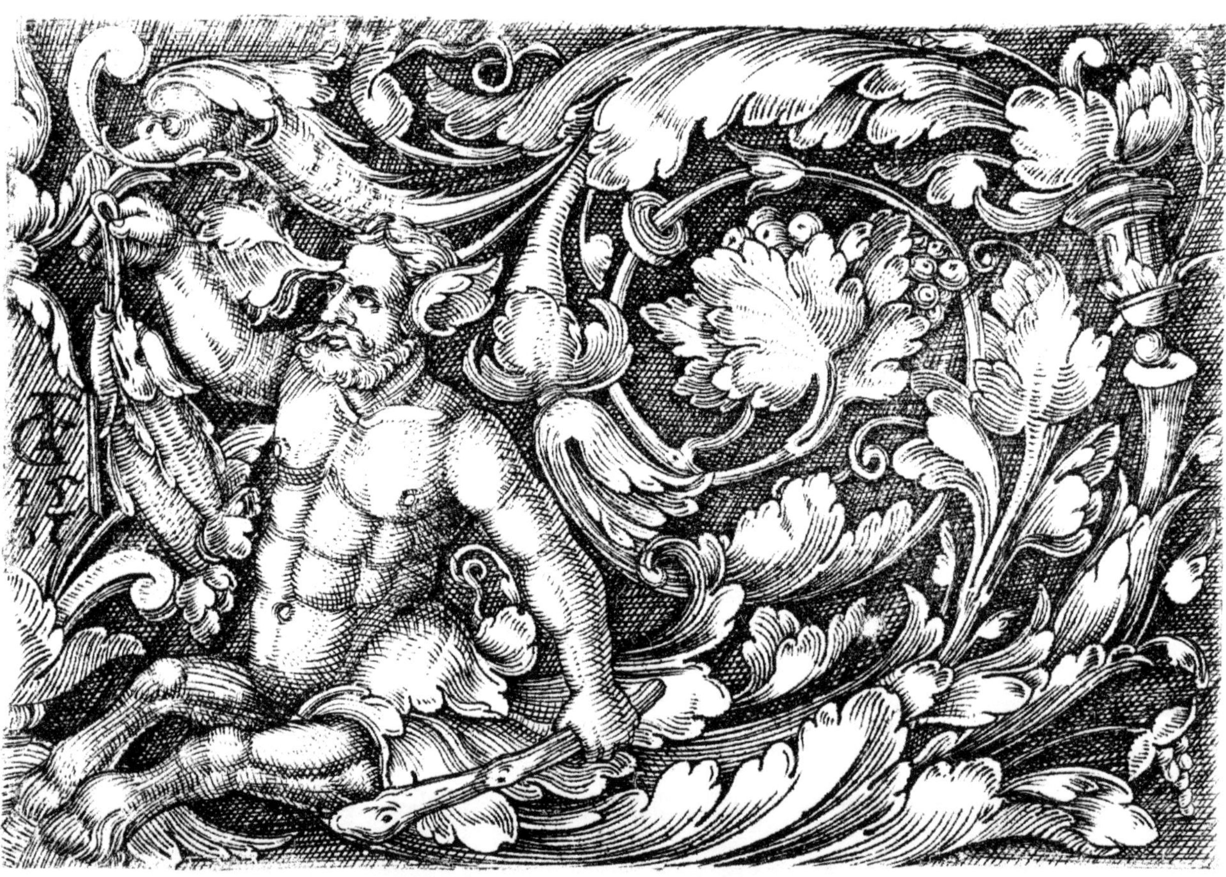

84: Ornament with centaur, Monogrammist FG, 1536.

85: Ornament with centaur, Monogrammist FG, 1537.

86

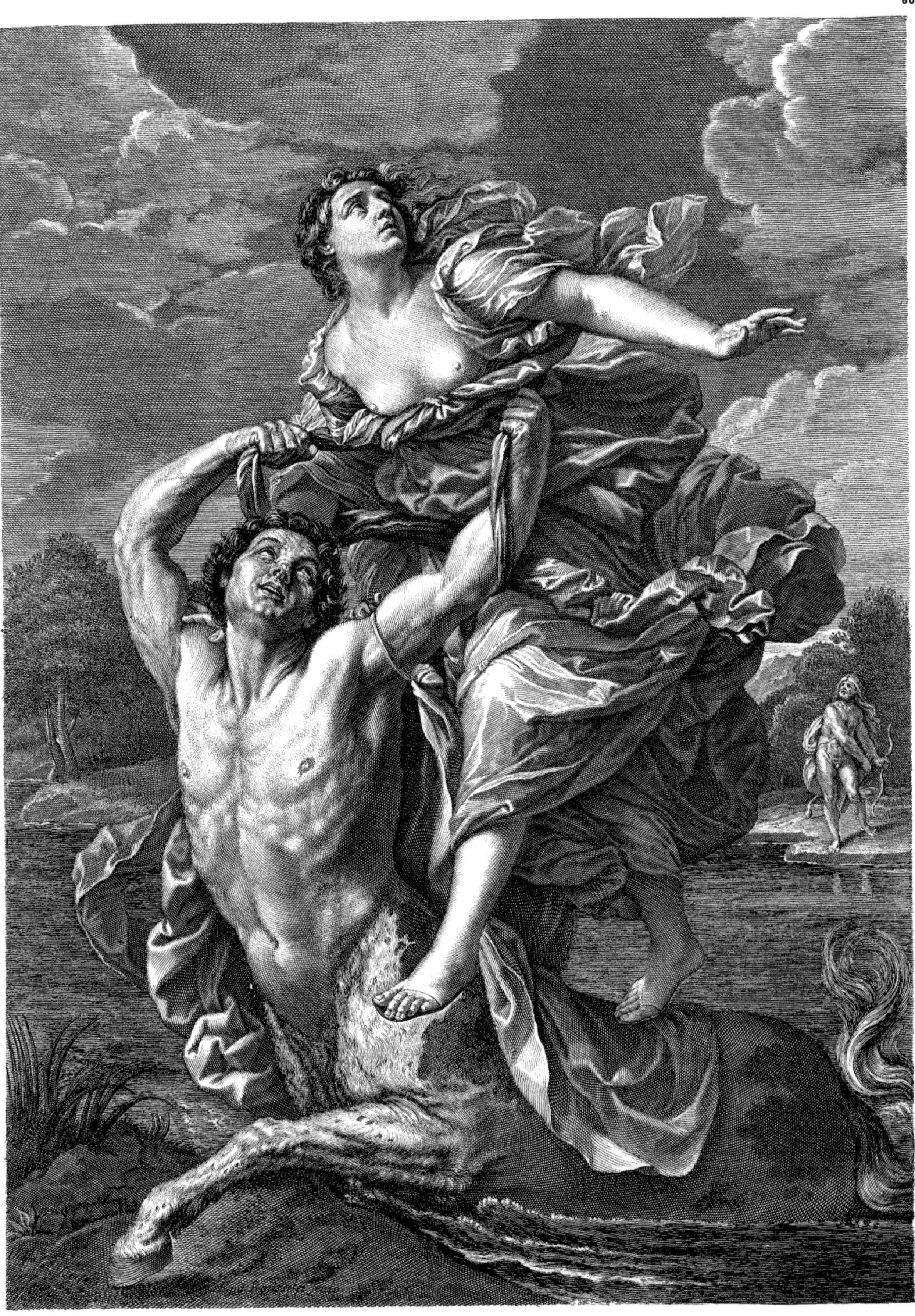

86: Deianeira kidnapped by the centaur Nessus, in the background Hercules with bow and arrow, Gilles Rousselet, after Guido Reni, 1620 – 1686.

87

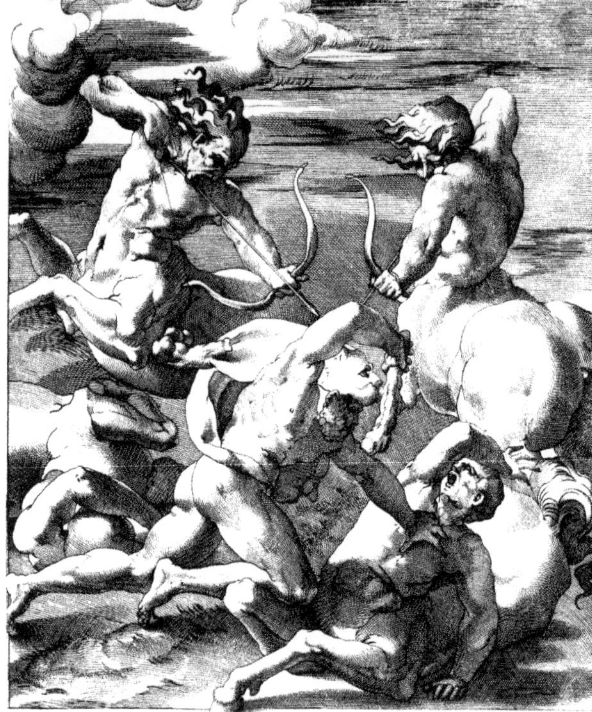

88

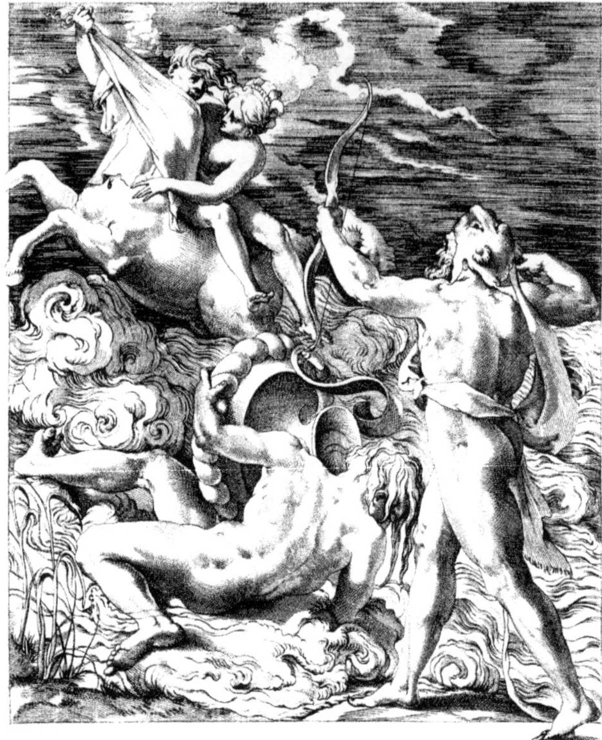

89

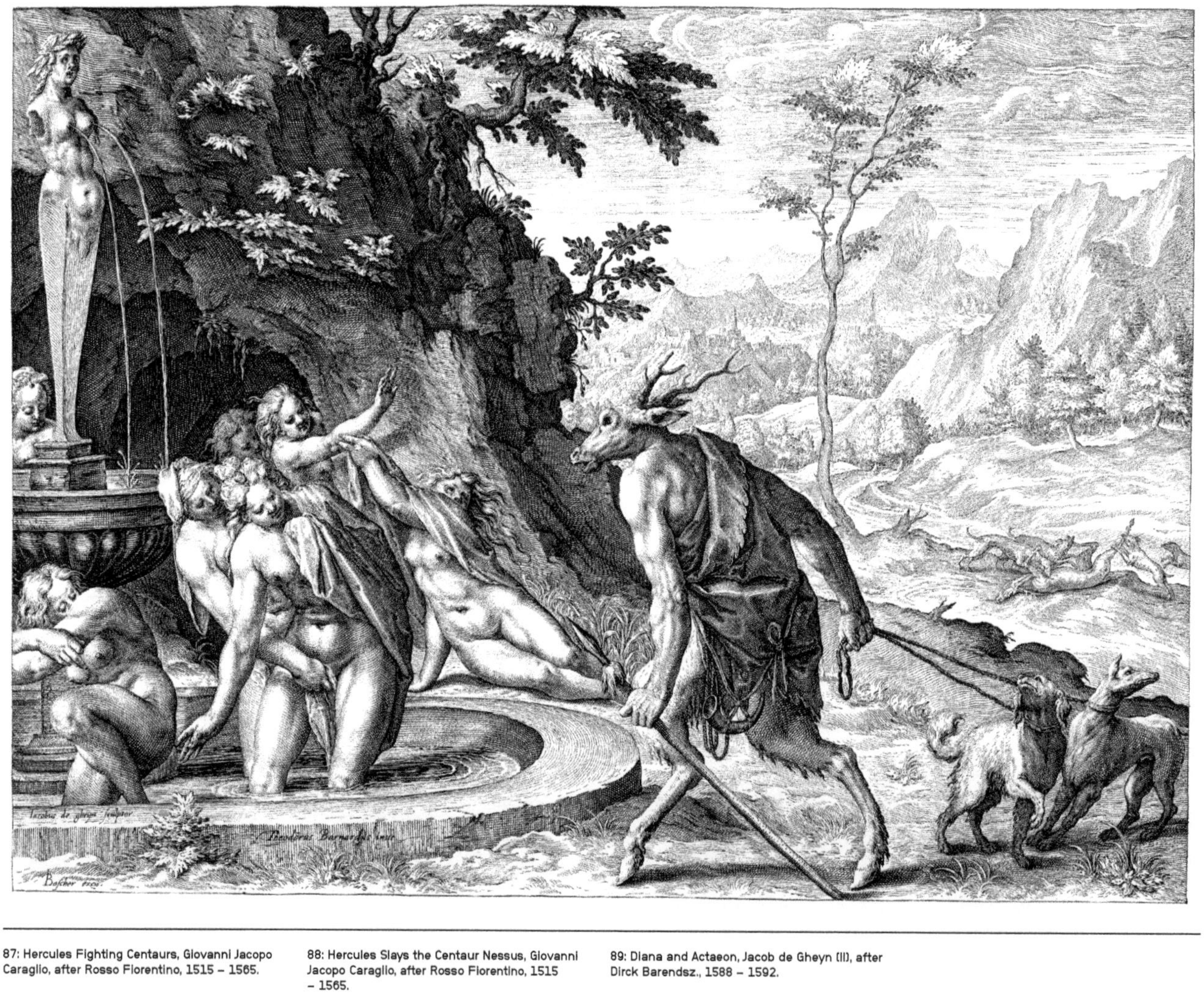

87: Hercules Fighting Centaurs, Giovanni Jacopo Caraglio, after Rosso Fiorentino, 1515 – 1565.

88: Hercules Slays the Centaur Nessus, Giovanni Jacopo Caraglio, after Rosso Fiorentino, 1515 – 1565.

89: Diana and Actaeon, Jacob de Gheyn (II), after Dirck Barendsz., 1588 – 1592.

90

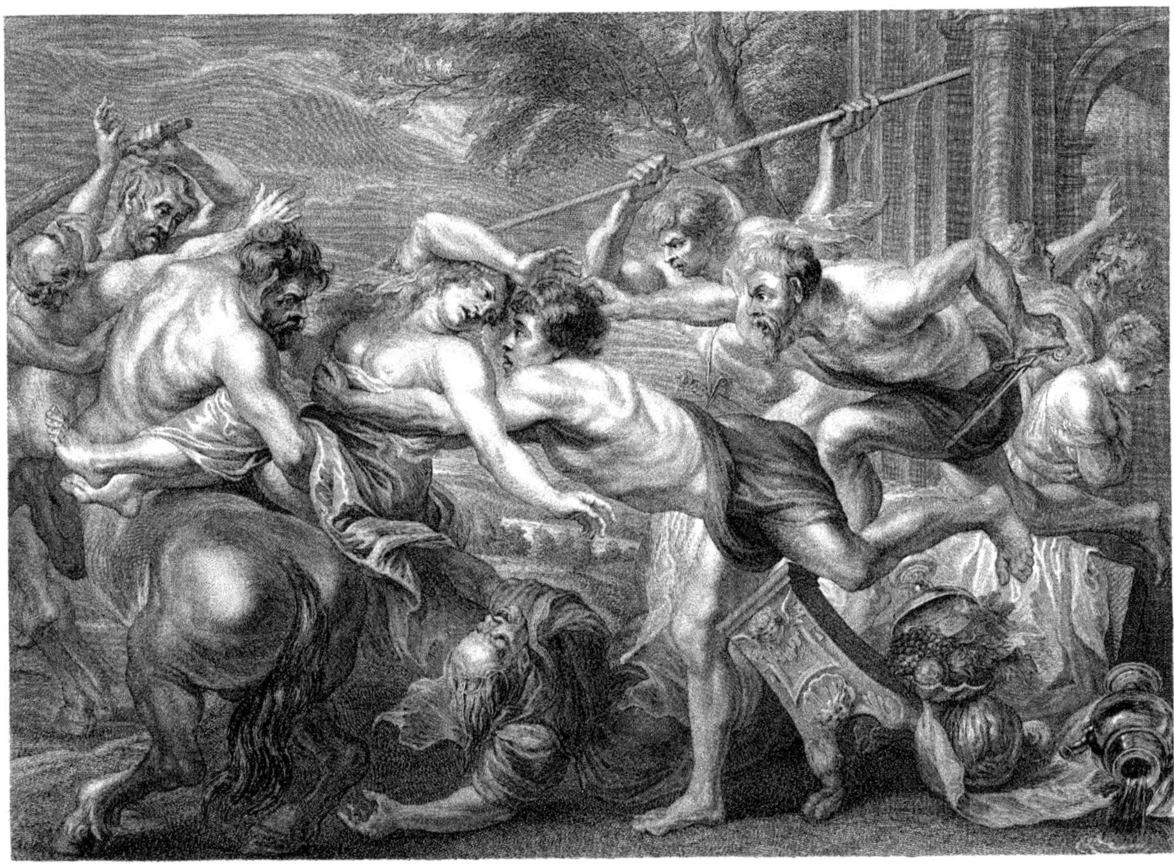

91

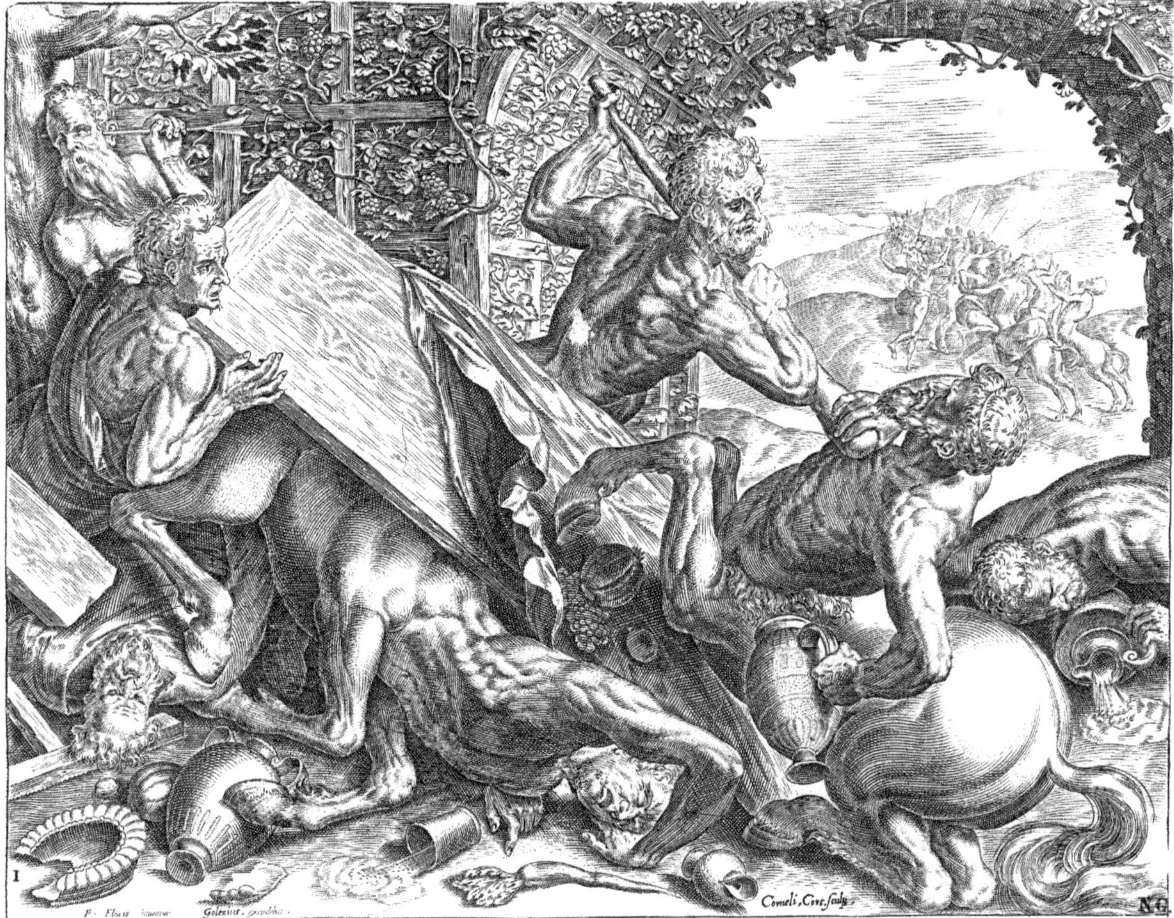

90: Centaur Eurytus kidnaps Hippodamea, Pieter de Bailliu (I), after Peter Paul Rubens, 1623 – 1660.

91: Hercules voorkomt de roof van Hippodamia door de centauren, Cornelis Cort, after Frans Floris (I), in or after 1563 – before 1595.

92

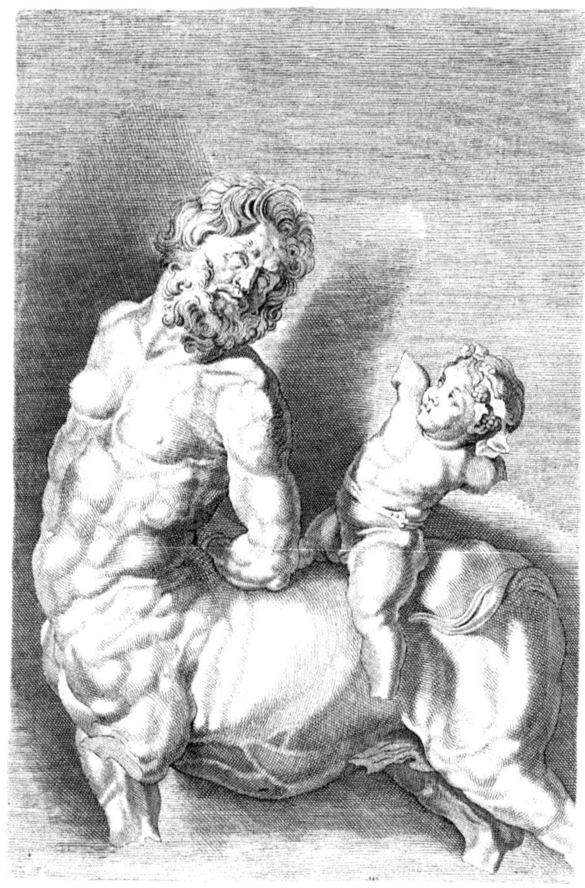

93

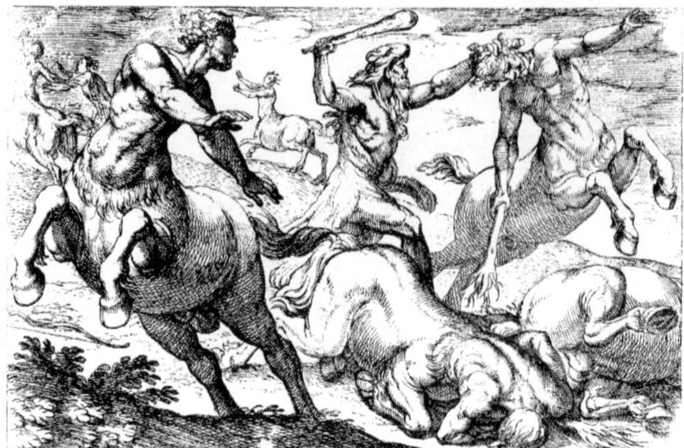

94

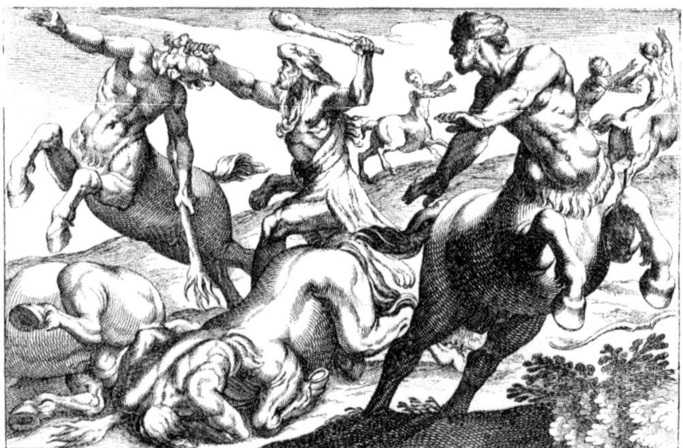

95

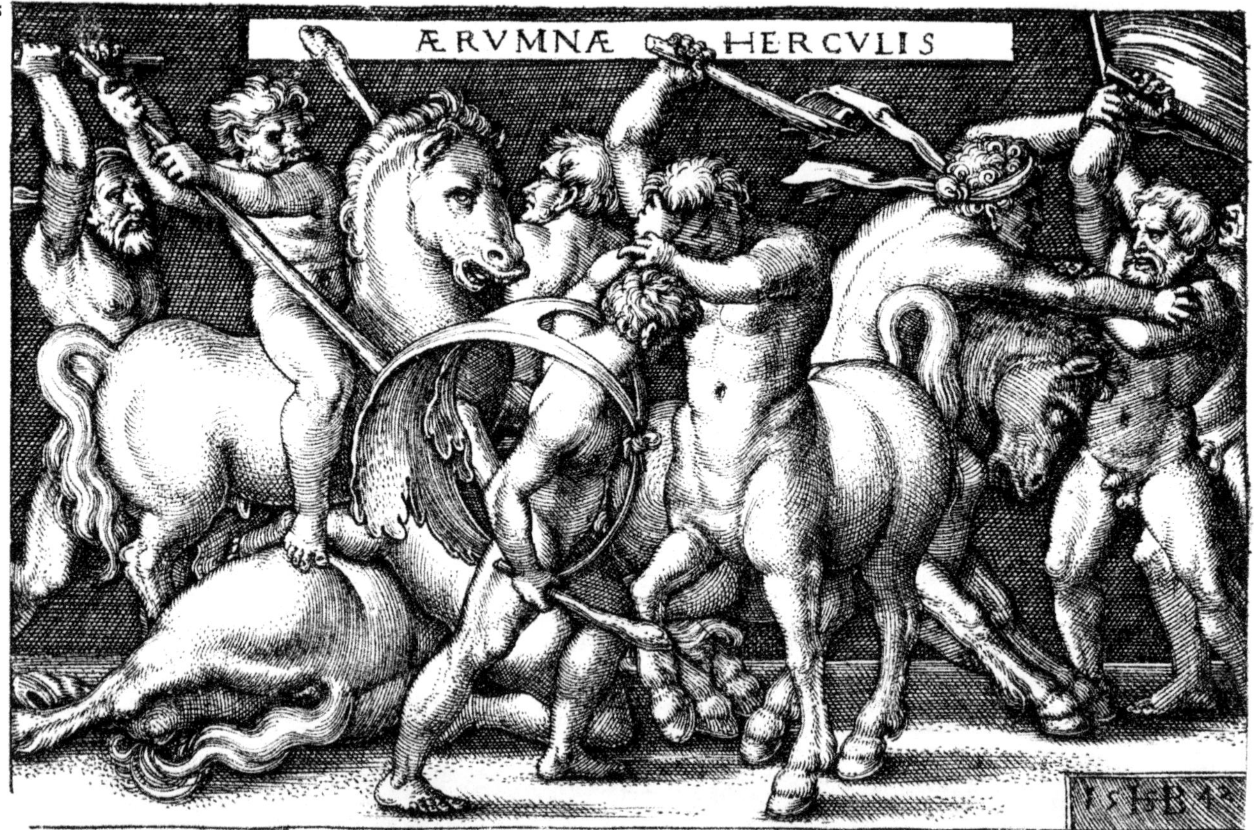

92: Antique statue 'The Tamed Centaur', Paulus Pontius, after Peter Paul Rubens, 1616 – 1657.

93: Hercules and the Centaurs, Antonio Tempesta, 1608.

94: Hercules fighting the centaurs, Simon Frisius, after Antonio Tempesta, 1610 – 1664.

95: Hercules Fighting Centaurs, Hans Sebald Beham, 1542.

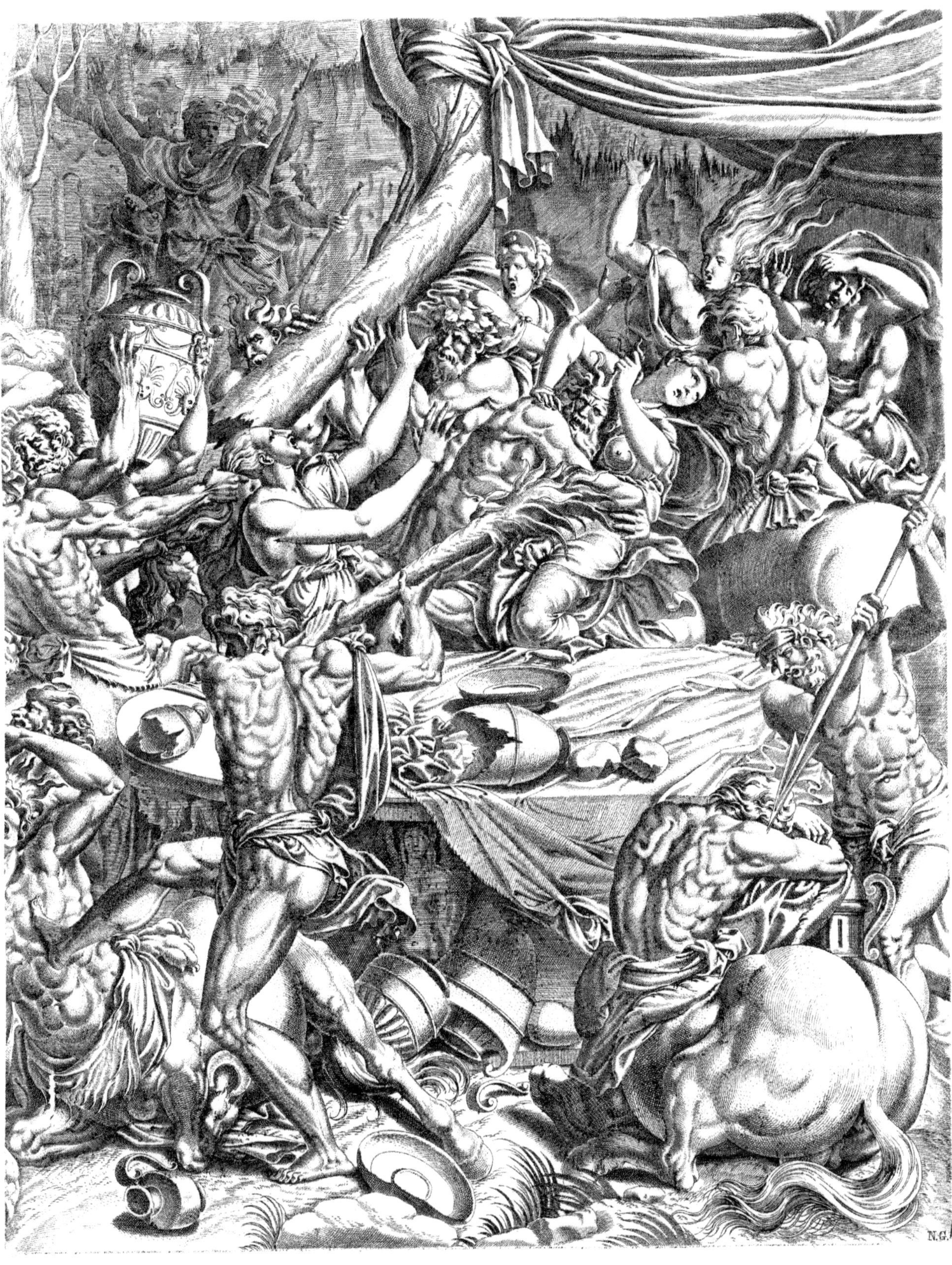

96: Battle between the Lapiths and Centaurs,
right part, Cornelis Bos, after Luca Penni, 1550.

97

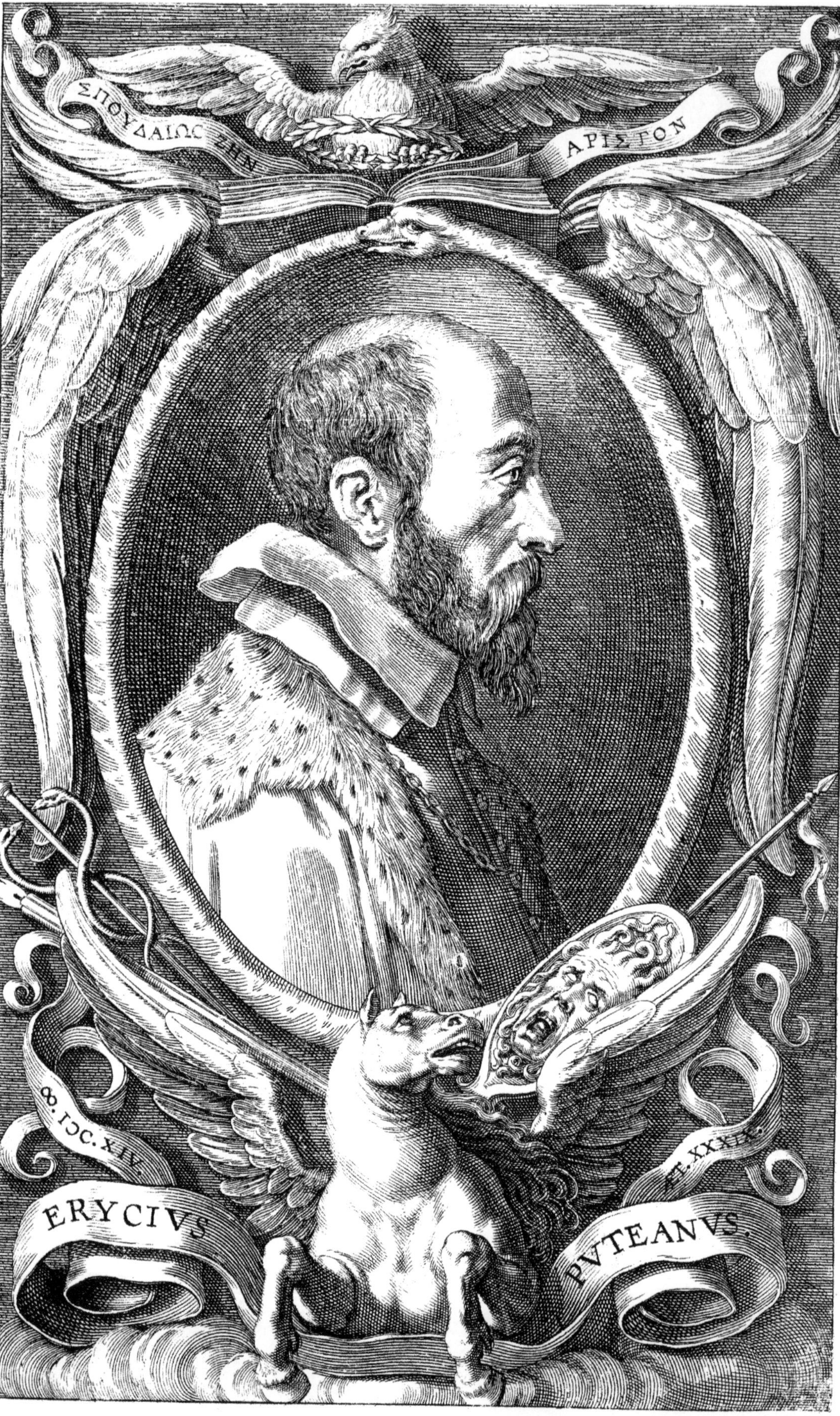

97: Portrait of Erycius Puteanus, Pieter de Jode (I), 1590 – 1632.

98

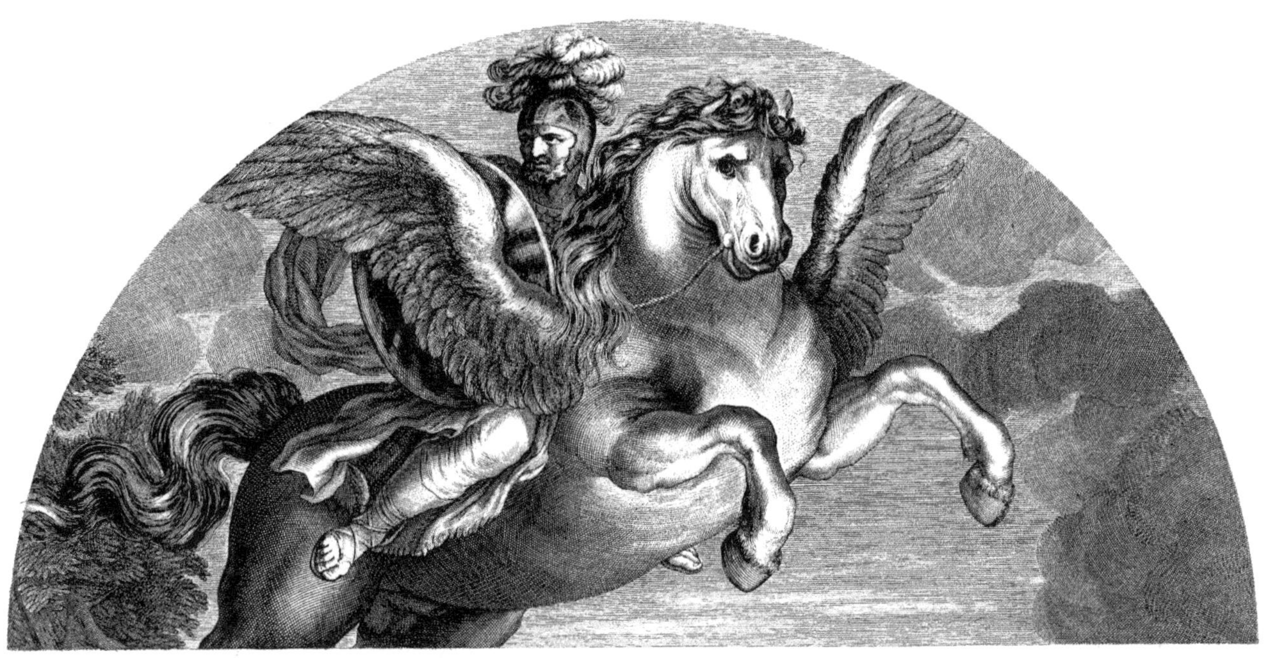

99

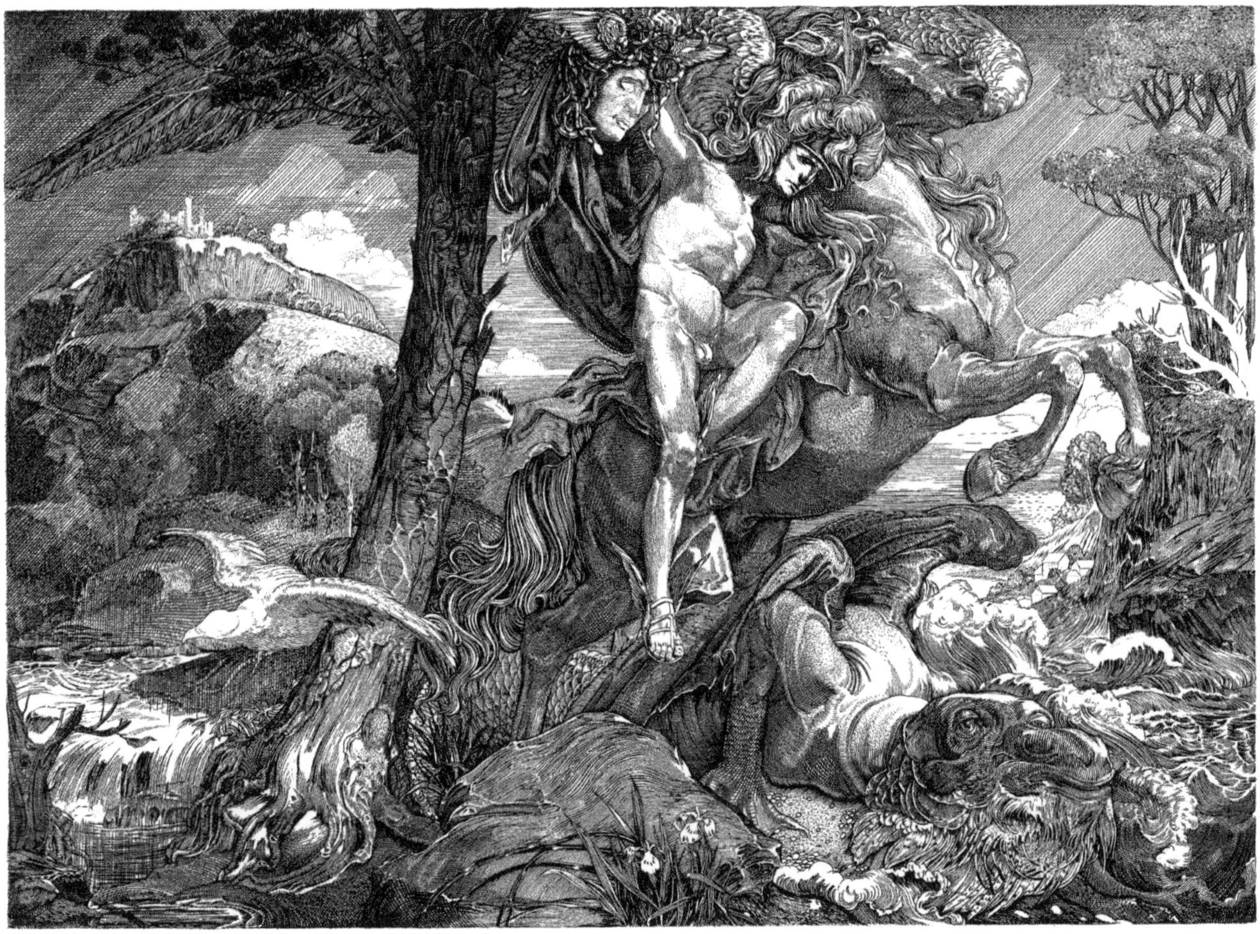

98: Perseus op Pegasus, Charles de La Haye, after Pietro da Cortona, 1651 – 1691.

99: Perseus and the Sea Monster, Johannes Josephus Aarts, 1907.

100

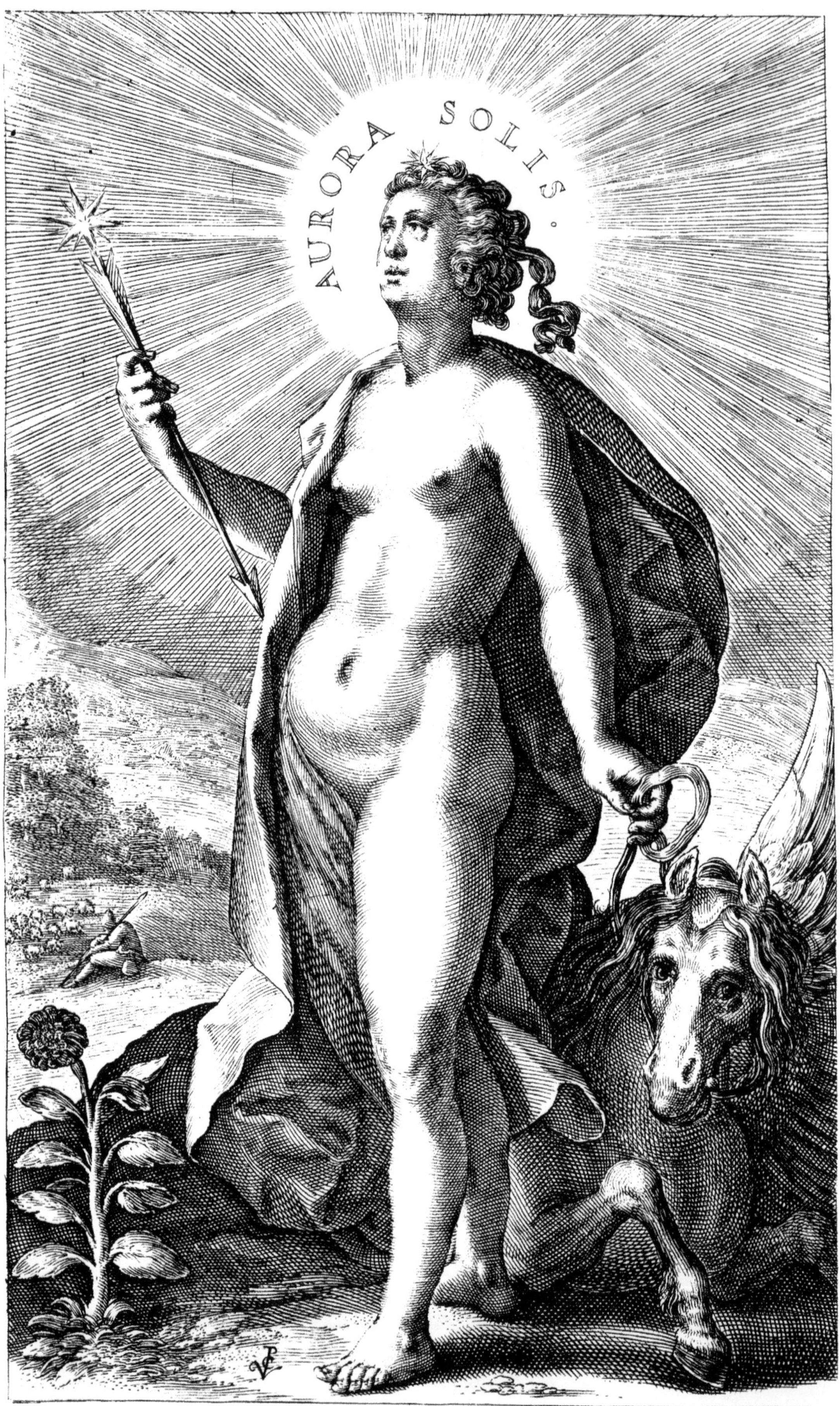

100: Morning, Crispijn van de Passe (I), 1611
– 1637.

101

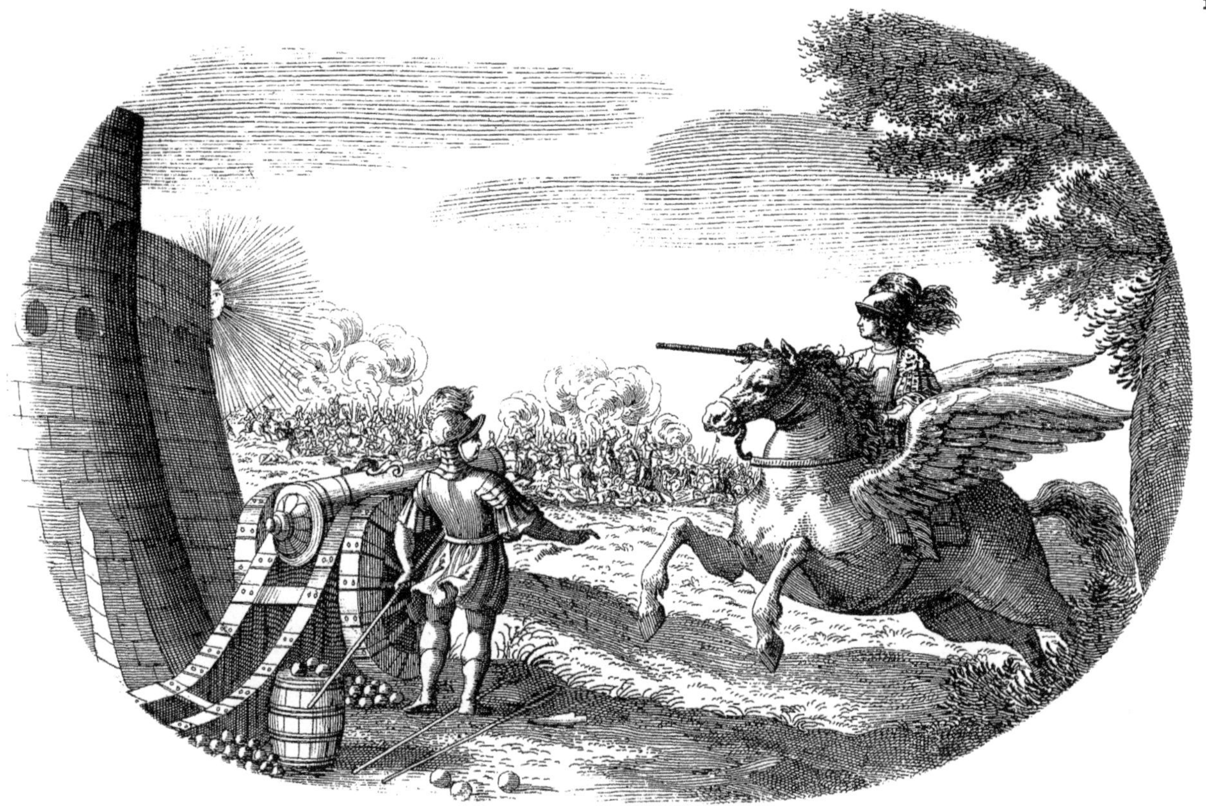

102

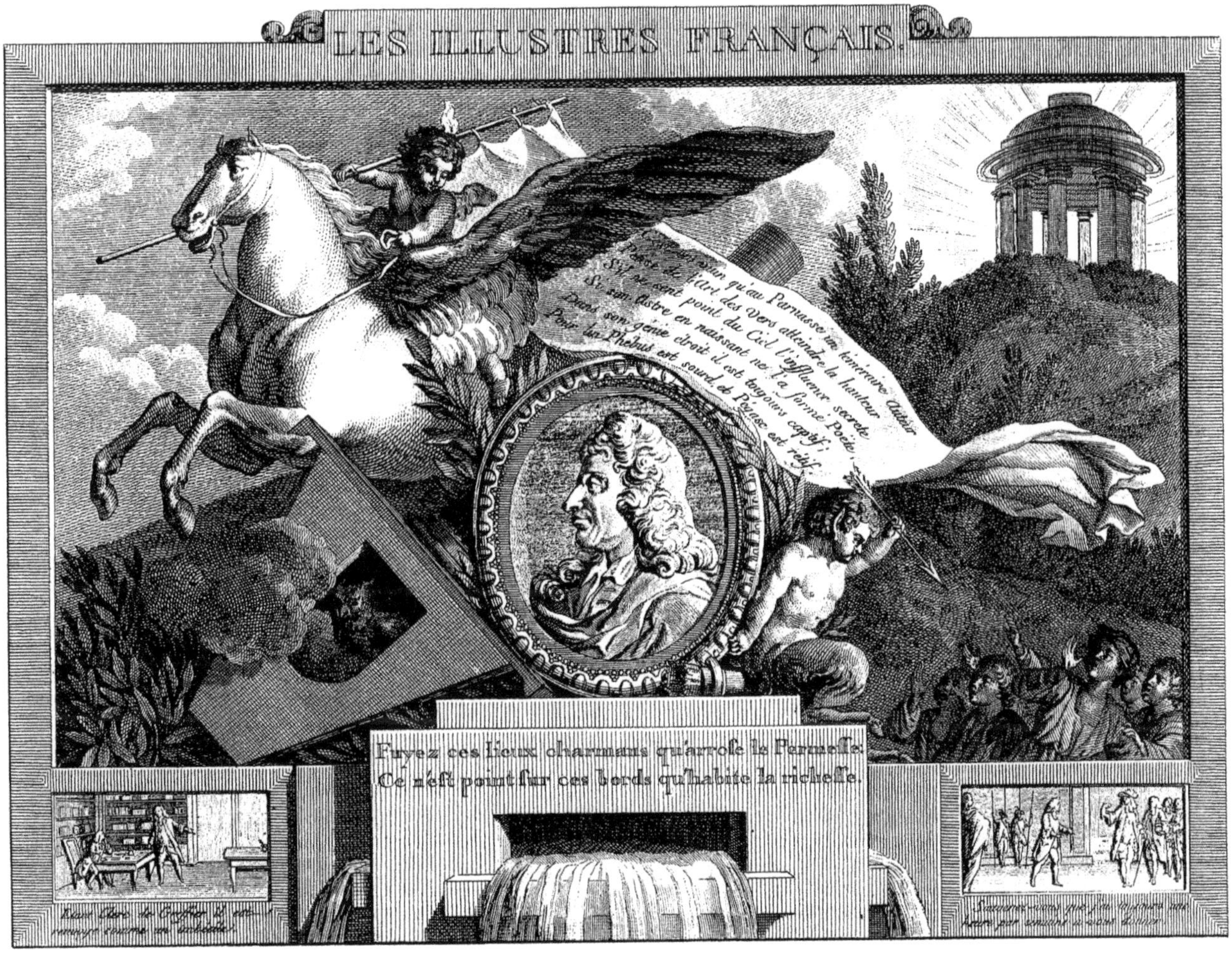

101: Time verse on the year 1704 and the battle of Höchstädt, anonymous, 1704.

102: An Allegorical portrait of Nicolas Boileau, Nicolas Ponce, after Clément Pierre Marillier, 1790 – 1816.

103

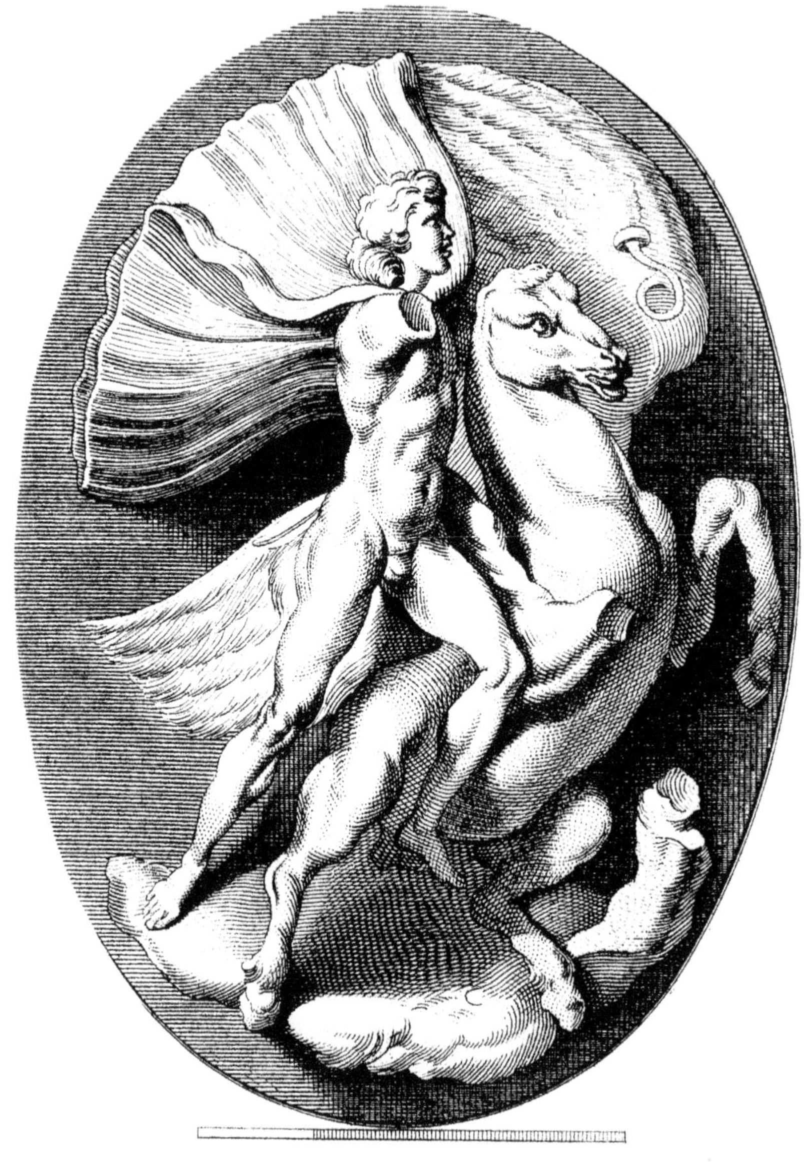

104

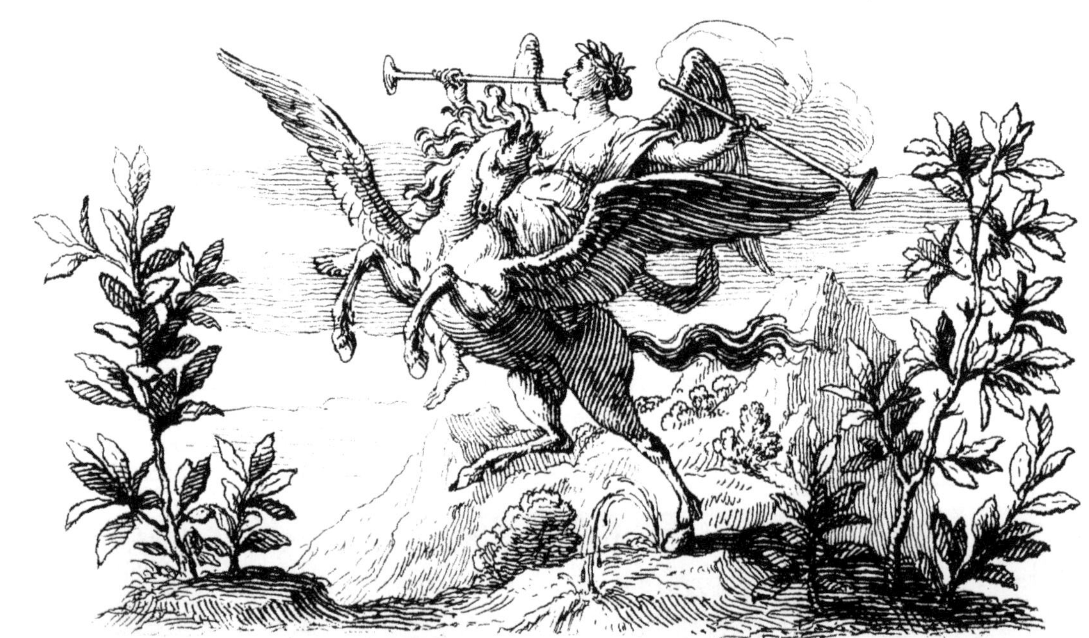

103: Camee met Perseus en Pegasus, anonymous, 1771 – 1822.

104: Fame worn by Pegasus, Bernard Picart, 1721.

105

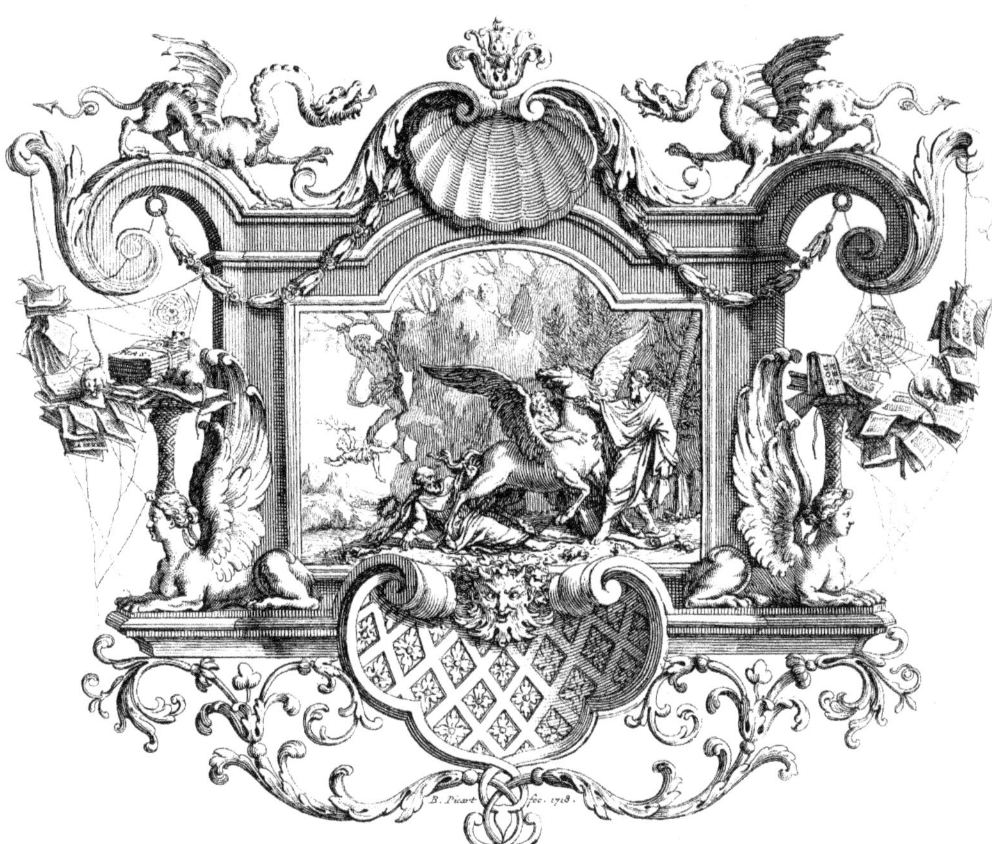

106

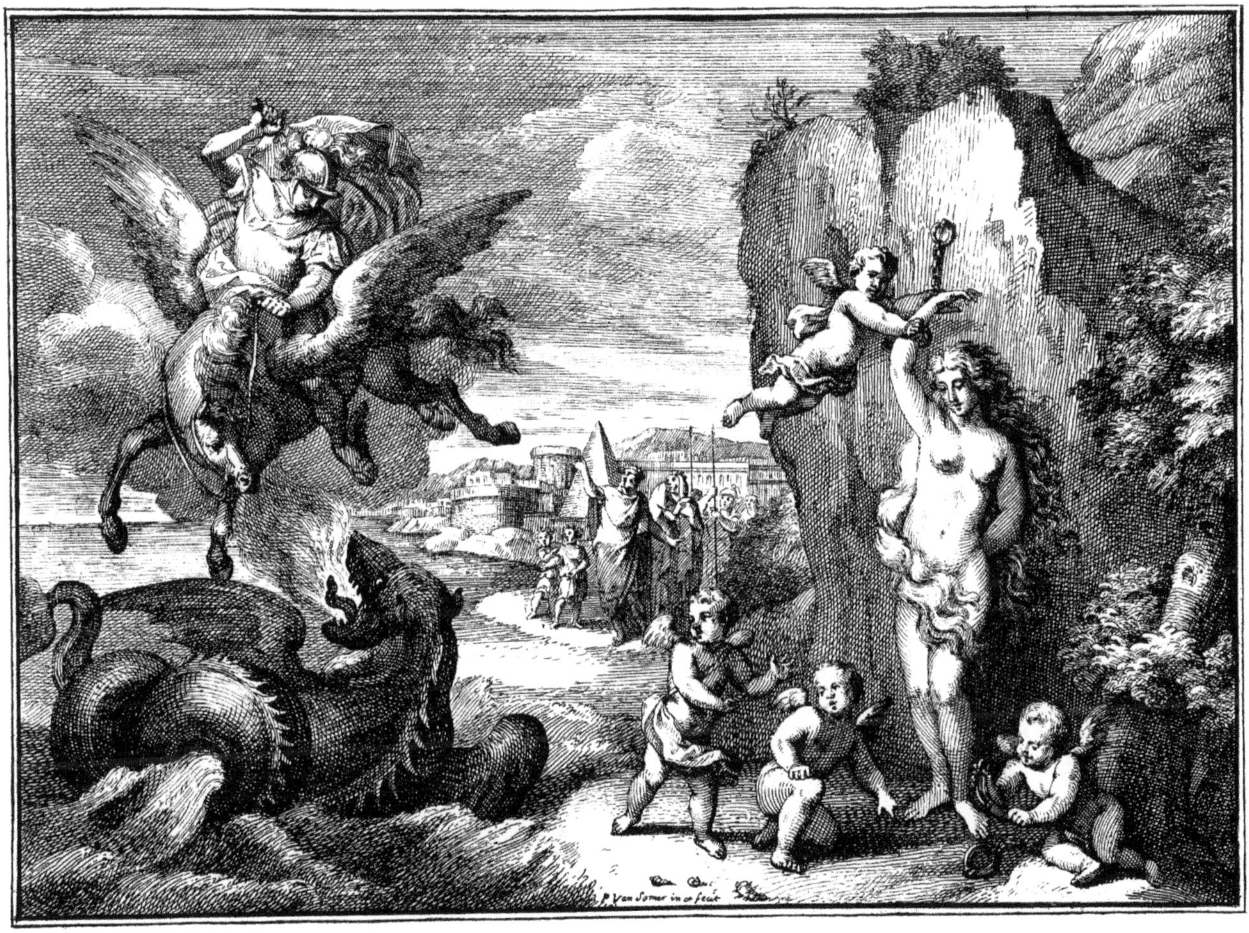

105: Restraining Pegasus, Bernard Picart, 1718.

106: Perseus and Andromeda, Paul van Somer (II), 1670 – 1697.

107

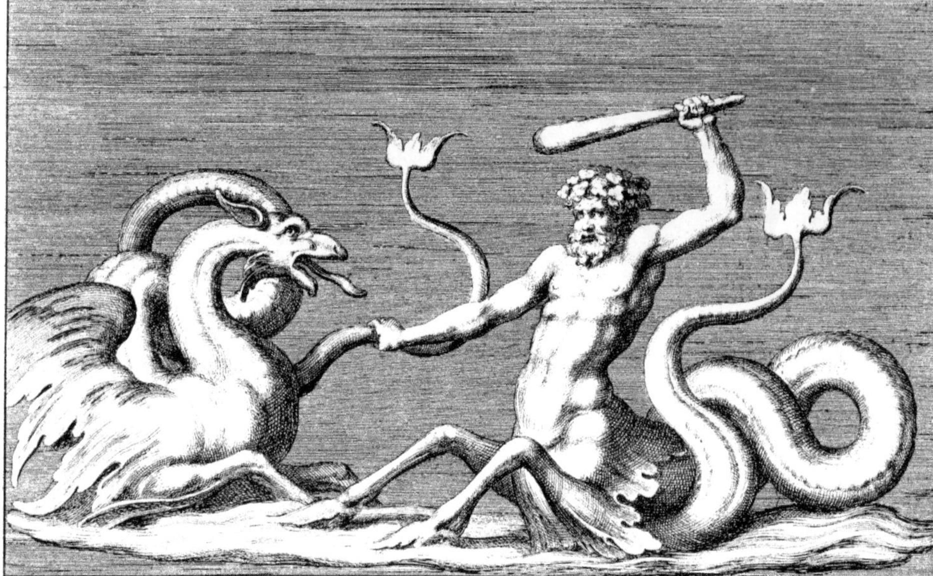

108

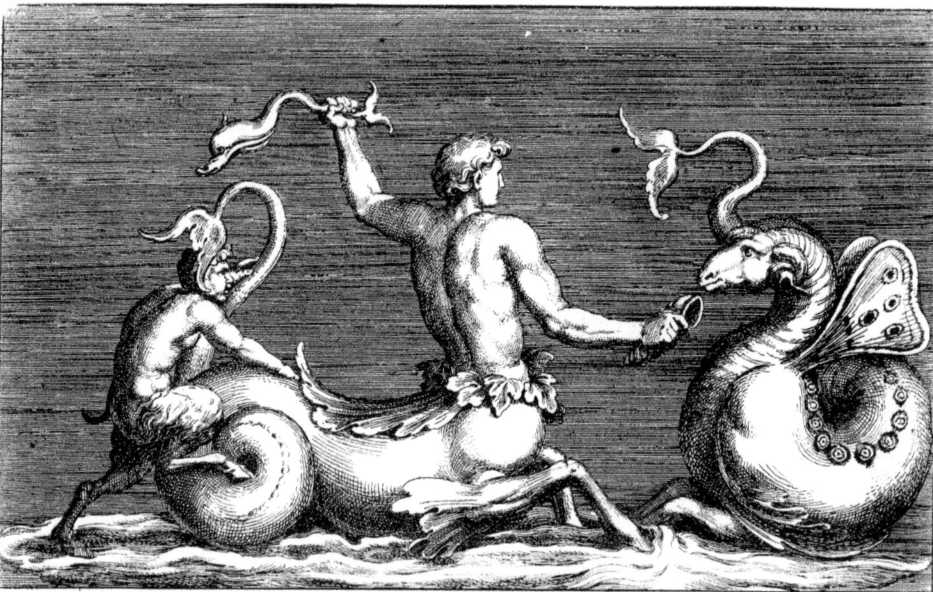

109

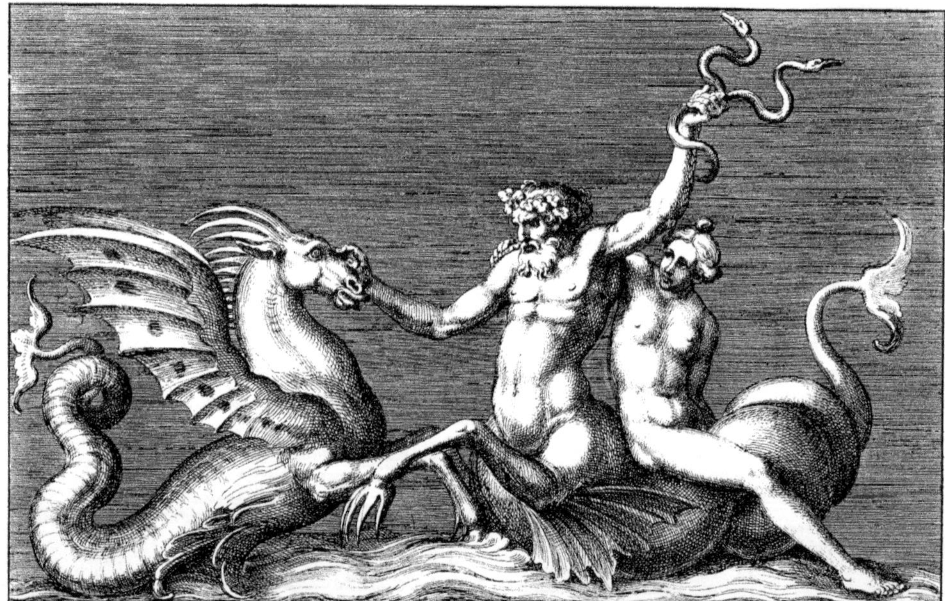

107: Triton fighting a sea monster, Pietro Sante Bartoli, after Rafaël, 1645 – 1700.

108: Triton fighting a sea monster, Pietro Sante Bartoli, after Rafaël, 1645 – 1700.

109: Triton fighting a sea monster, Pietro Sante Bartoli, after Rafaël, 1645 – 1700.

110

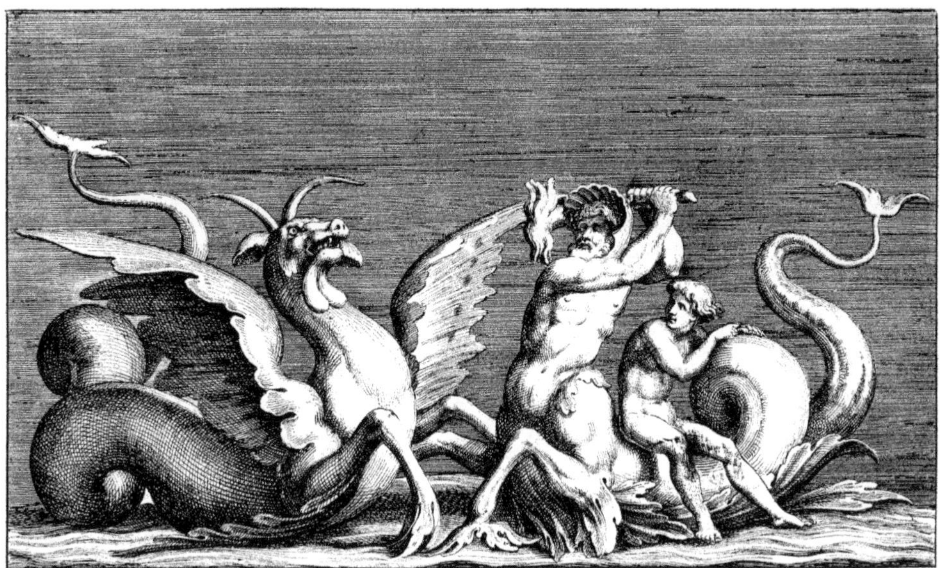

111

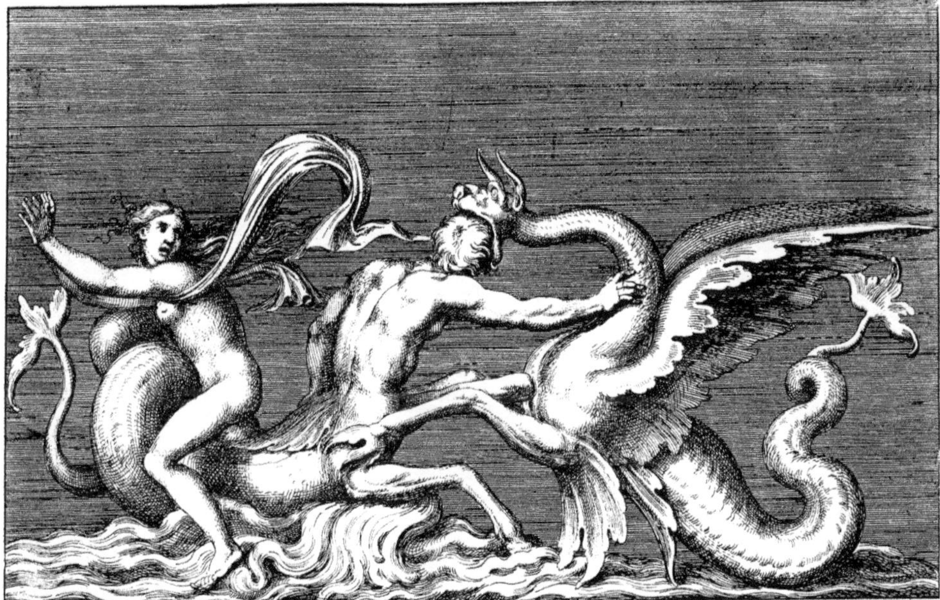

112

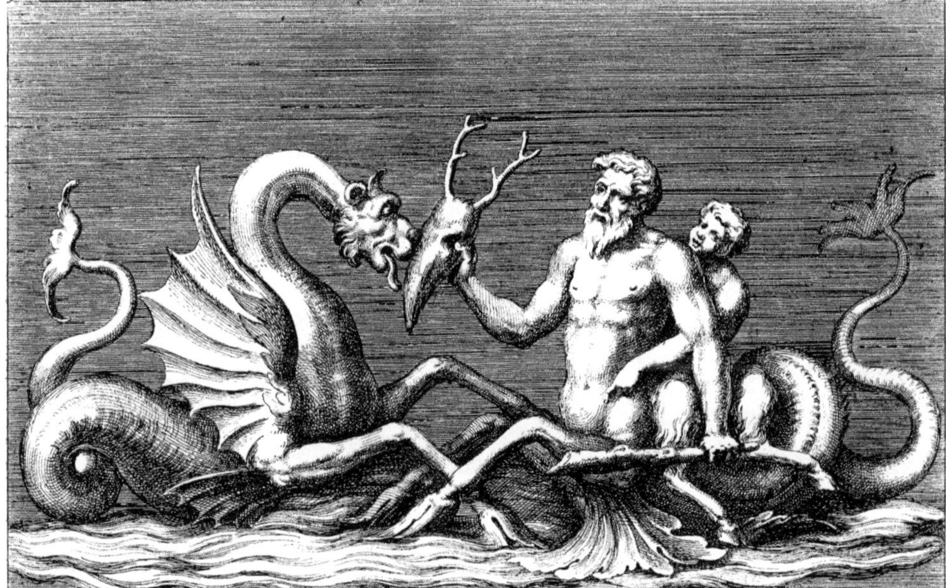

110: Triton fighting a sea monster, Pietro Sante Bartoli, after Rafaël, 1645 – 1700.

111: Triton fighting a sea monster, Pietro Sante Bartoli, after Rafaël, 1645 – 1700.

112: Triton fighting a sea monster, Pietro Sante Bartoli, after Rafaël, 1645 – 1700.

113

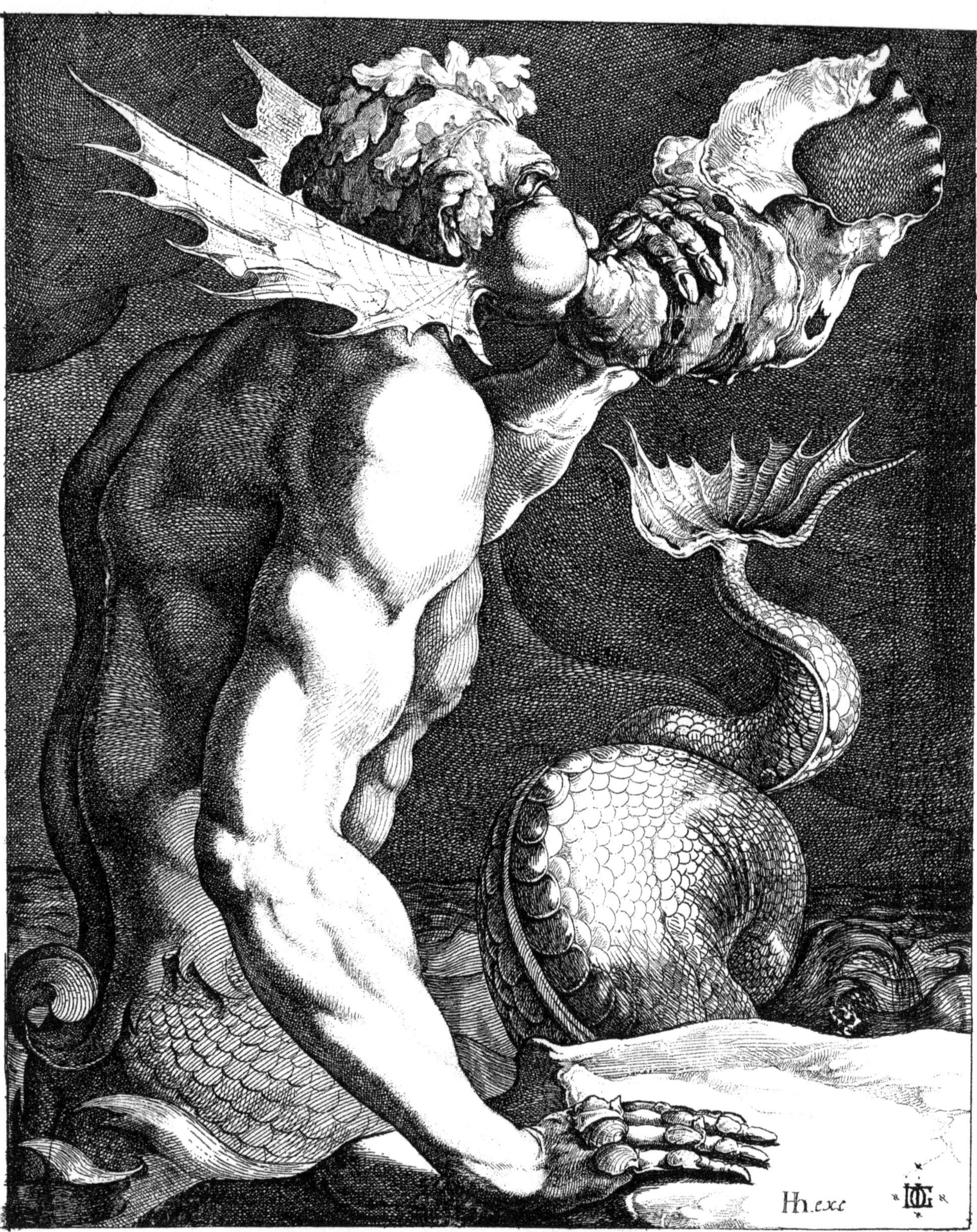

113: A triton blowing on a shell, Jacob de Gheyn
(III), 1616 – 1620.

114

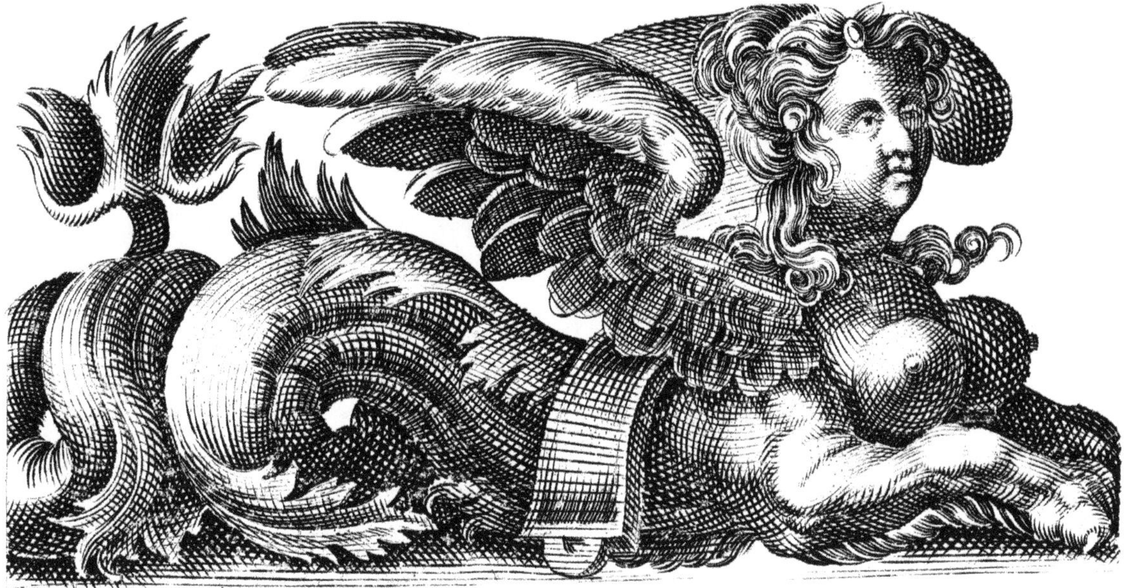

115

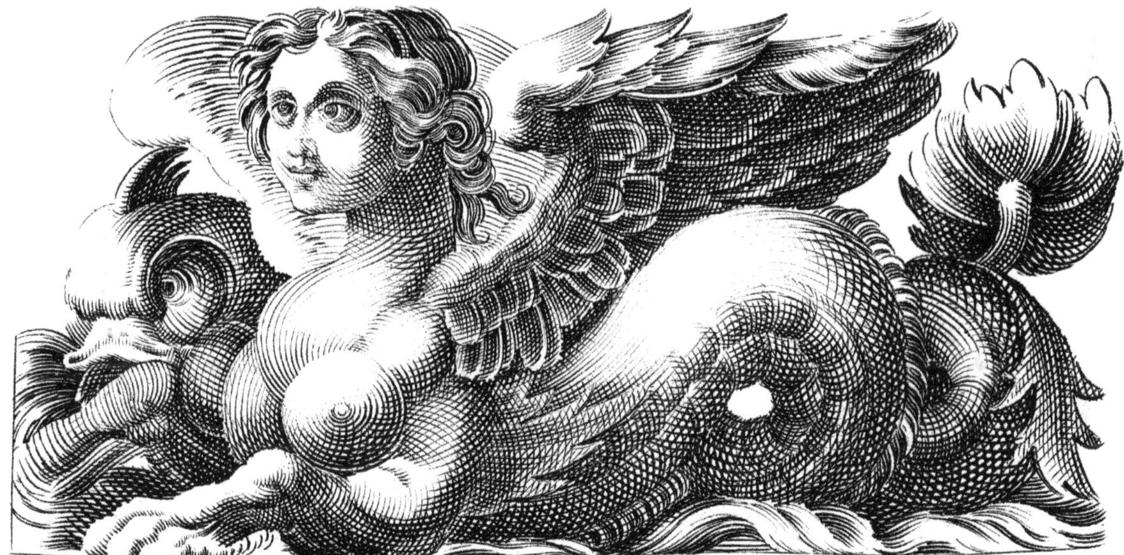

116

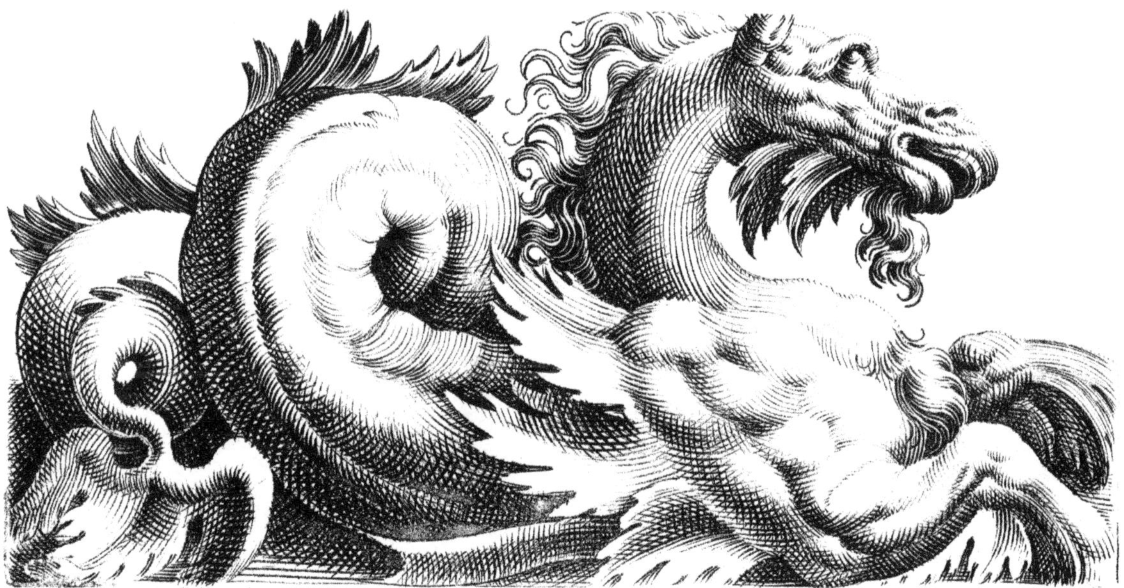

114: Sphinx with a fish tail and a sort of saddle on the back, Adam Fuchs, after Giovanni Andrea Maglioli, c. 1526–1606

115: Sphinx with a Fish Tail, Adam Fuchs, after Giovanni Andrea Maglioli, c. 1526–1606.

116: Seahorse with Leaf Fins and a Goatee, Giovanni Andrea Maglioli, 1580 – 1610.

117

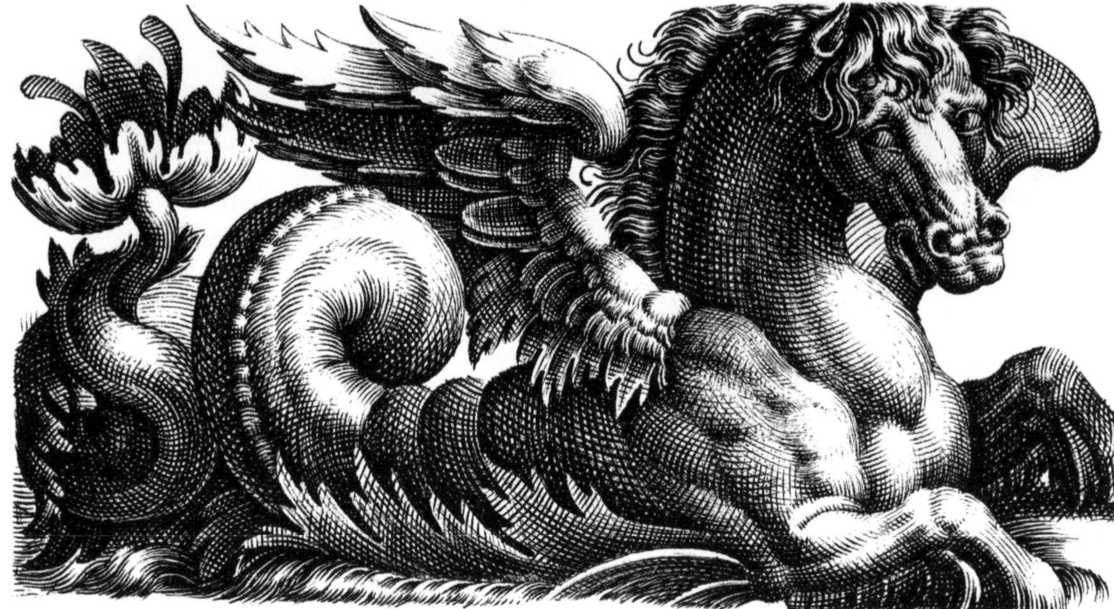

118

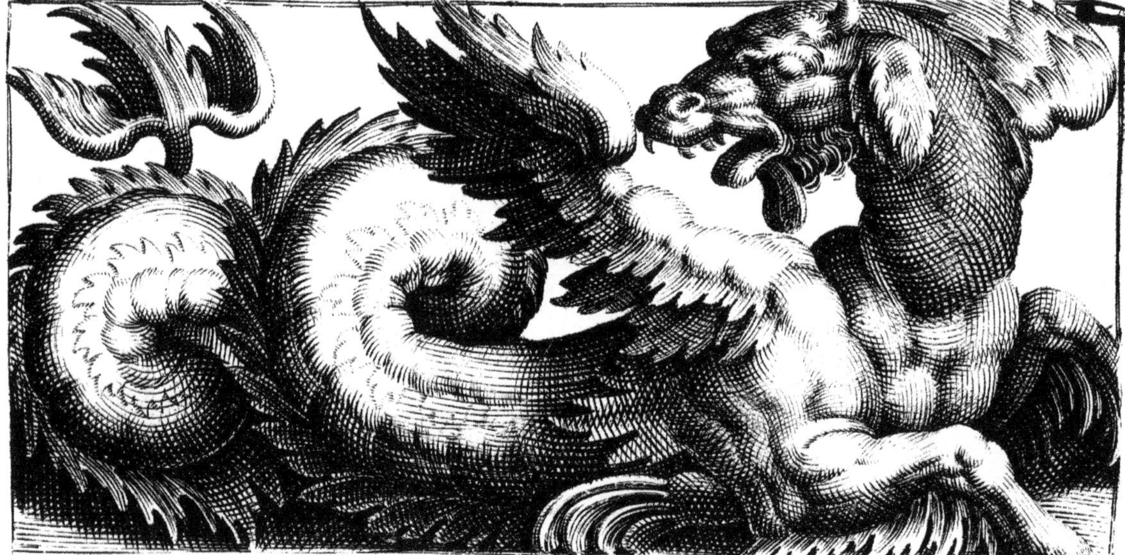

119

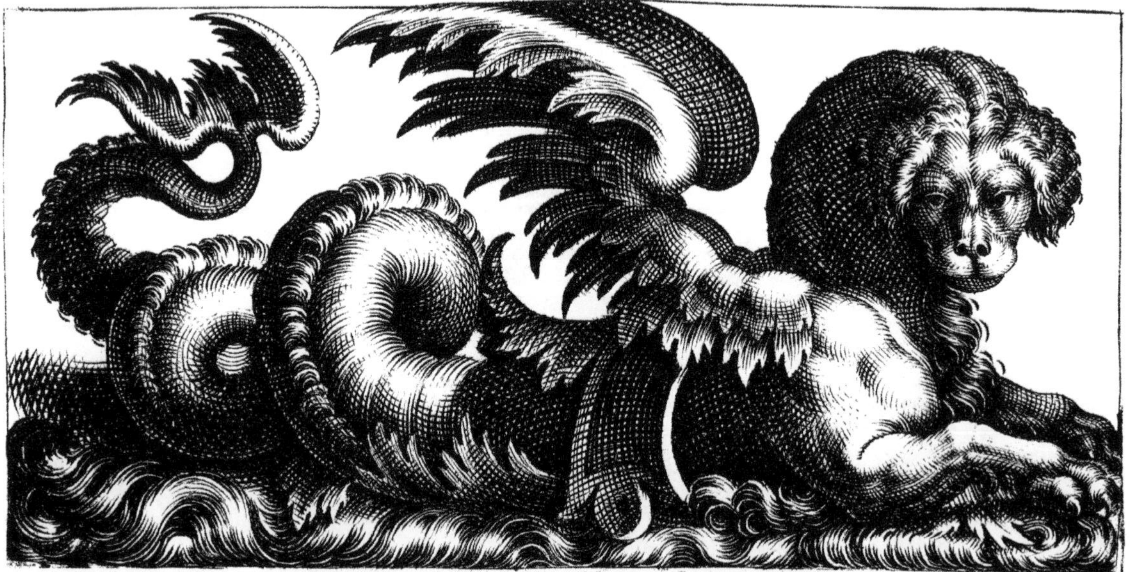

117: Winged seahorse with an open blade at the end of its tail from which two pistils protrude, Giovanni Andrea Maglioli, 1580 – 1610.

118: Winged Seal Looking Back, Giovanni Andrea Maglioli, 1580 – 1610.

119: Winged seal with a kind of saddle on its back, Giovanni Andrea Maglioli, 1580 – 1610.

120

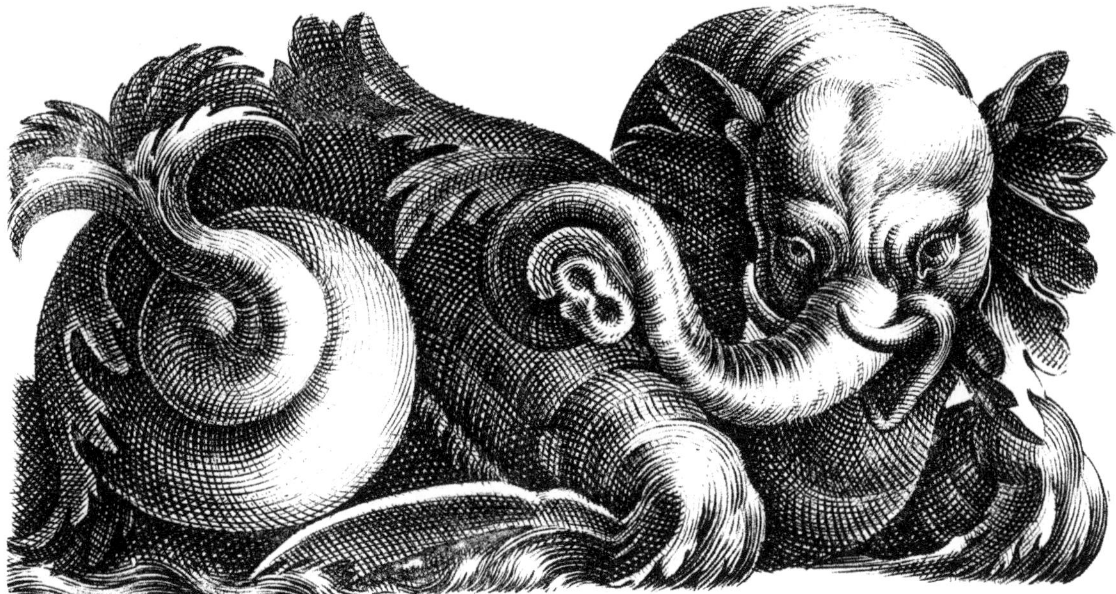

121

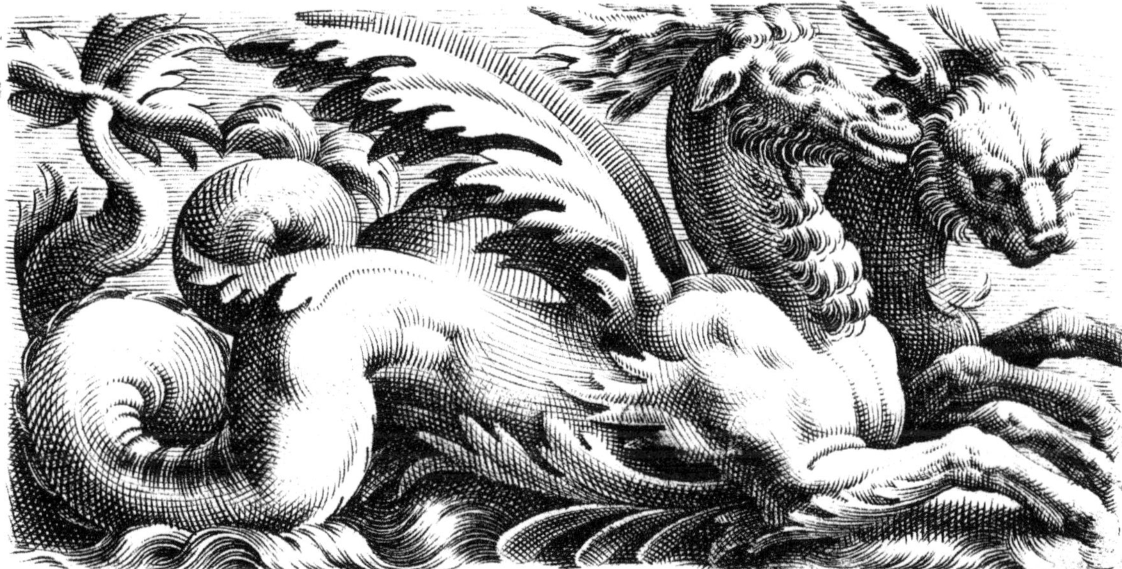

122

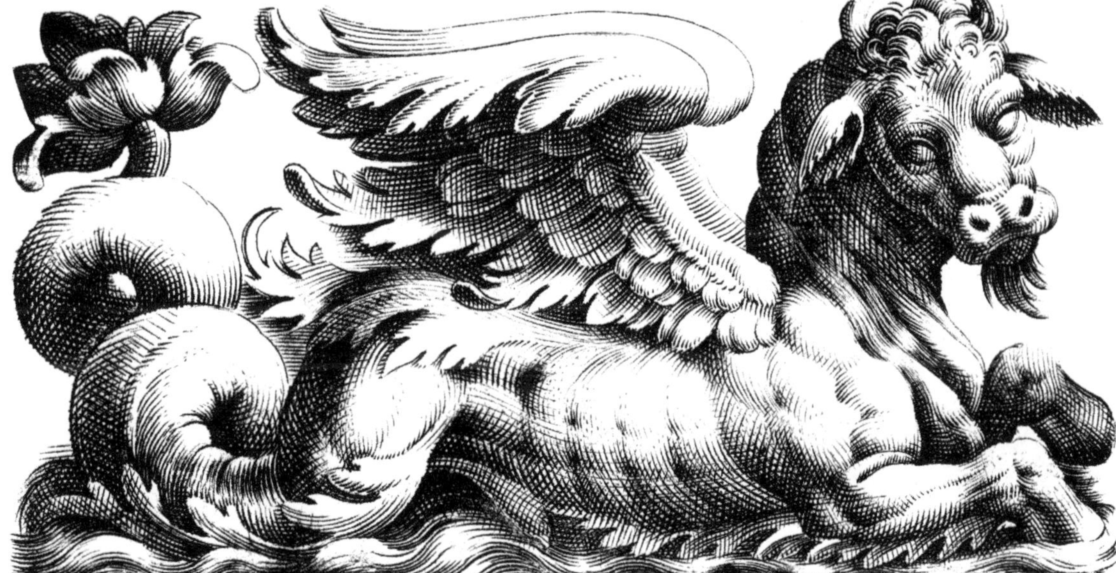

120: Sea elephant with ears made of leaves, Giovanni Andrea Maglioli, 1580 – 1610.

121: Two sea creatures side by side, Giovanni Andrea Maglioli, 1580 – 1610.

122: Winged sea bull with a goatee, Giovanni Andrea Maglioli, 1580 – 1610.

123

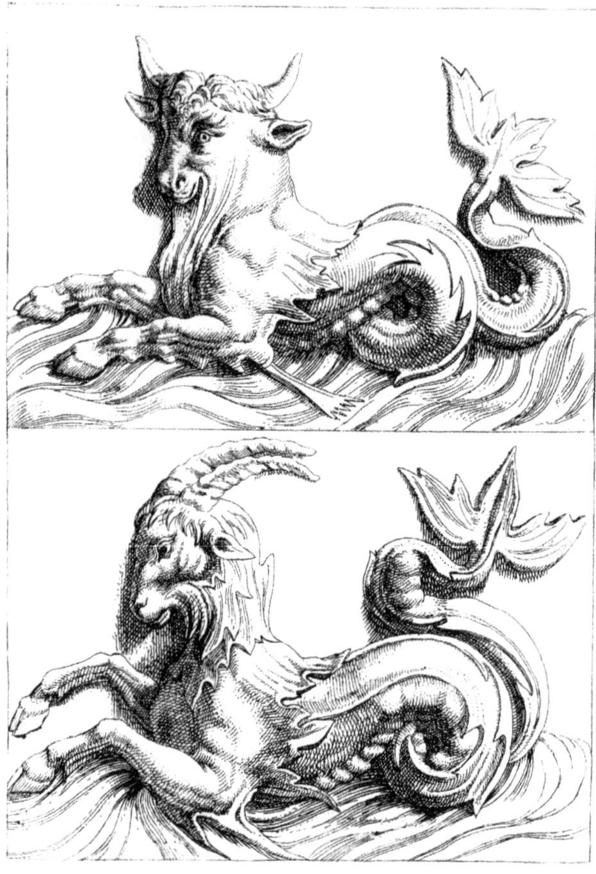

124

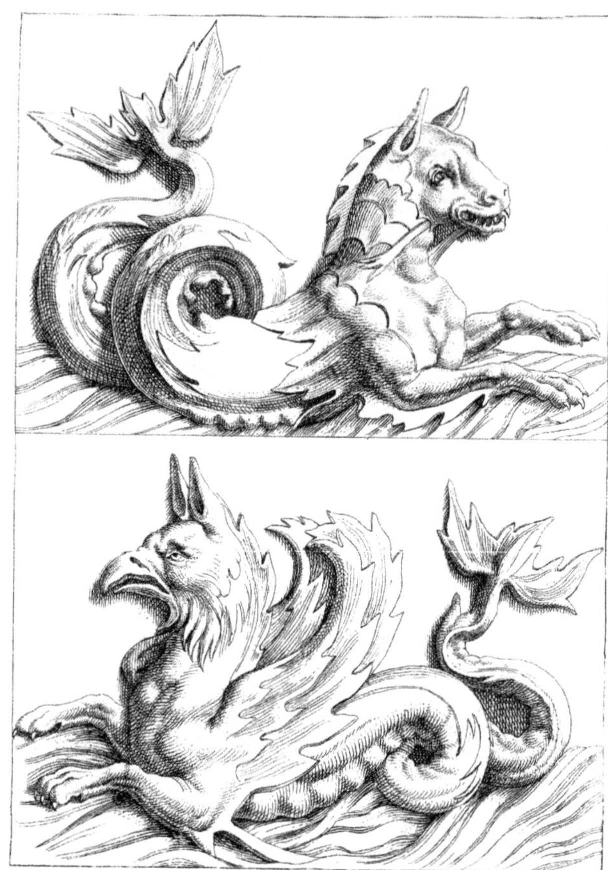

125

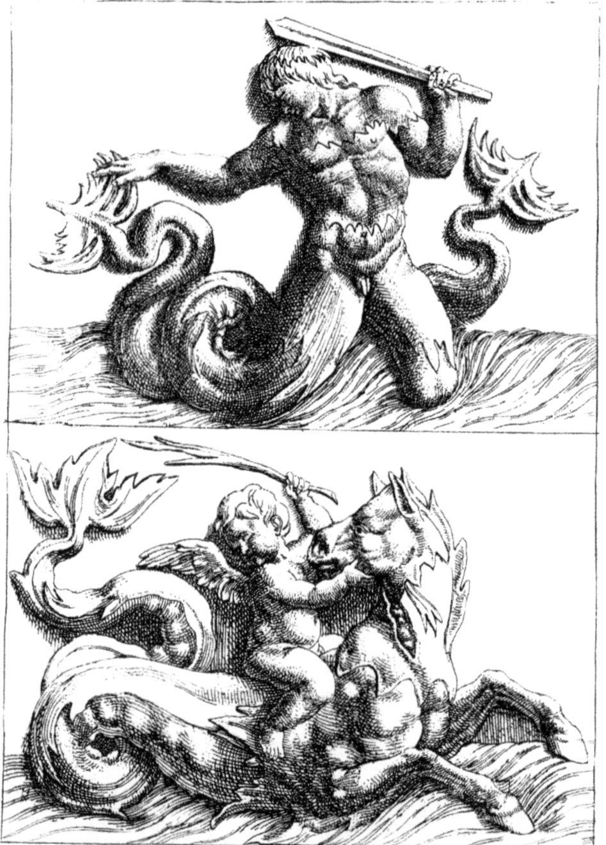

126

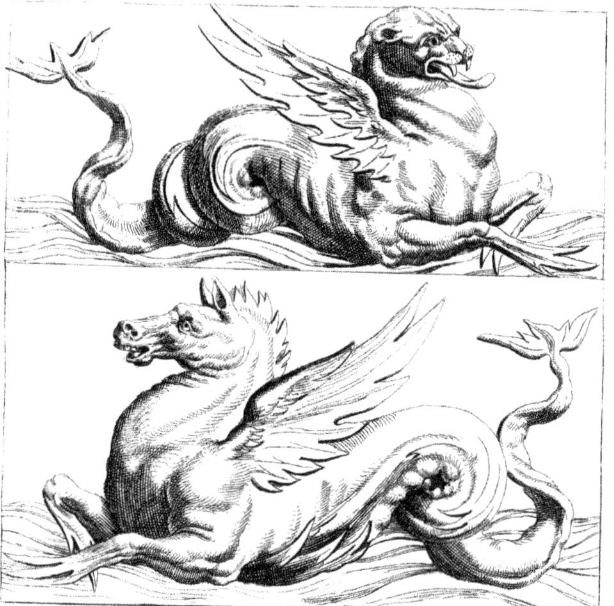

123: Sea bull and sea lamb, anonymous, c. 1688.

124: Two sea creatures, anonymous, c. 1688.

125: Triton and Cherub on Seahorse, anonymous, c. 1688

126: Sea leopard and sea horse, anonymous, c. 1688.

127

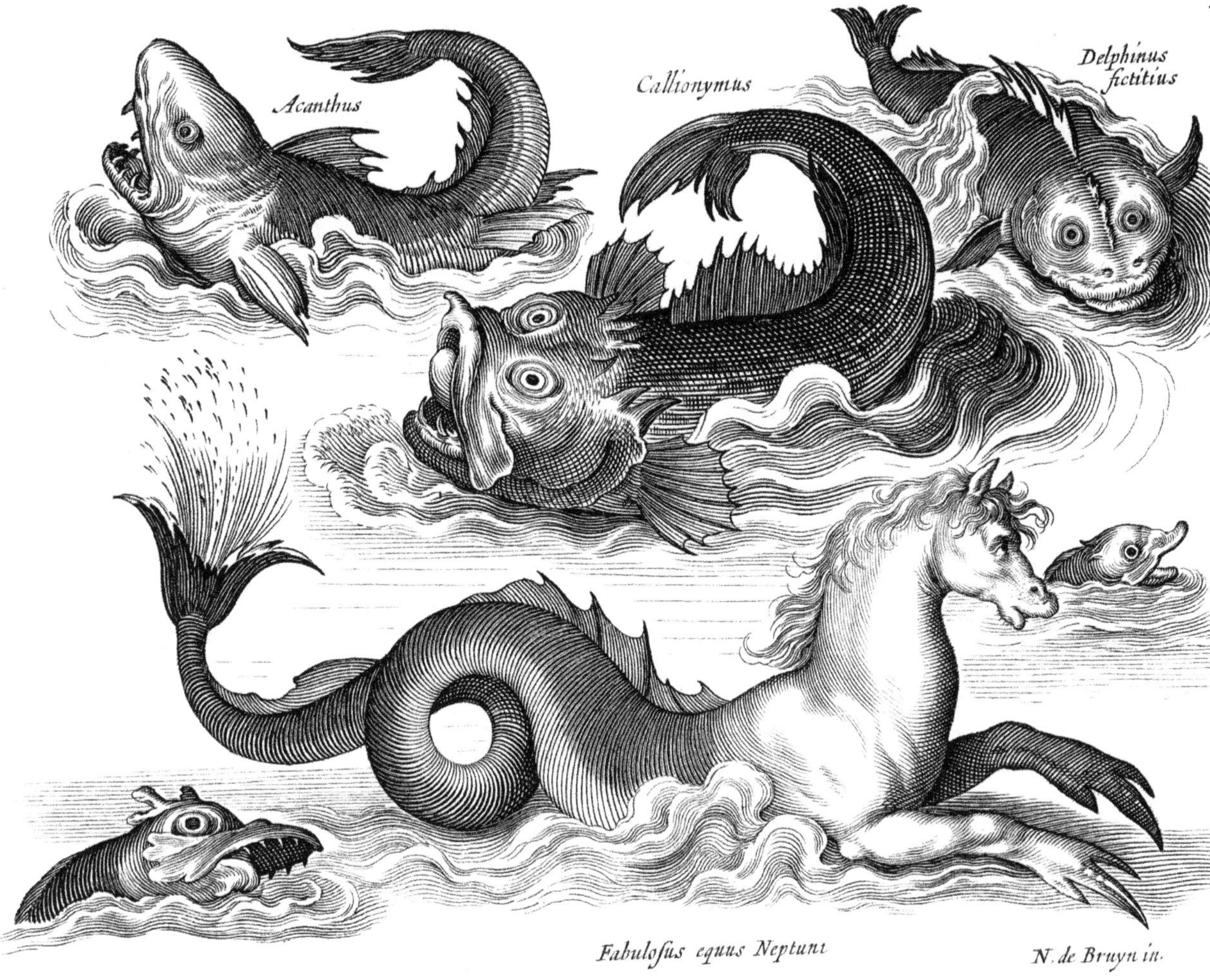

Acanthus

Callionymus

Delphinus fictitius

Fabulosus equus Neptuni

N. de Bruyn in.

128

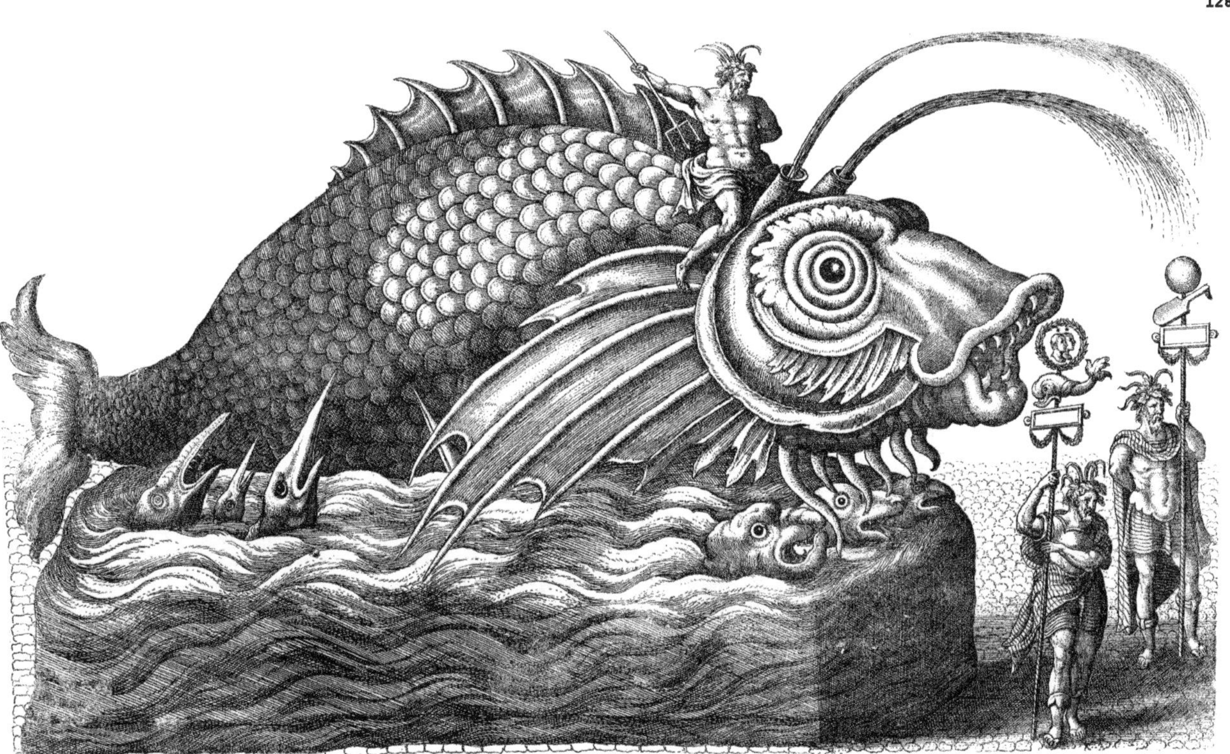

127: Fantastic aquatic animals, including sea horse, Nicolaes de Bruyn, 1581 – 1652.

128: Float with a sea monster, 1594, Pieter van der Borcht (I), 1594 – 1595.

129

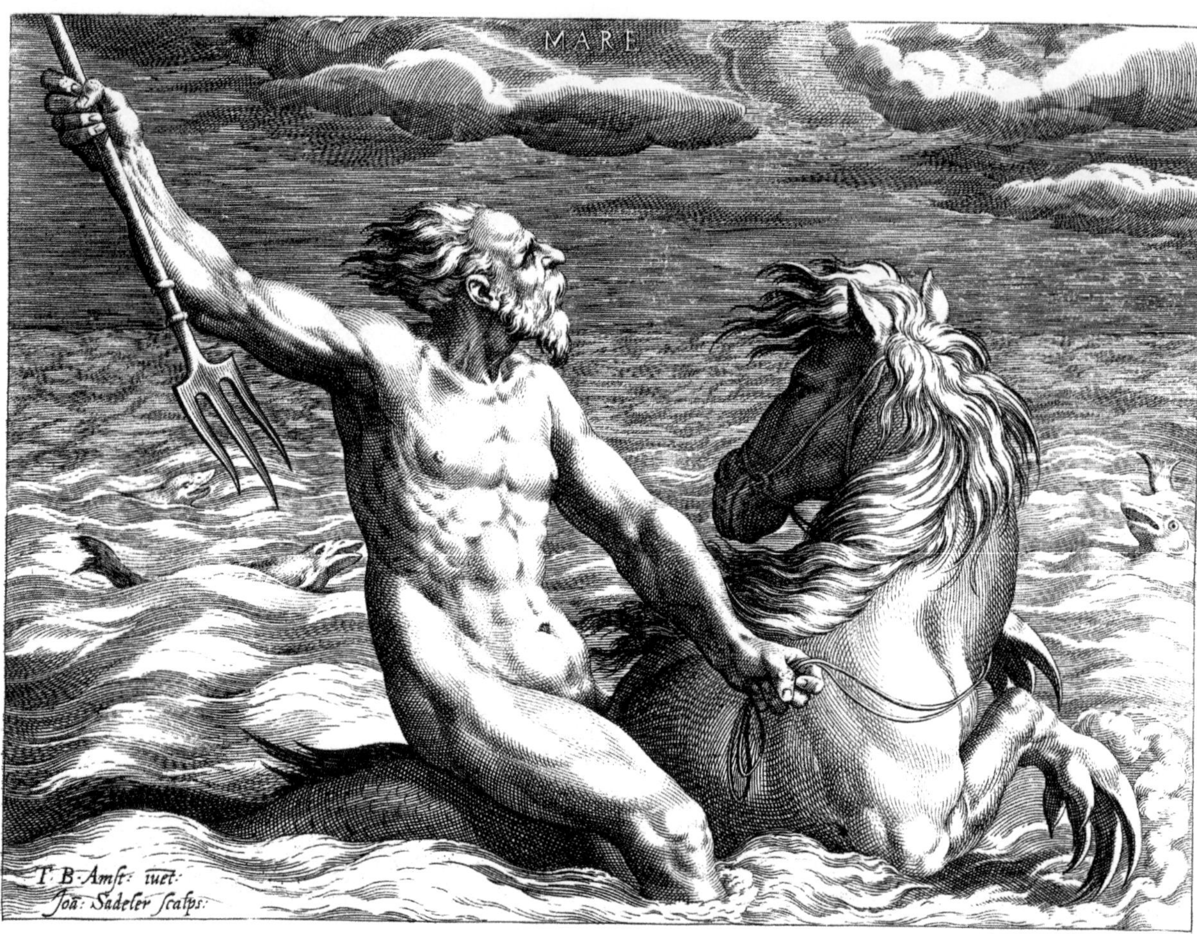

130

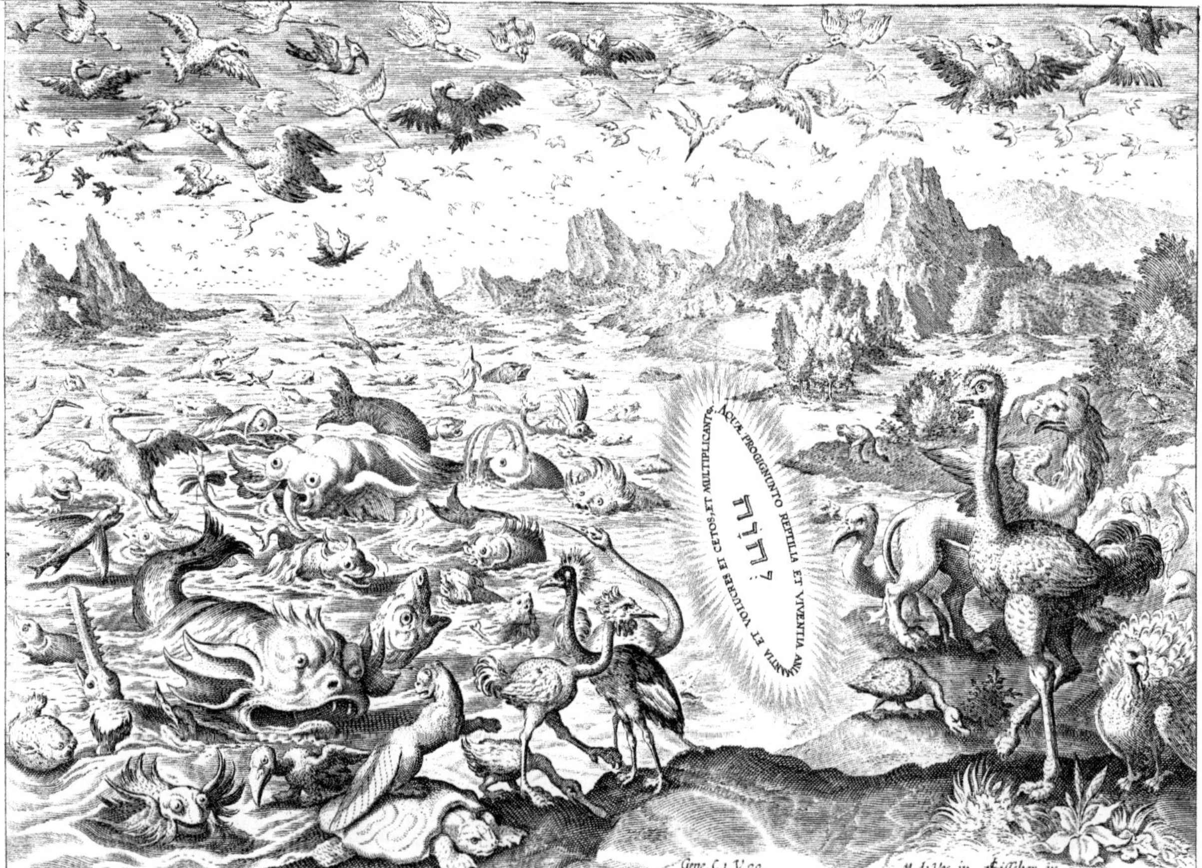

129: Water personified by the god Neptune, Johann Sadeler (I), after Dirck Barendsz., 1587.

130: Creation of Birds and Sea Creatures, Johann Sadeler (I), after Maerten de Vos, 1639.

131

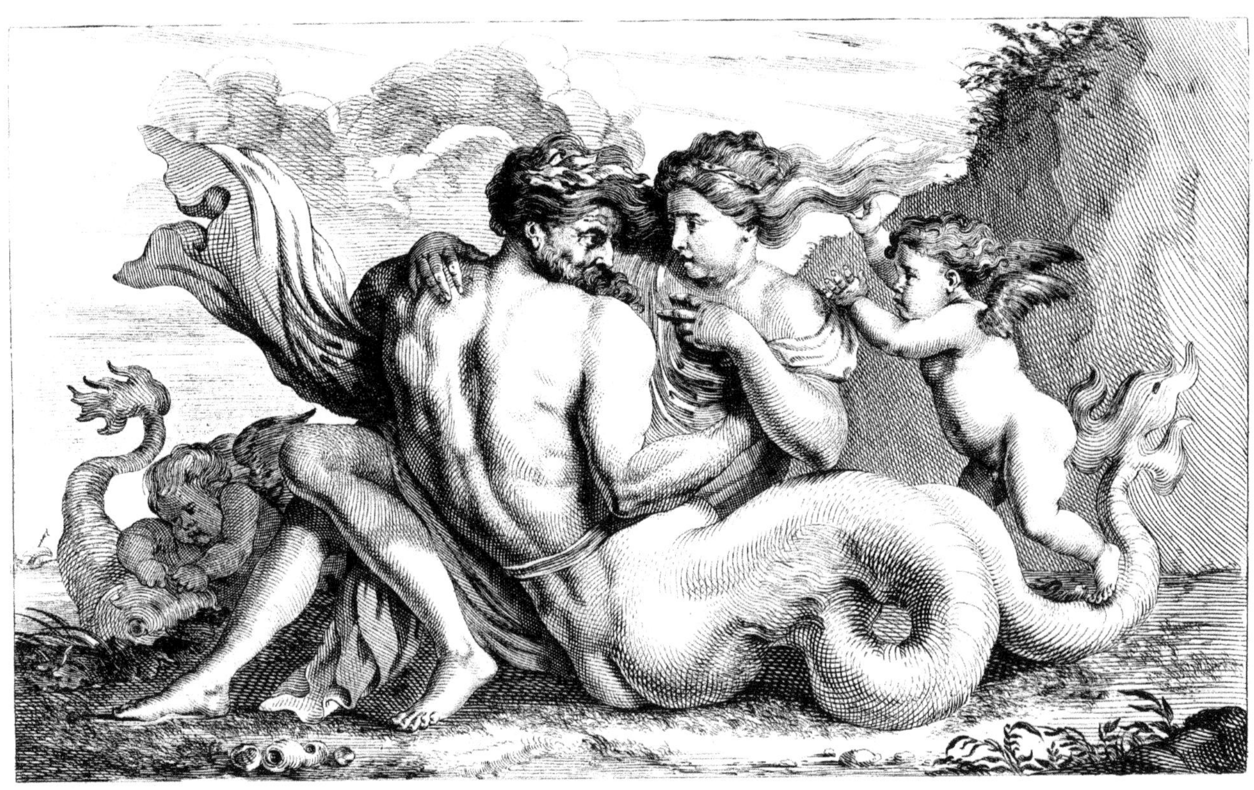

132

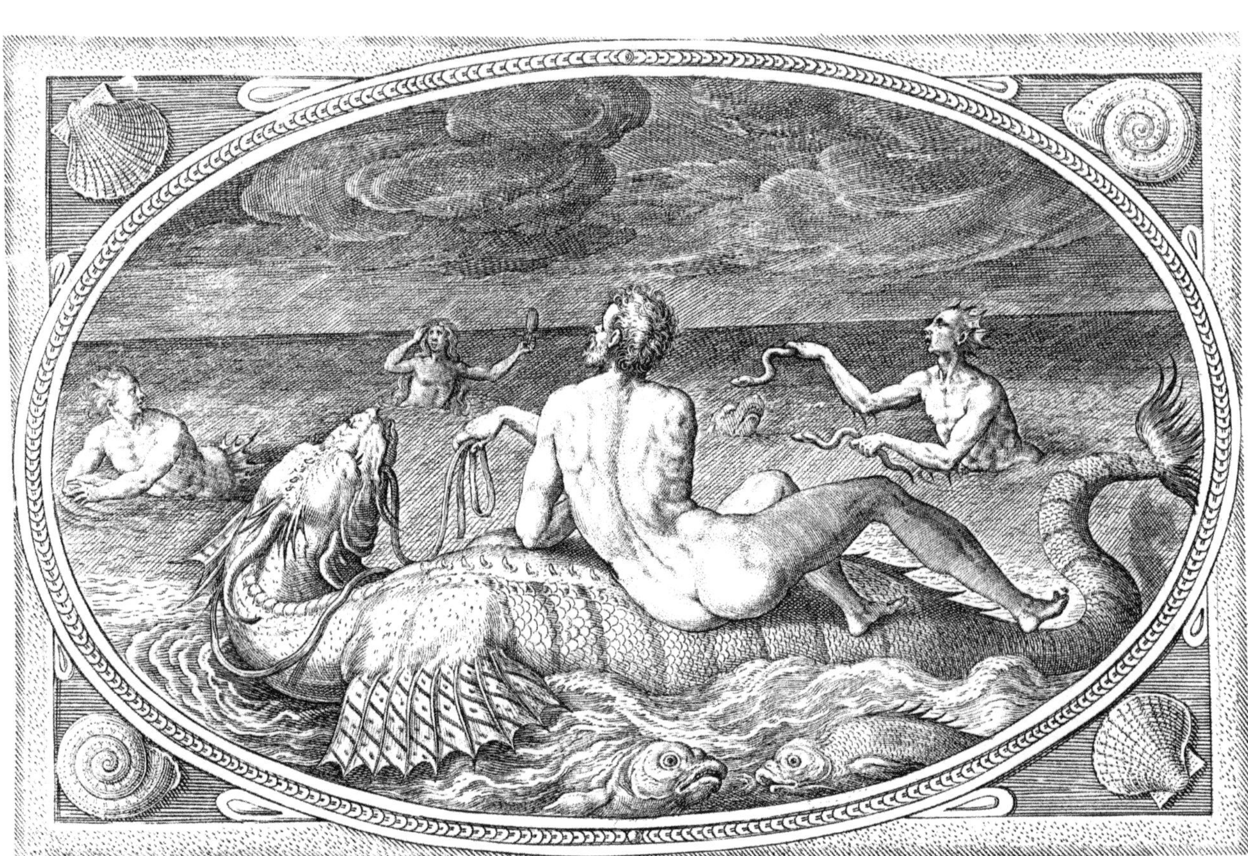

131: Siren and triton, Theodorus van Kessel, after Peter Paul Rubens, 1630 – 1660.

132: Acis on a fish, Adriaen Collaert, after Philips Galle, 1570 – 1618.

133

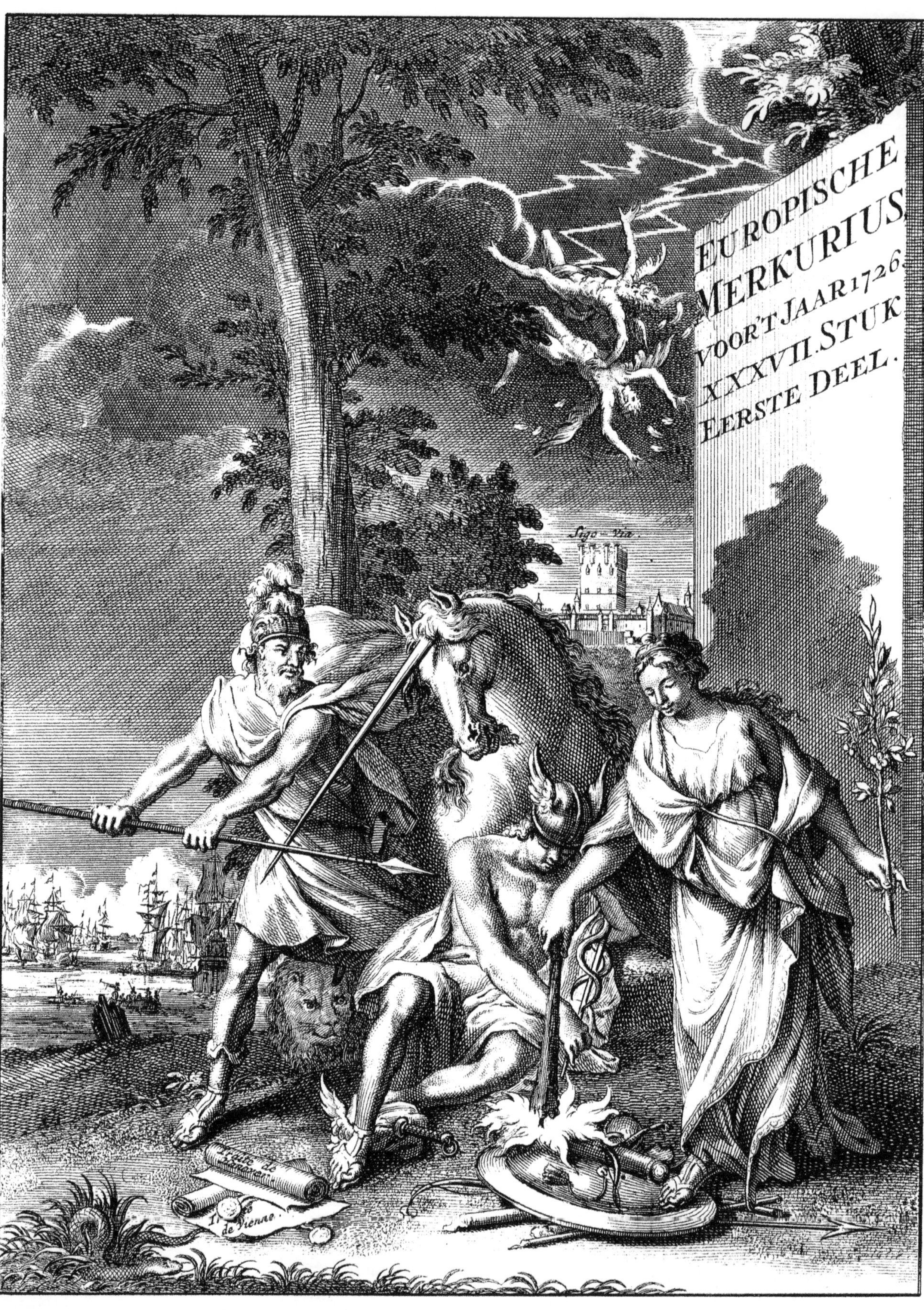

133: Dream of Mercury with Unicorn and Peace, anonymous, 1726.

134

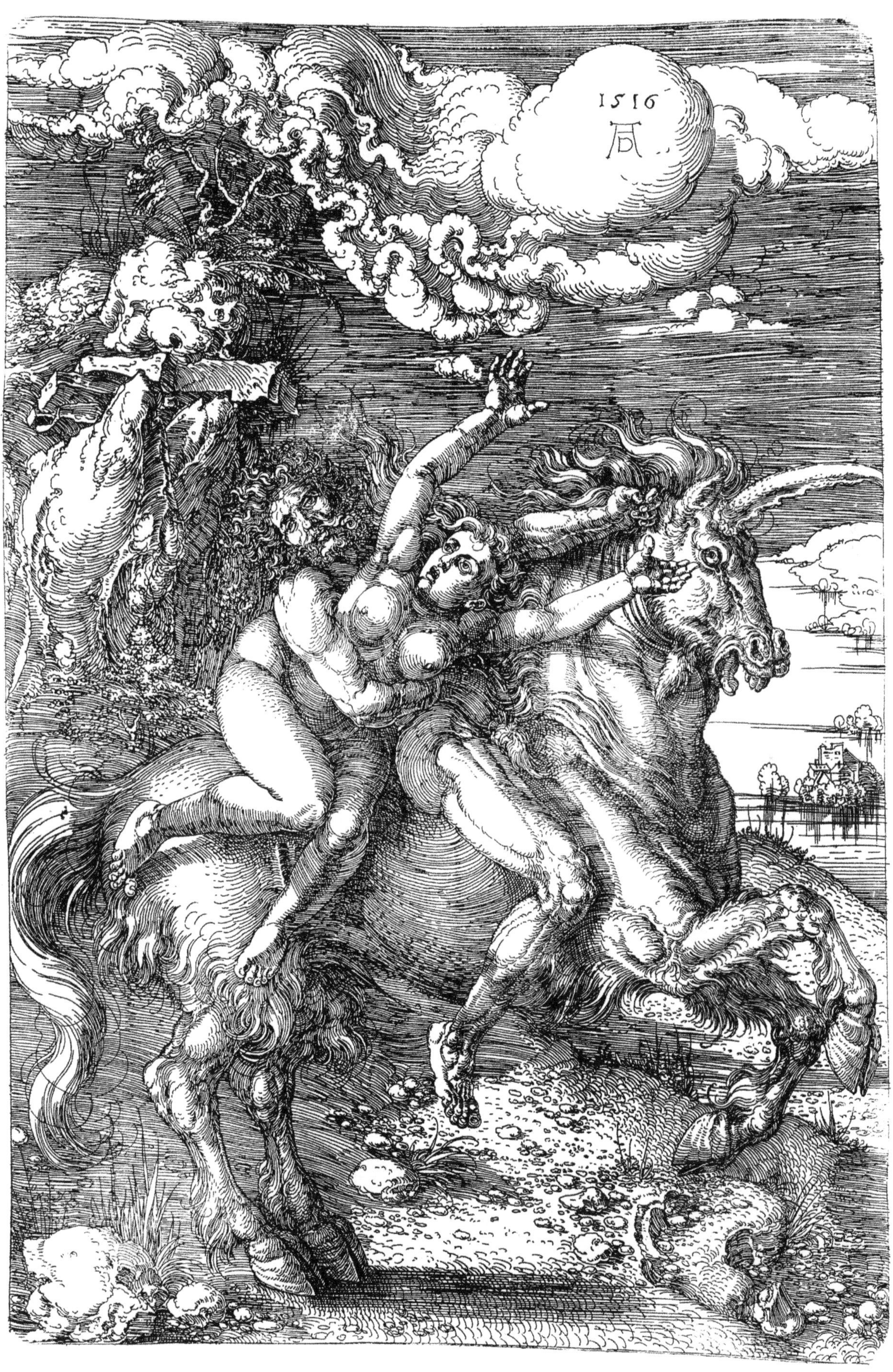

134: Abduction of Proserpine, 1516.

135

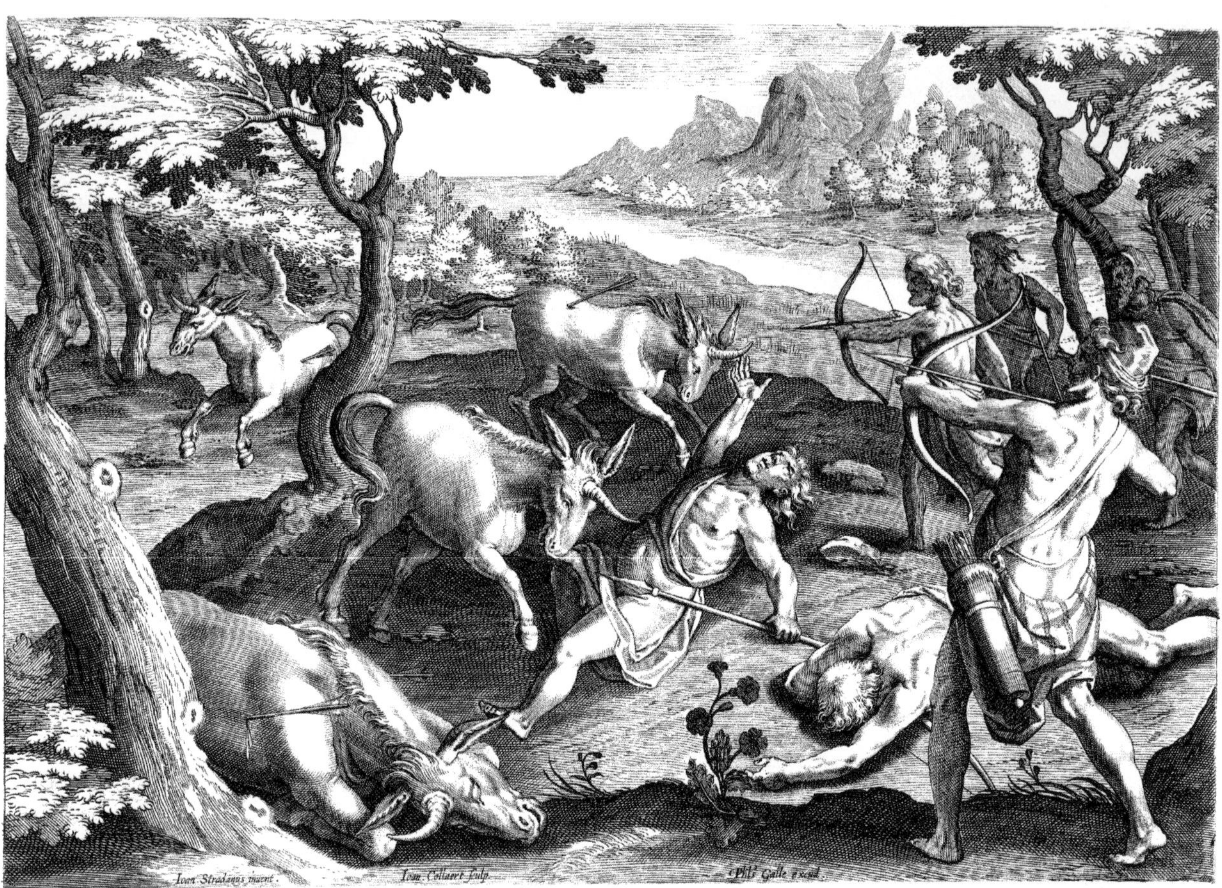

136

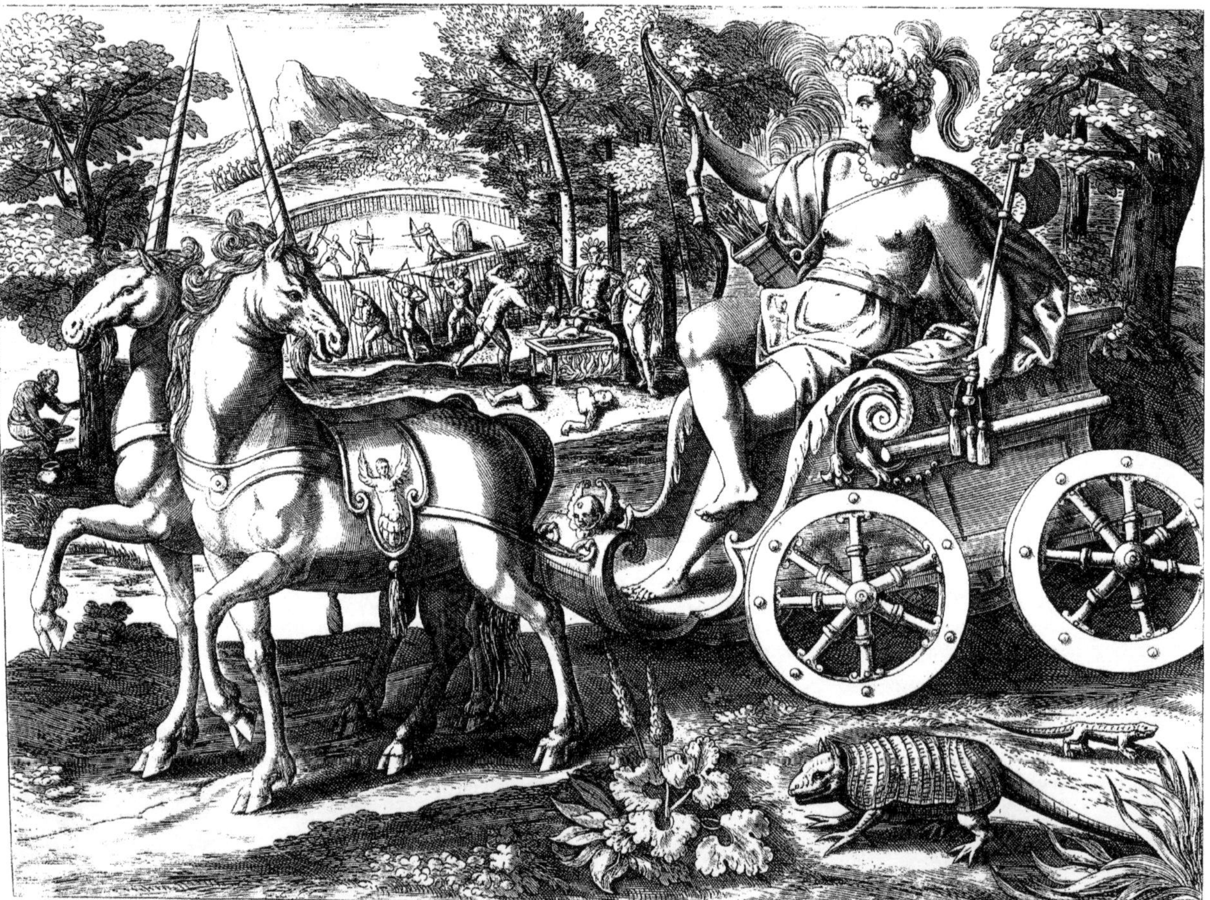

135: Hunting for unicorns, Jan Collaert (II), after Jan van der Straet, 1594 – 1598.

136: Allegory of America, from The Four Continents ca. 1560-1590.

137

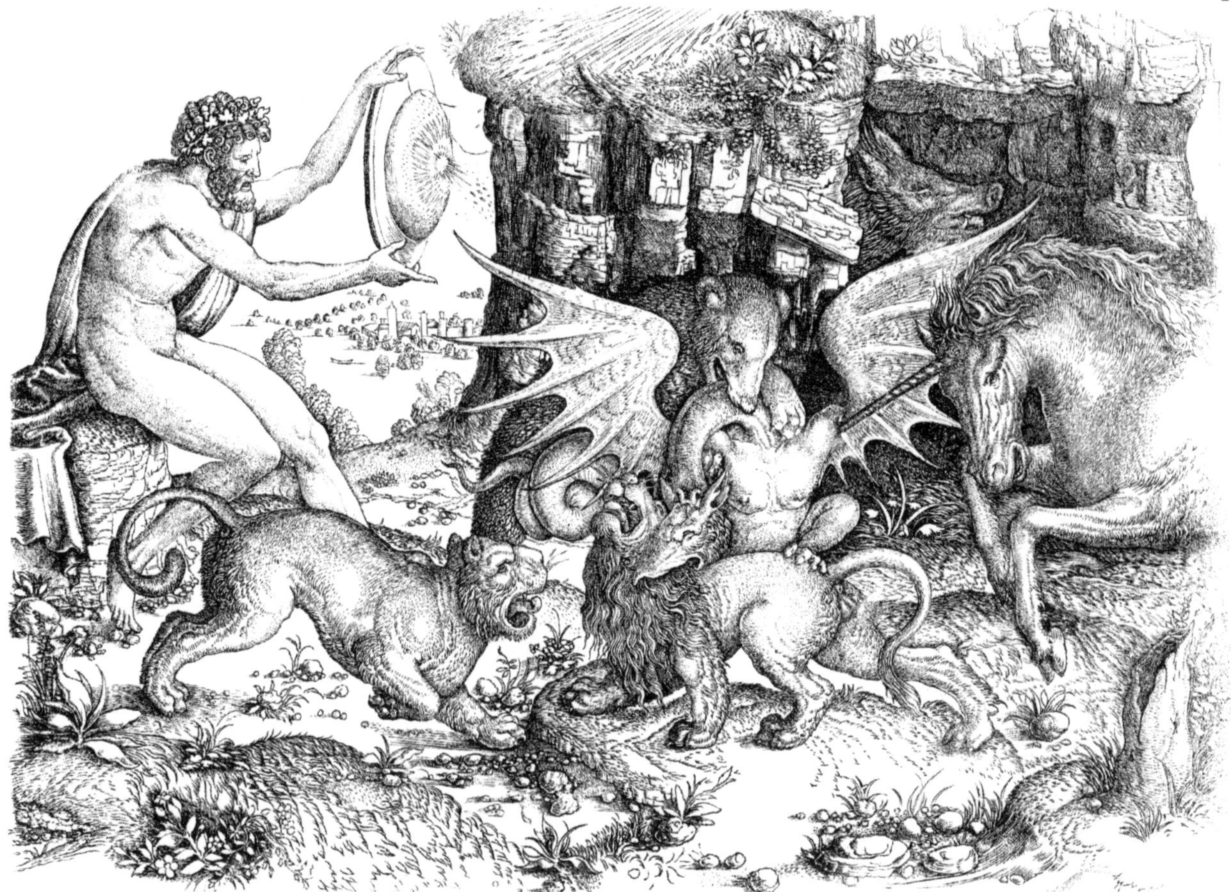

138

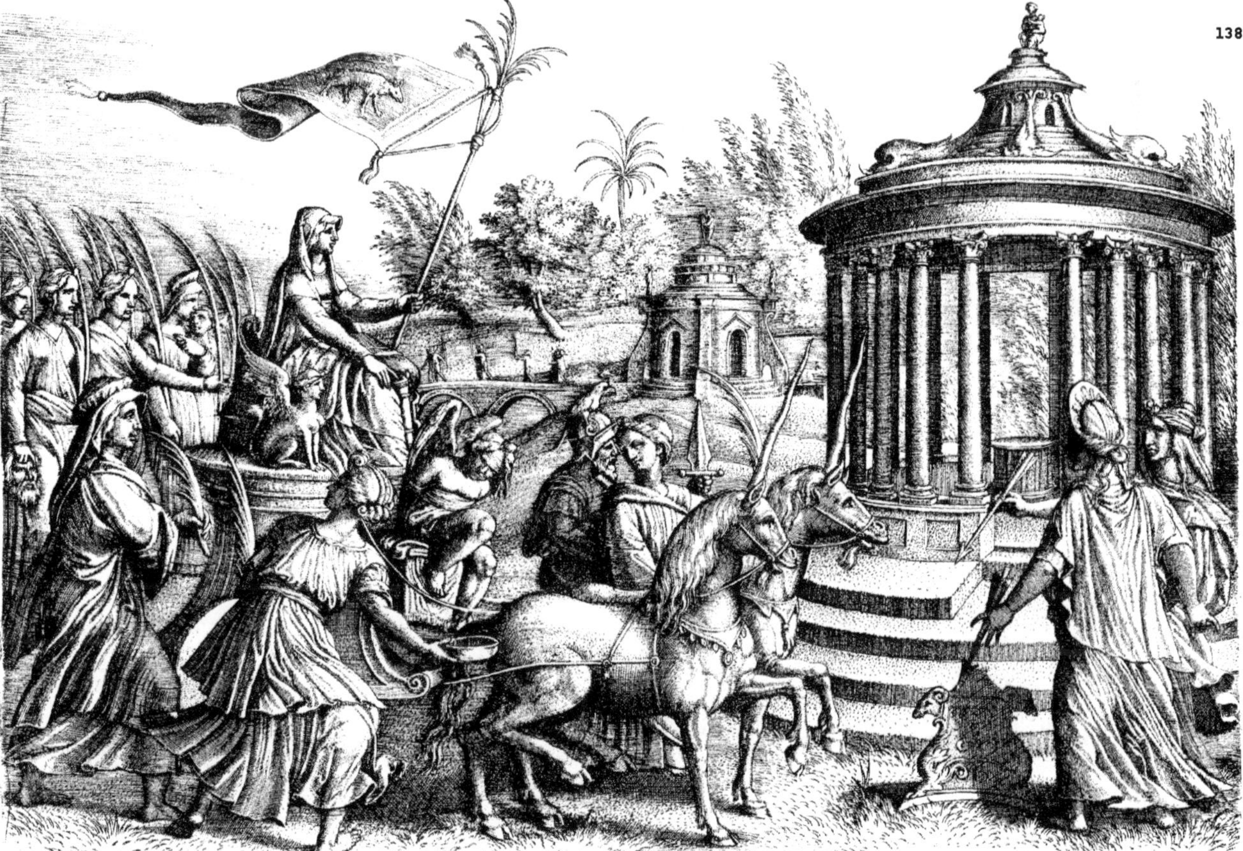

137: Allegory with fight between animals and dragon with a seated man with shield, Master of the Decapitation of John the Baptist.

138: Triumph of Chastity, Georg Pencz, 1539.

139

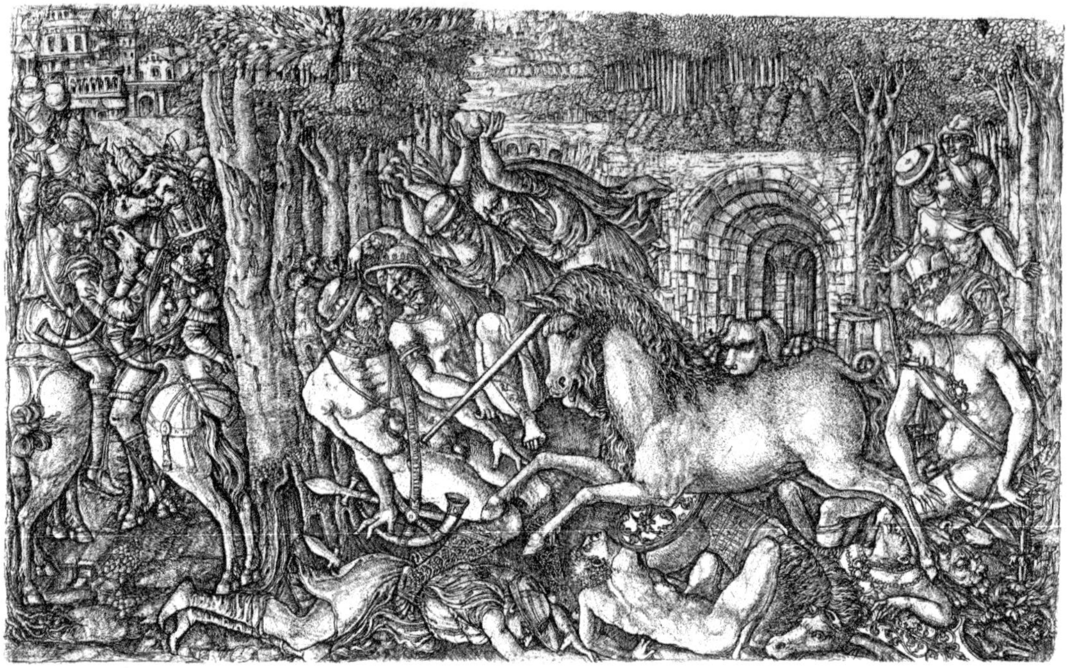

140

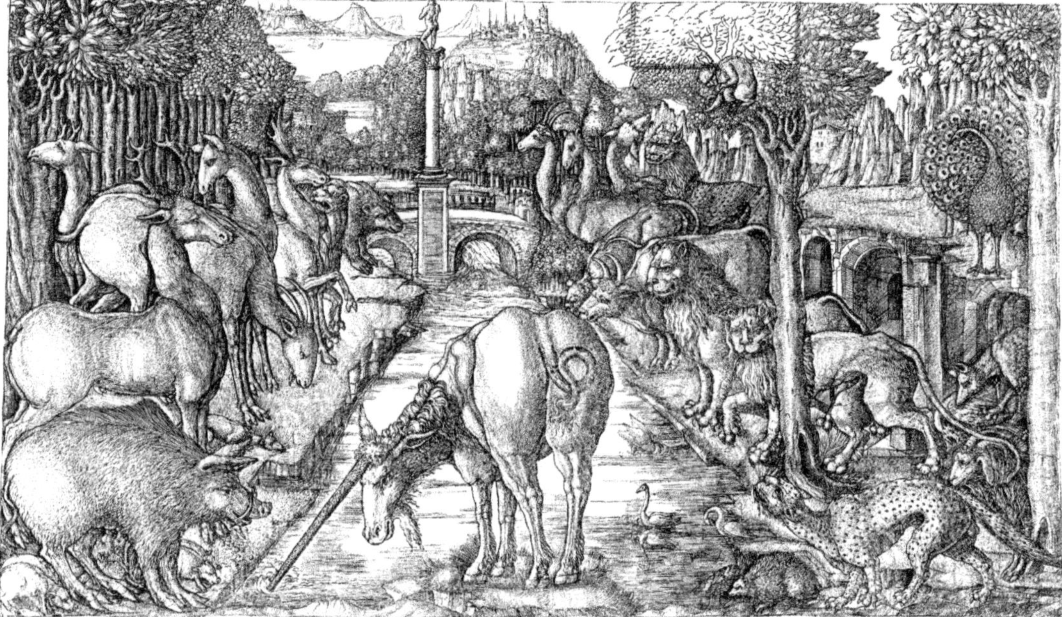

141

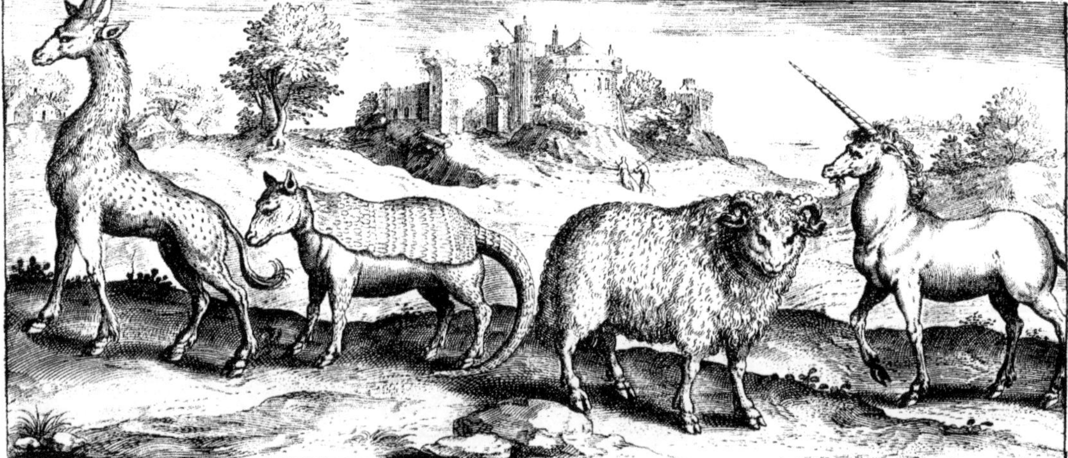

139: The king flees from the unicorn, Jean duvet, 1540–1551.

140: The unicorn purifies the water with its horn, Jean Duvet, 1540 – 1551.

141: Giraffe, civet, ram and unicorn in a landscape, Marcus Gheeraerts (I), 1583.

142

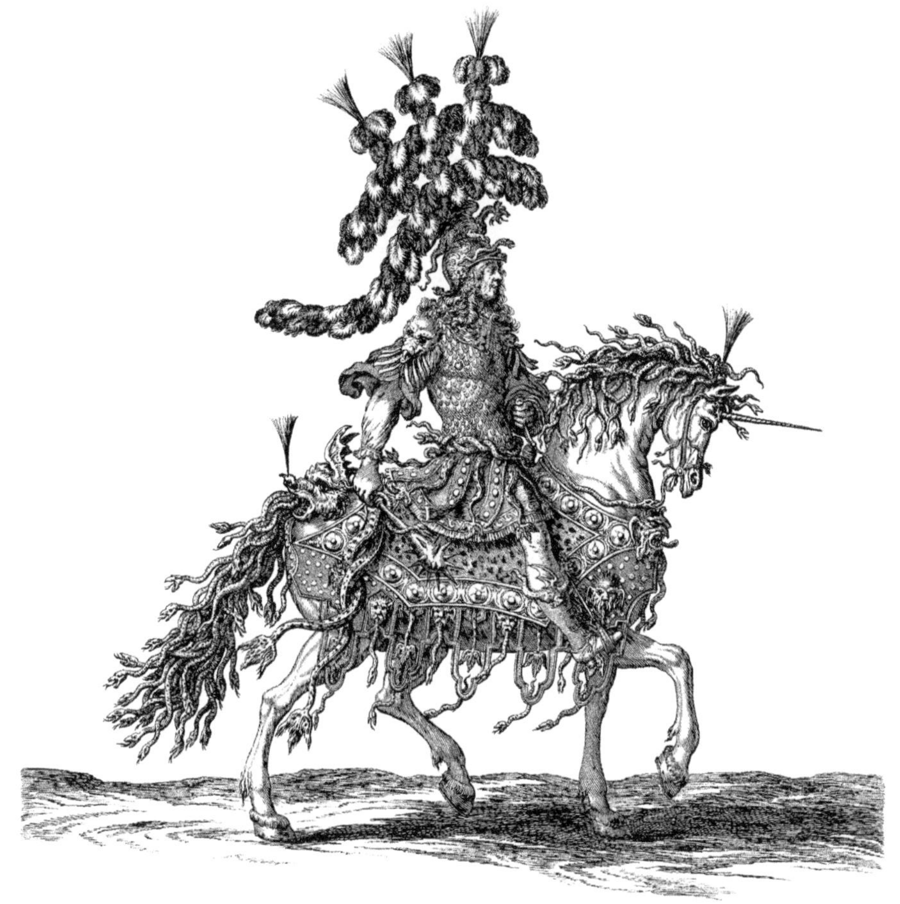

143

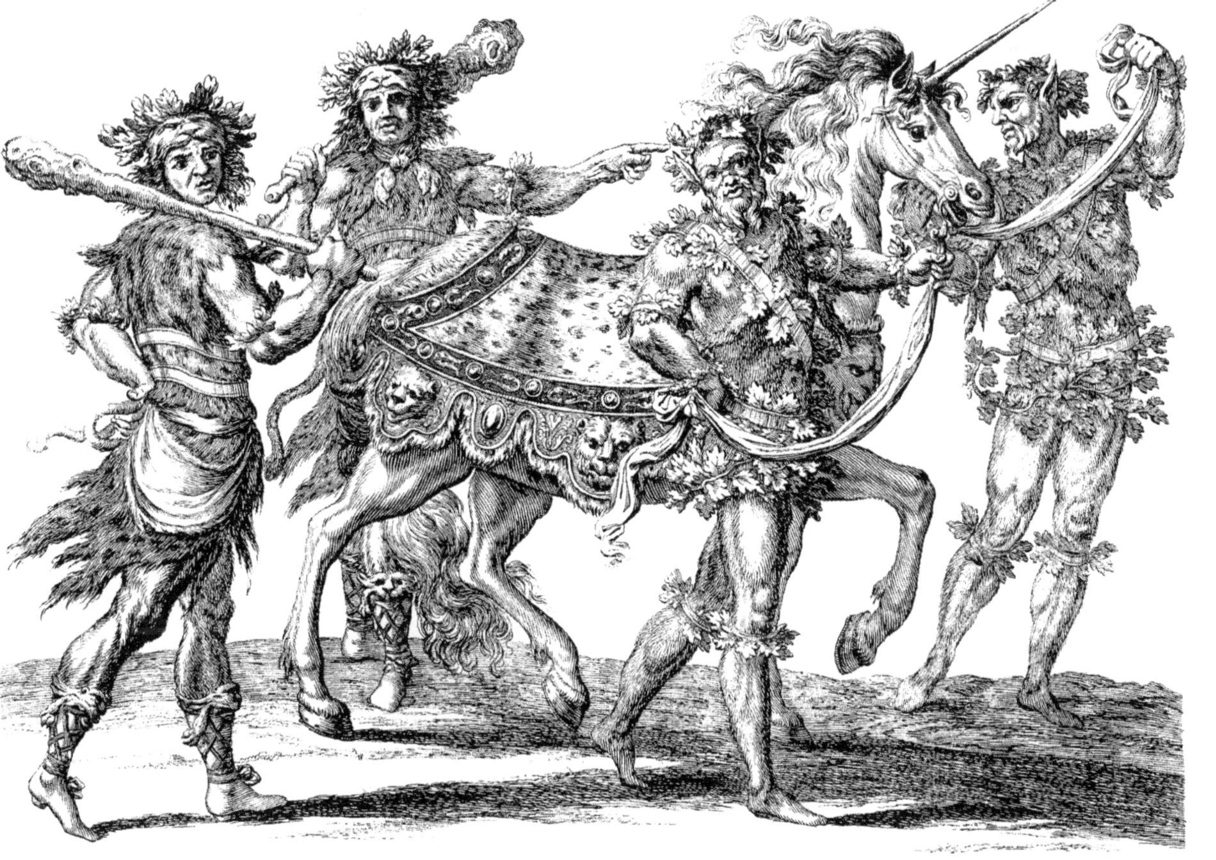

142: Perrault's 'Courses de Testes et la Bague made by Roy, Courtesy National Gallery of Art, Washington.

143: Stipatores, Equus Ductitius, Agasones and Americani. 1662.

144

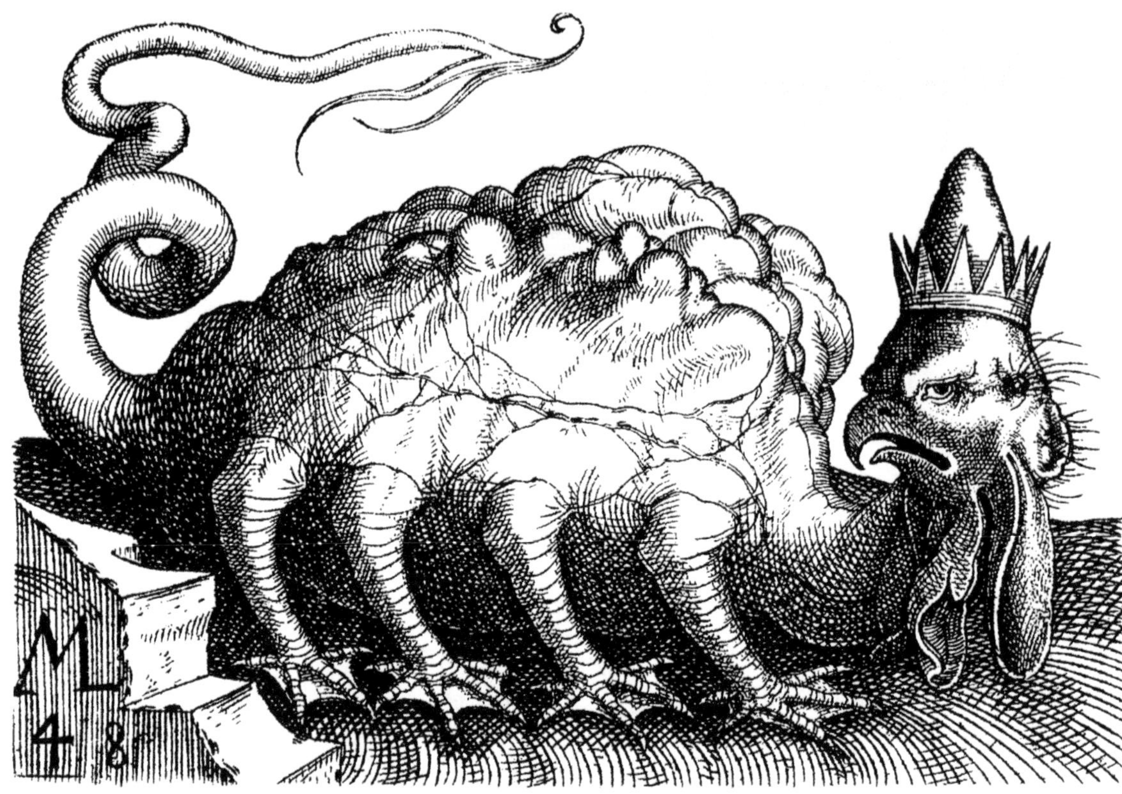

145

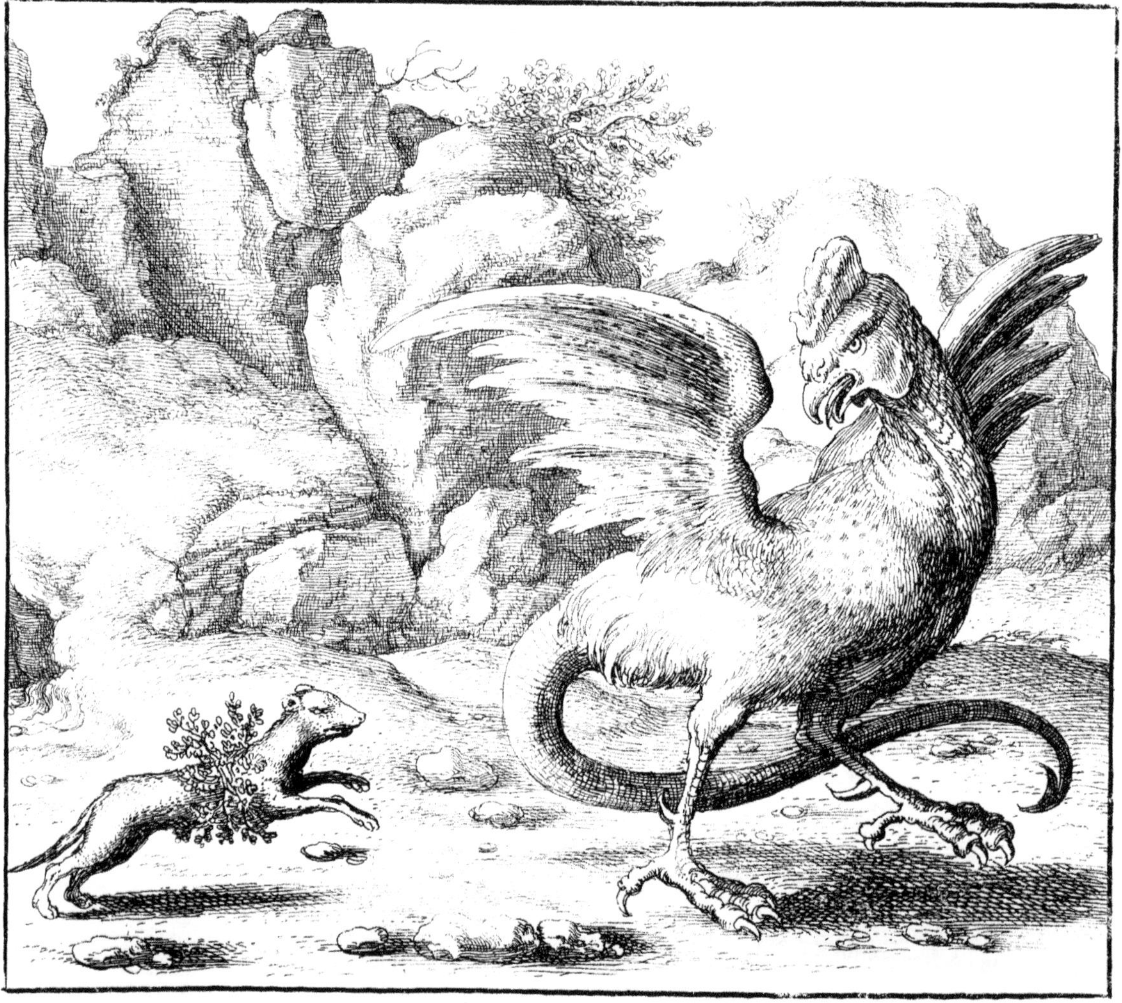

144: Melchior Lorck, Basilisk, 1548.

145: Fable of the Basilisk and the Weasel, Wenceslaus Hollar, after Aegidius Sadeler, after Marcus Gheeraerts, 1644 – 1652.

146

147

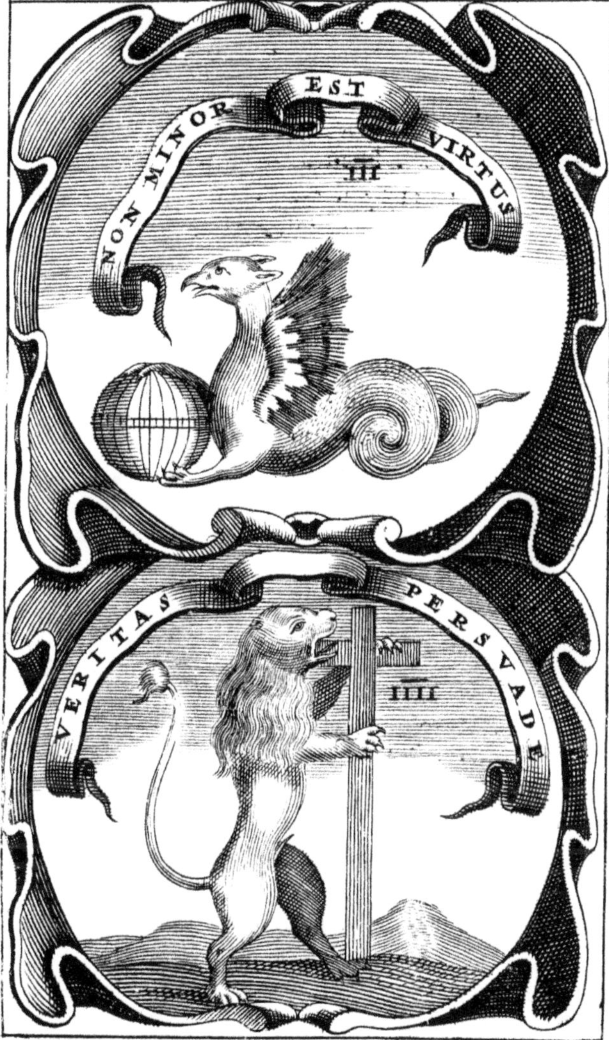

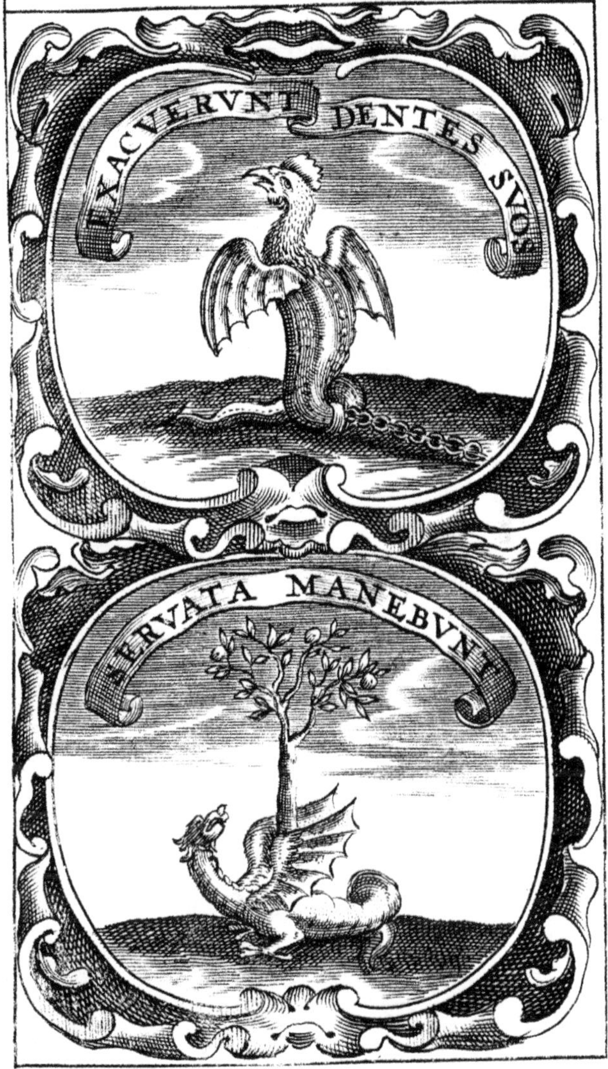

148

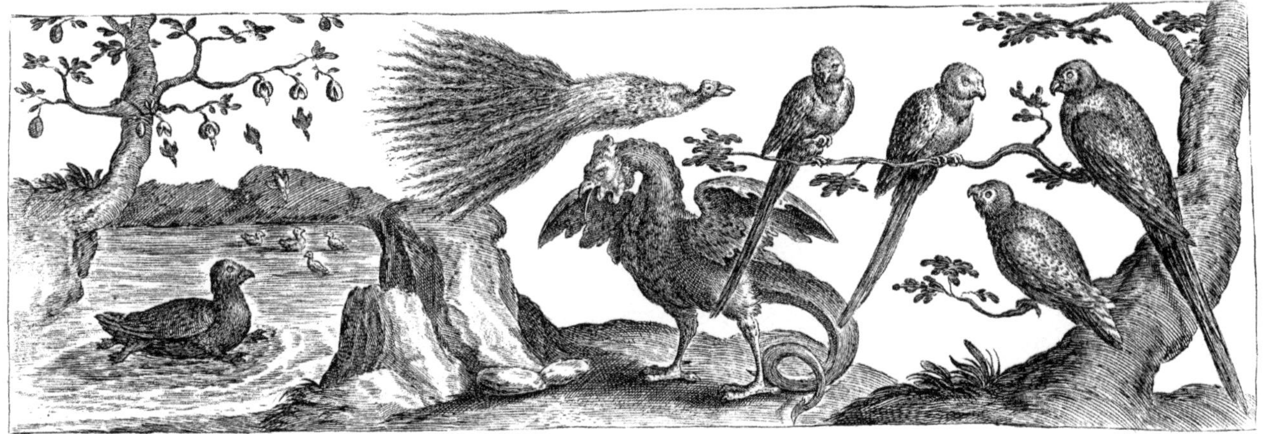

146: Basilisk met globe / Leeuw bijtend aan een kruis, anonymous, after Aegidius Sadeler, 1666.

147: Chained Basilisk / Dragon Under a Fruit Tree, anonymous, after Aegidius Sadeler, 1666.

148: Parrots and Fantastic Beasts, Philips Galle (attributed to workshop of), after Marcus Gheeraerts (I), 1547 – 1590.

149

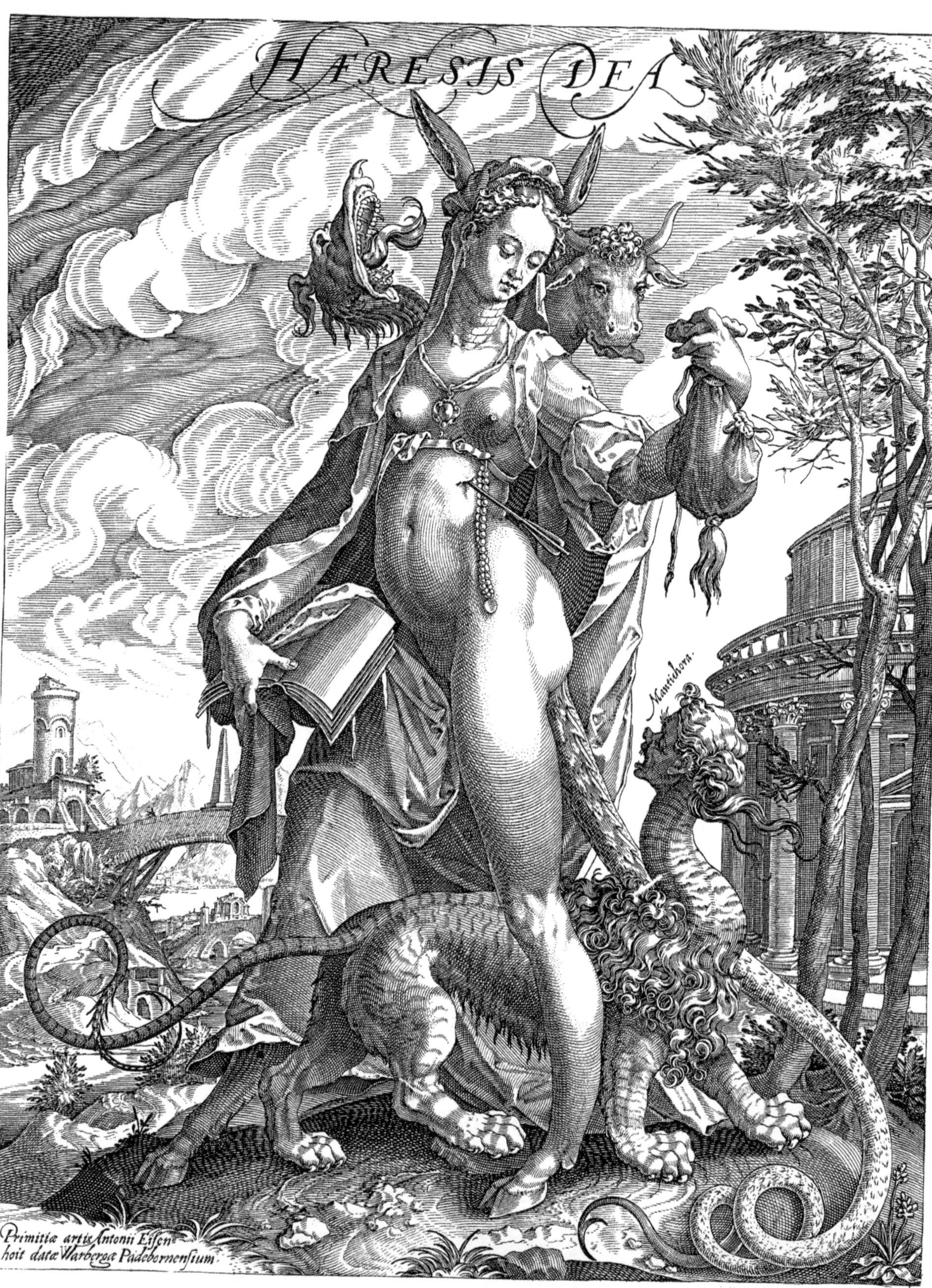

149: Heresy, Anton Eisenholt, 1589

150

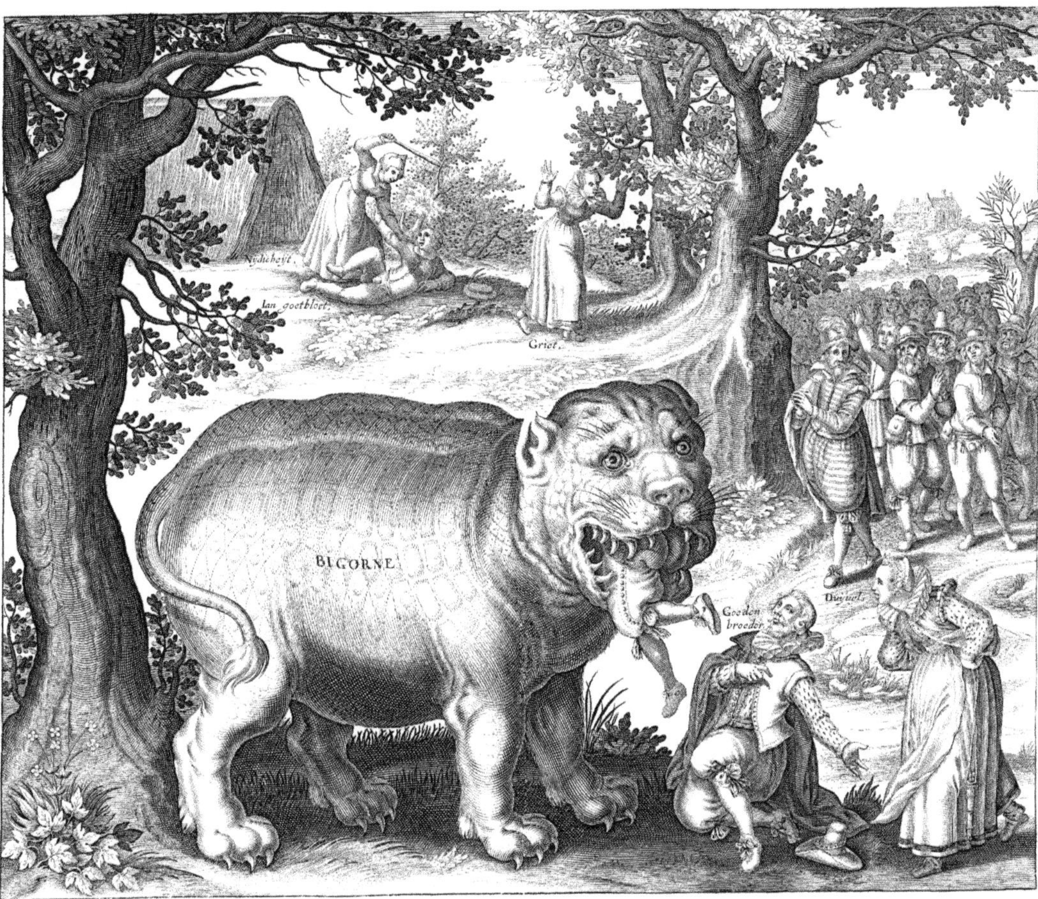

151

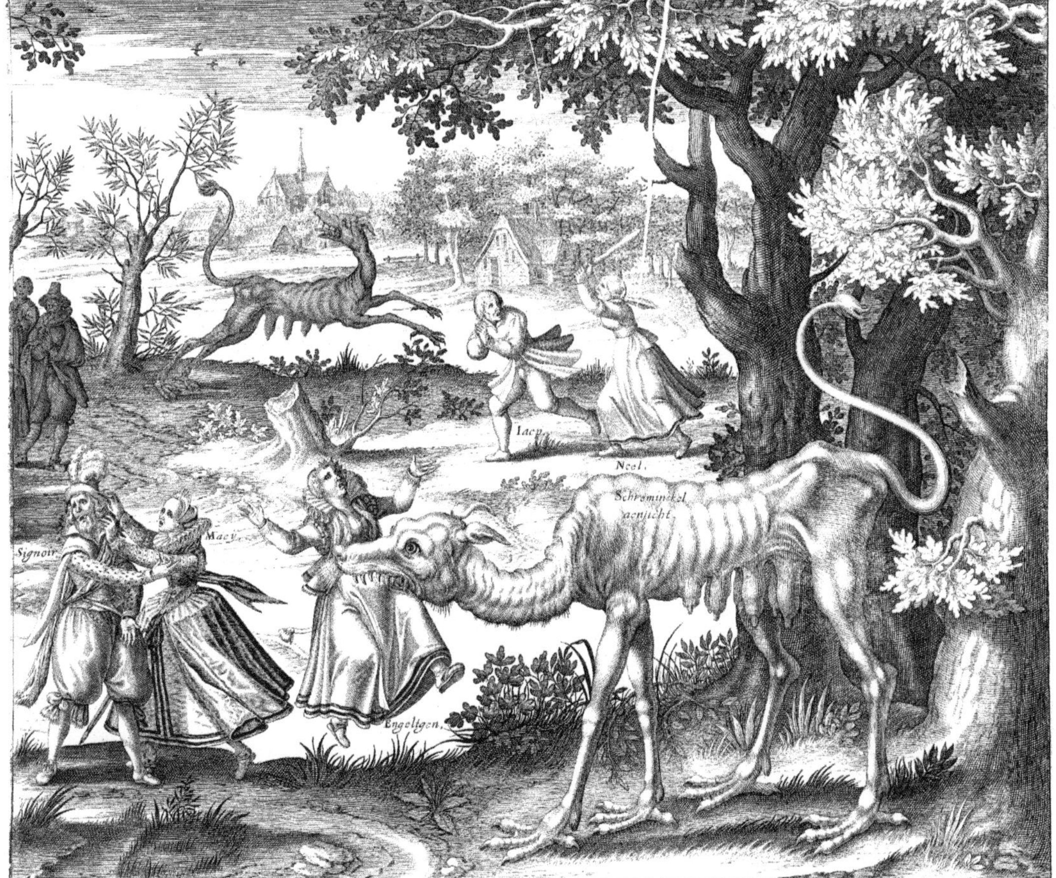

150: Bigorne, anonymous, 1600 – 1650.

151: Scharminkel, anonymous, 1600 – 1650.

152

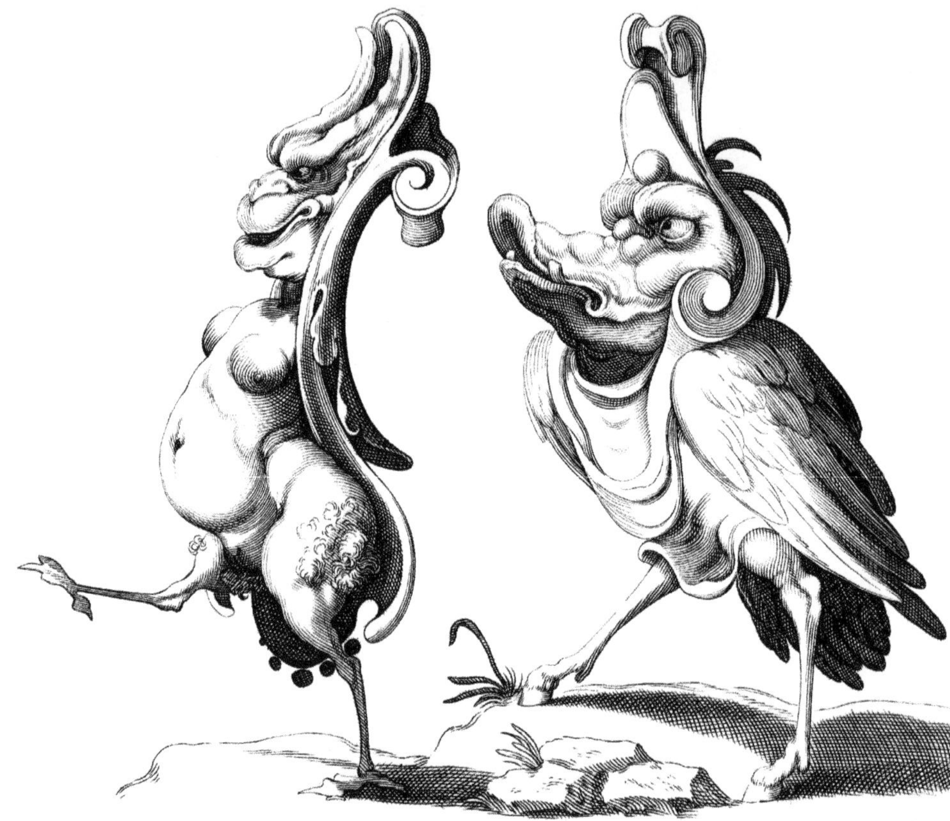

153

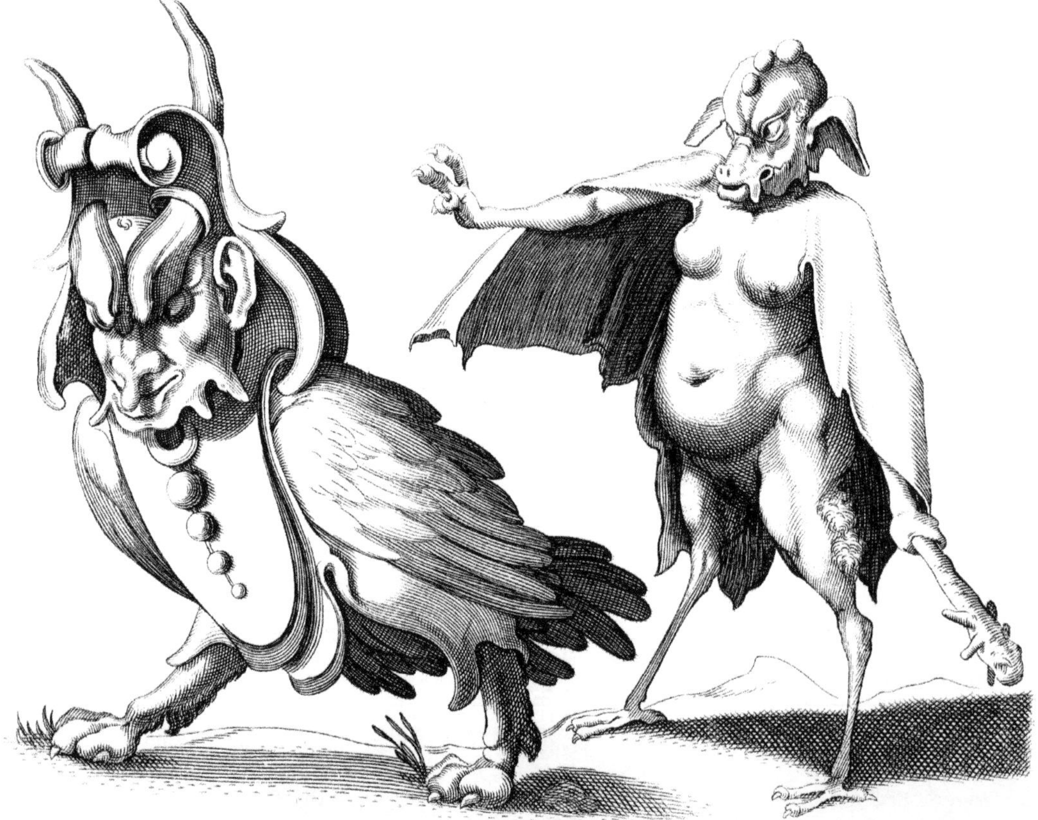

152: Two grotesques, walking to the left, anonymous, after Arent van Bolten.

153: Two grotesques, anonymous, after Arent van Bolten.

154

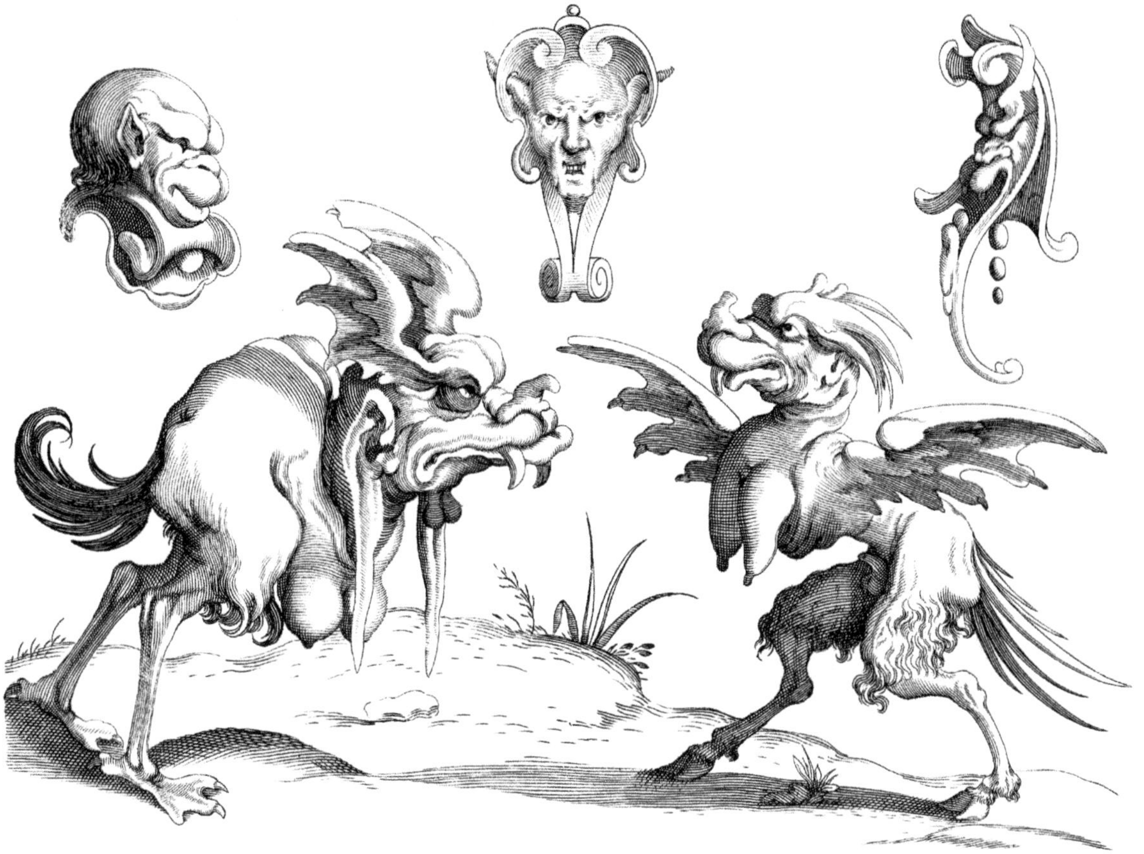

155

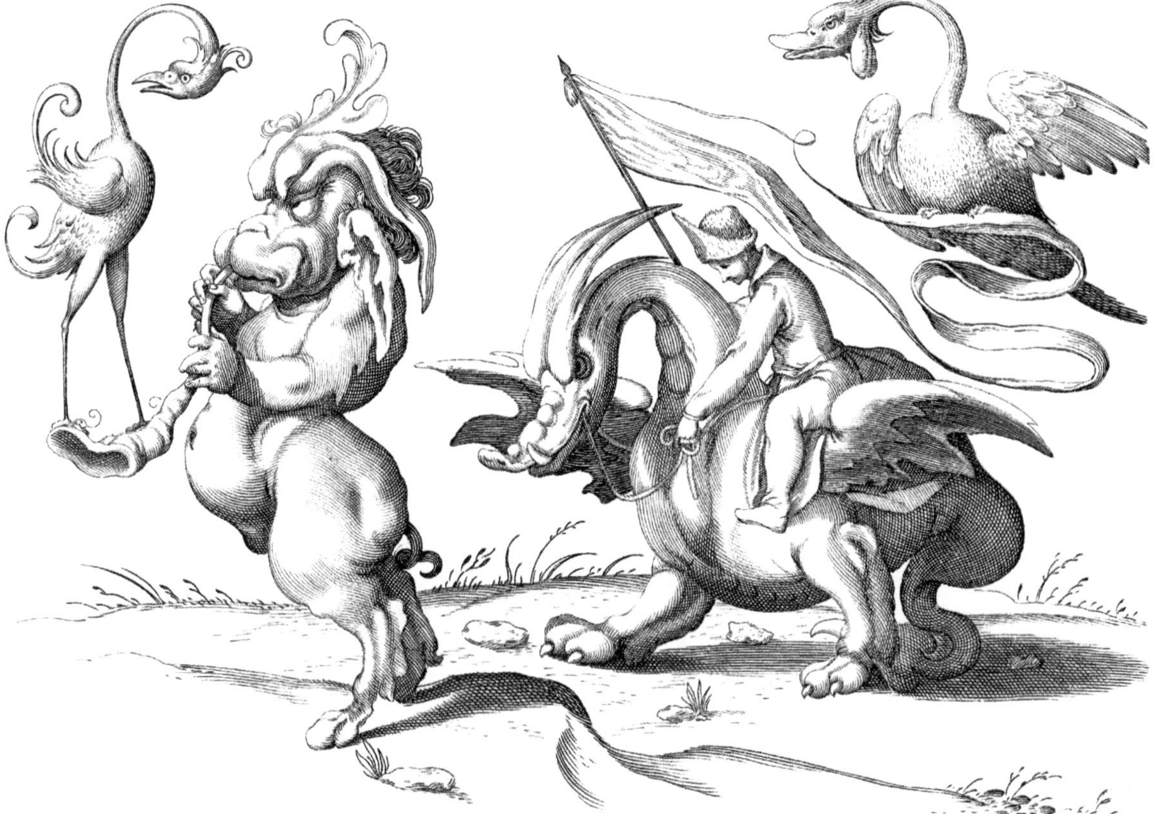

154: Two monsters surmounted by three masks, anonymous, after Arent van Bolten, c. 1604 – c. 1616.

155: Monster with trumpet and type of crane, anonymous, after Arent van Bolten, c. 1604 – c. 1616.

156

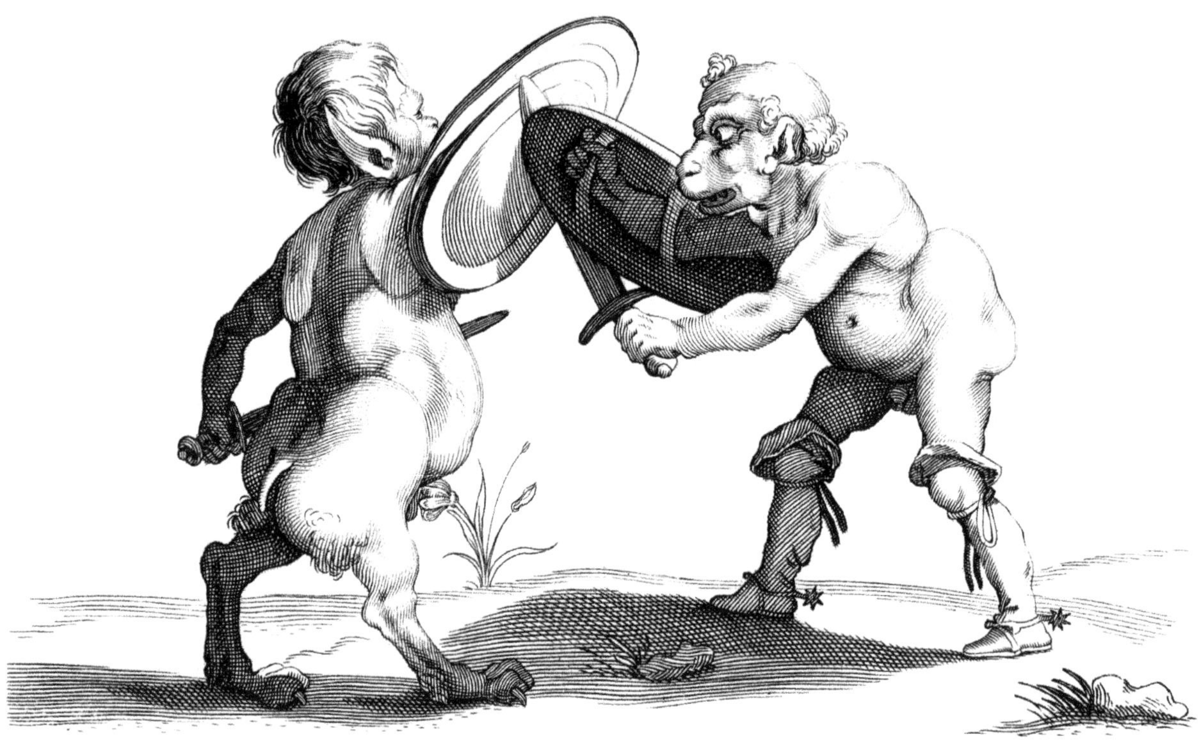

157

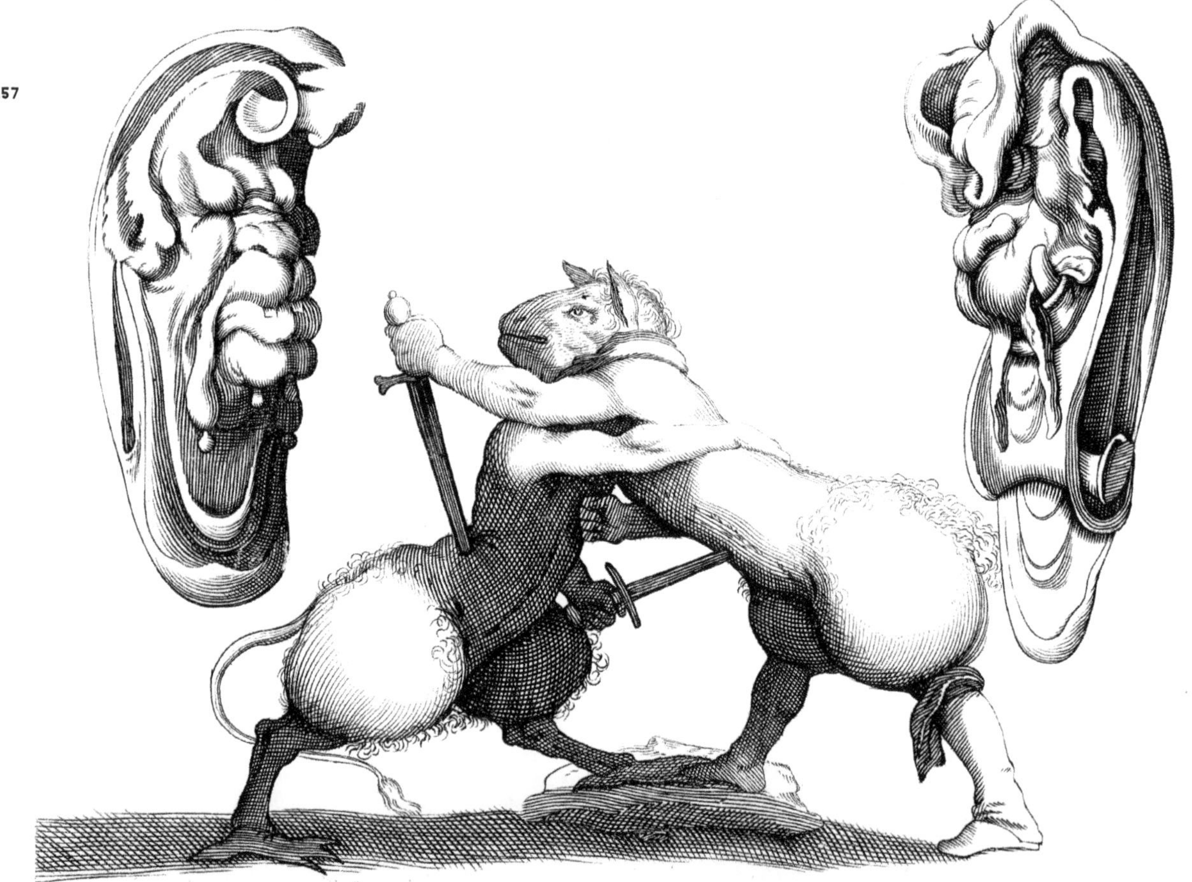

156: Two grotesques with sword and shield, anonymous, after Arent van Bolten.

157: Two fighting grotesque figures, anonymous, after Arent van Bolten.

158

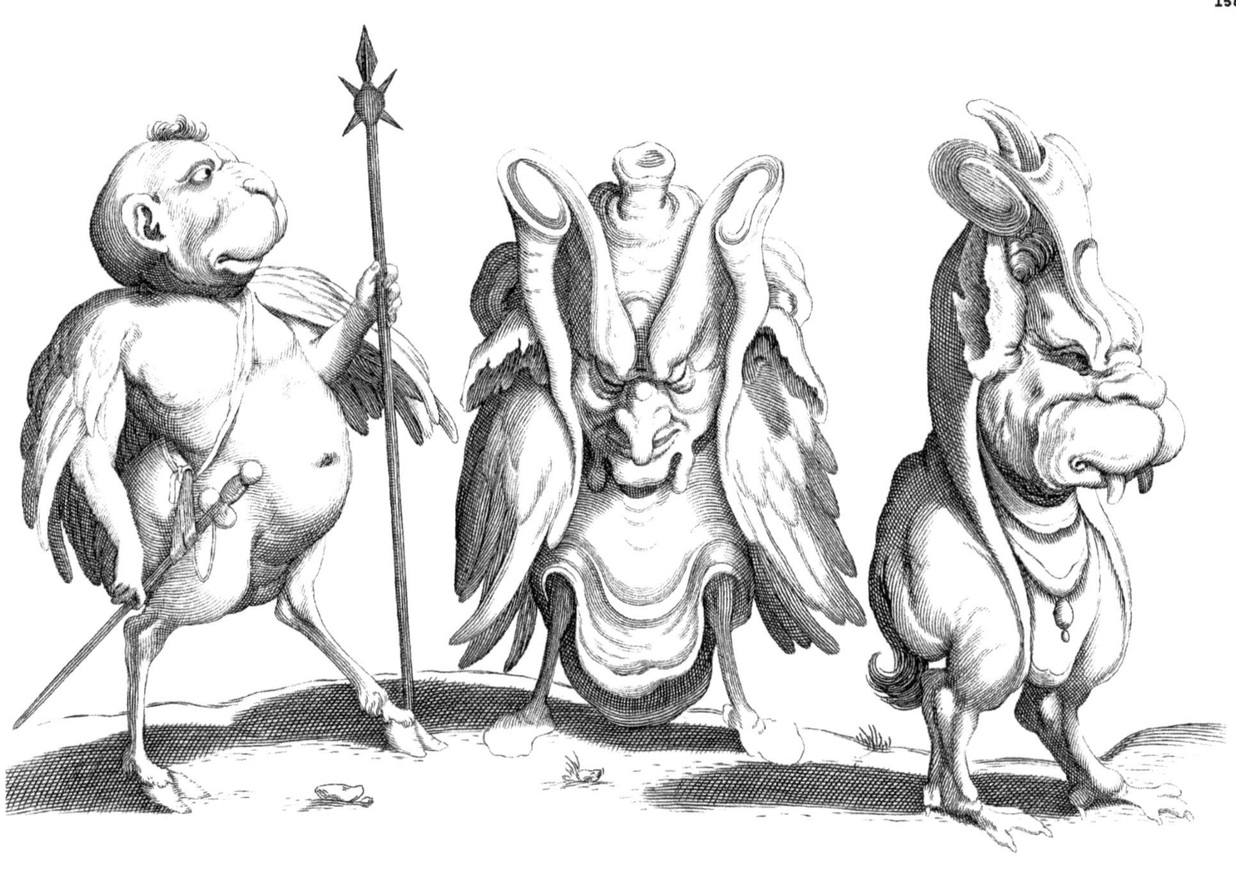

159

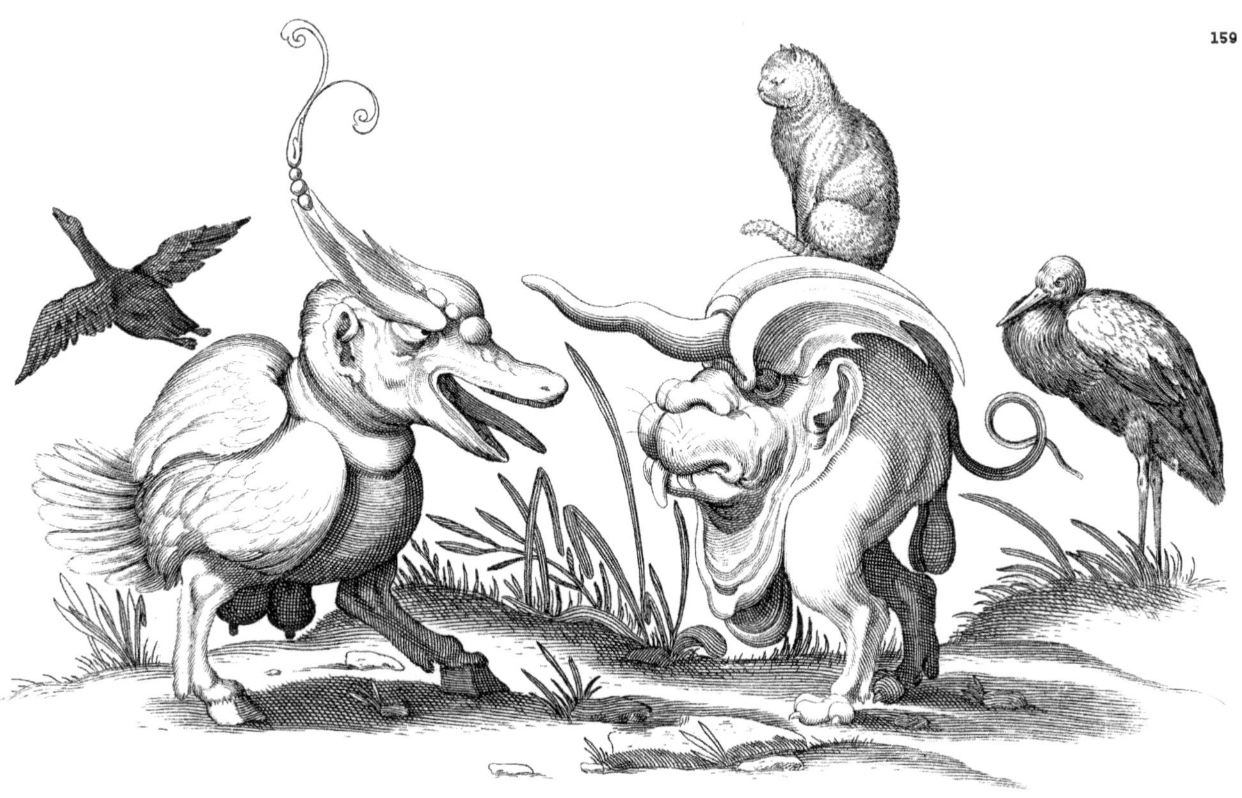

158: Three monsters, anonymous, after Arent van Bolten, c. 1604 – c. 1616.

159: Two Monsters with Cat, Goose and Stork., Anonymous, after Arent van Bolten, c. 1604 – c. 1616.

160

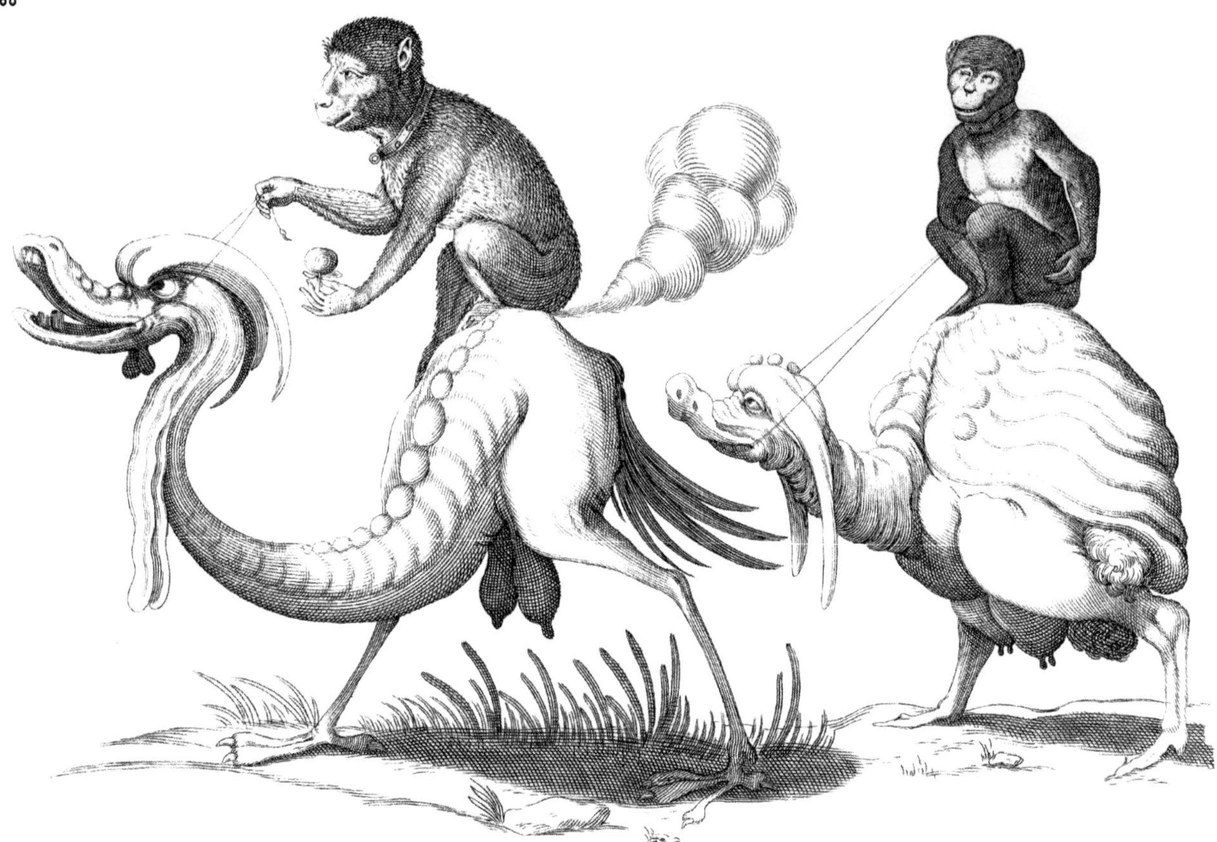

161

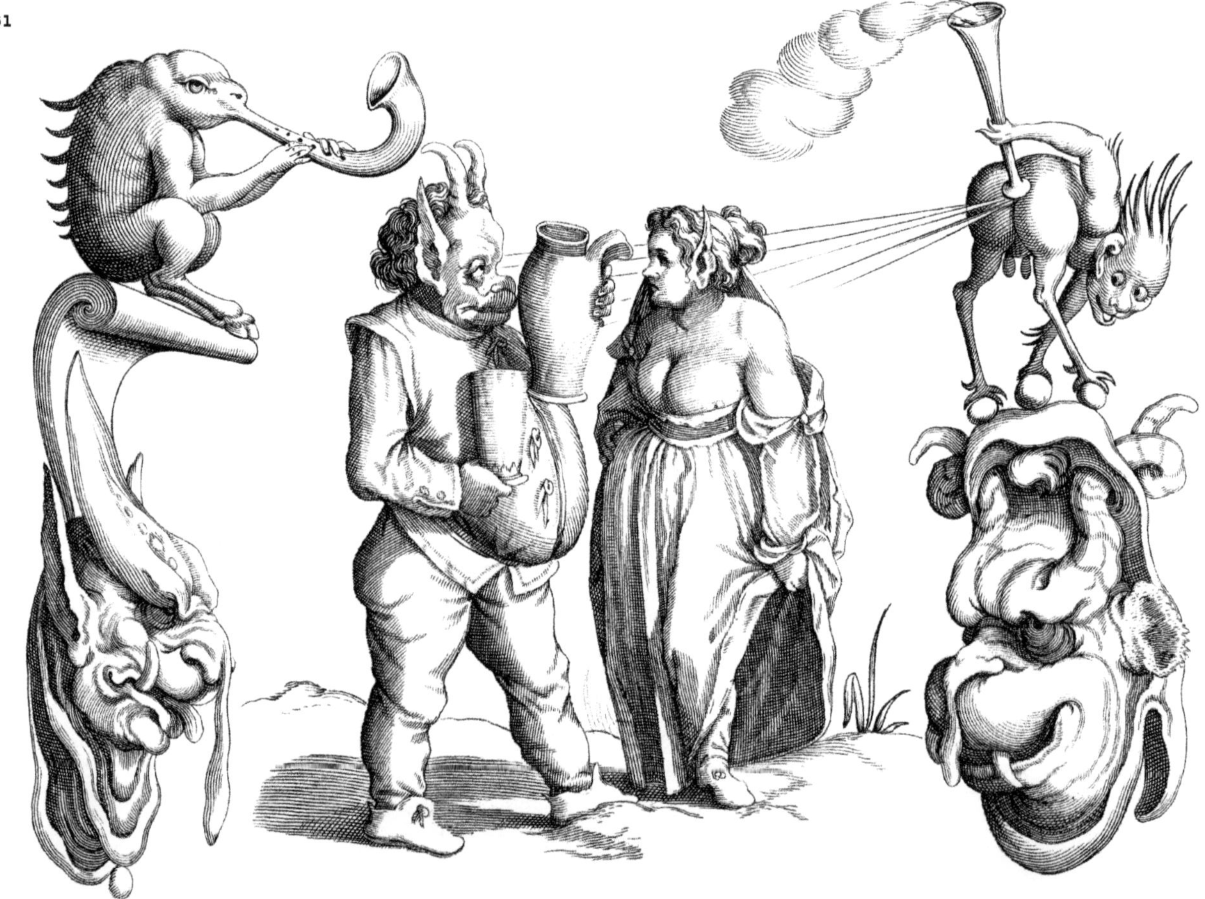

160: Two Monsters Ridden by Monkeys, Arent van Bolten, c. 1604 – c. 1616.

161: Woman and male monster with jug and cup, anonymous, after Arent van Bolten, c. 1604 – c. 1616.

162

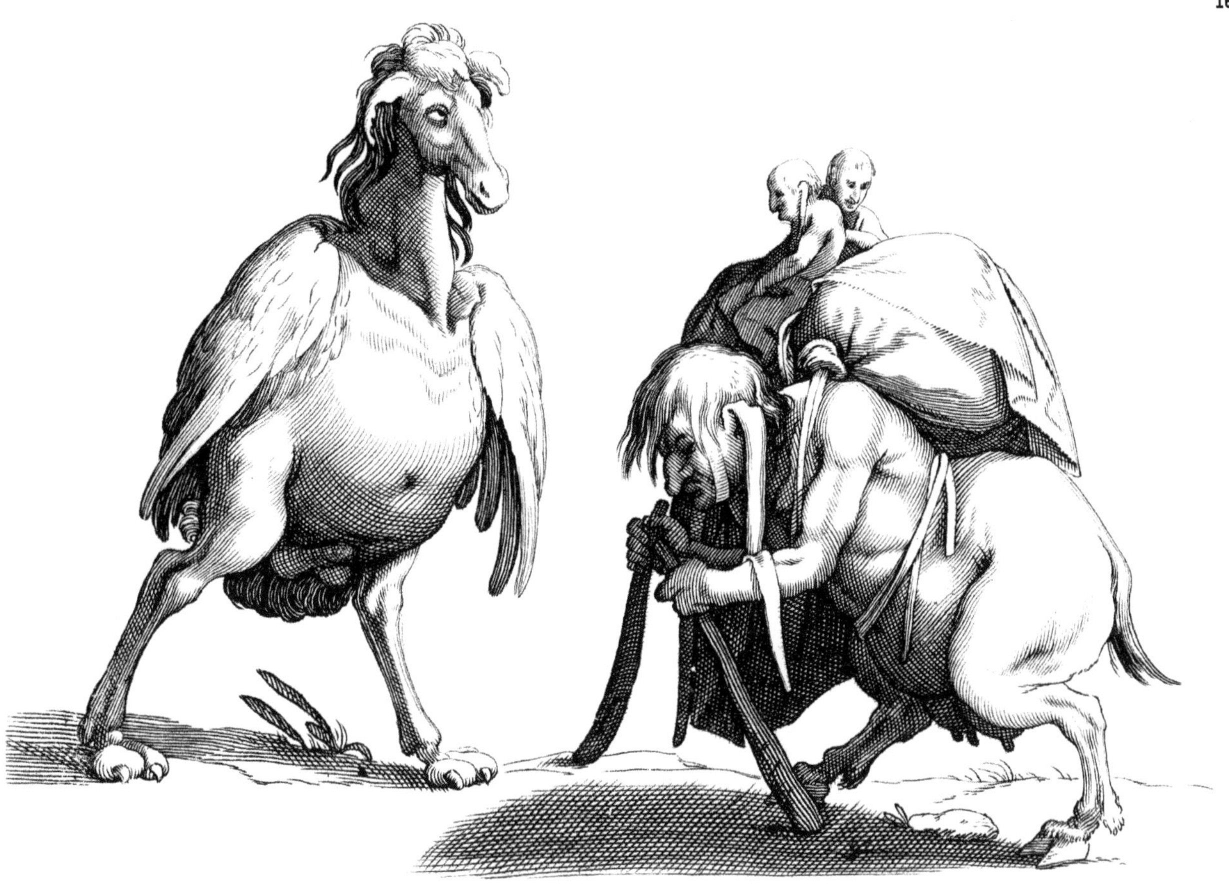

163

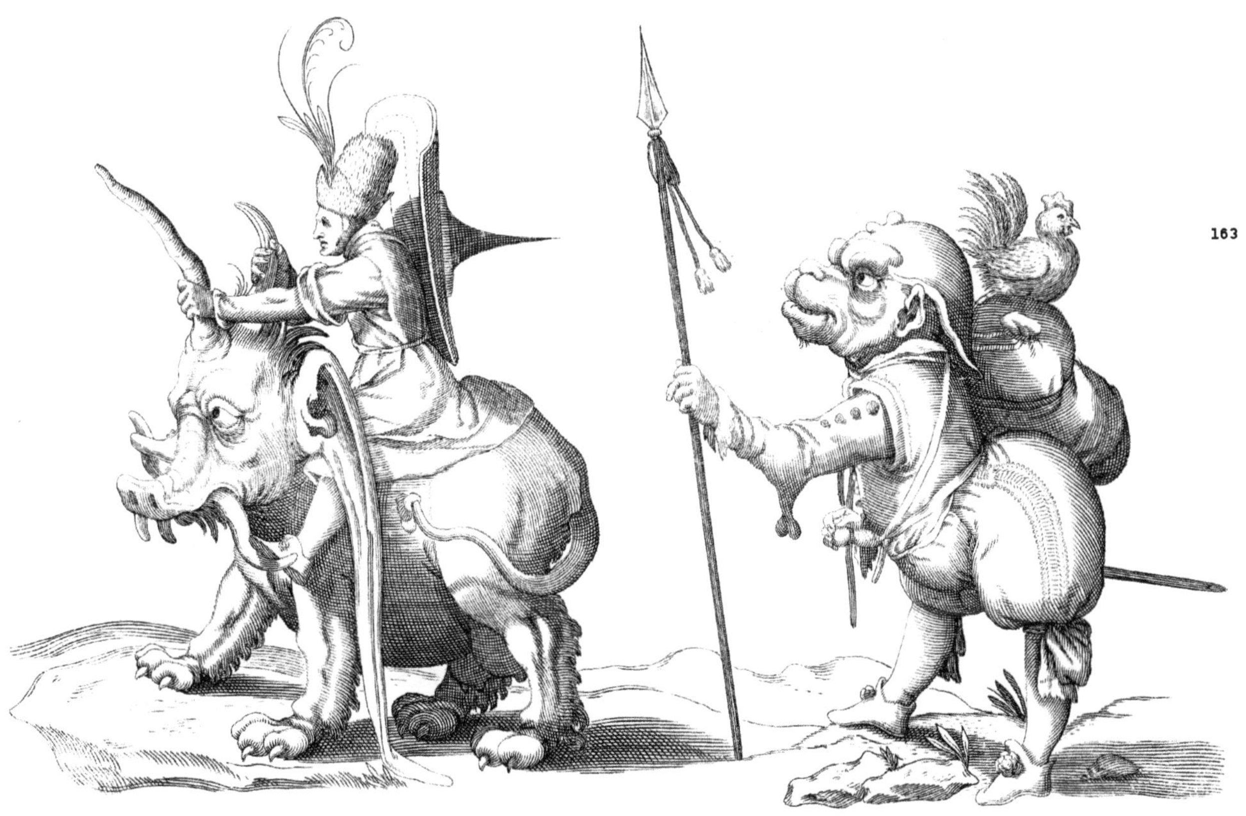

162: Two grotesques, anonymous, after Arent van Bolten.

163: Rider on an elephant-like monster, anonymous, after Arent van Bolten, c. 1604 – c. 1616.

164

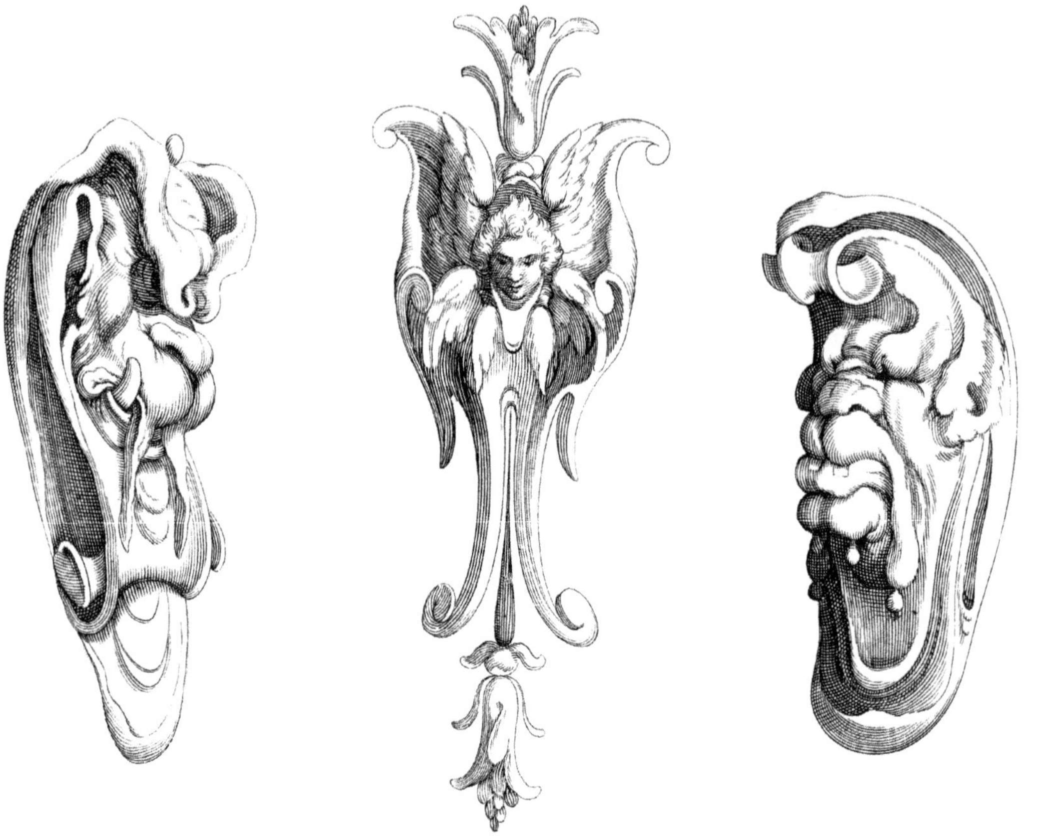

165

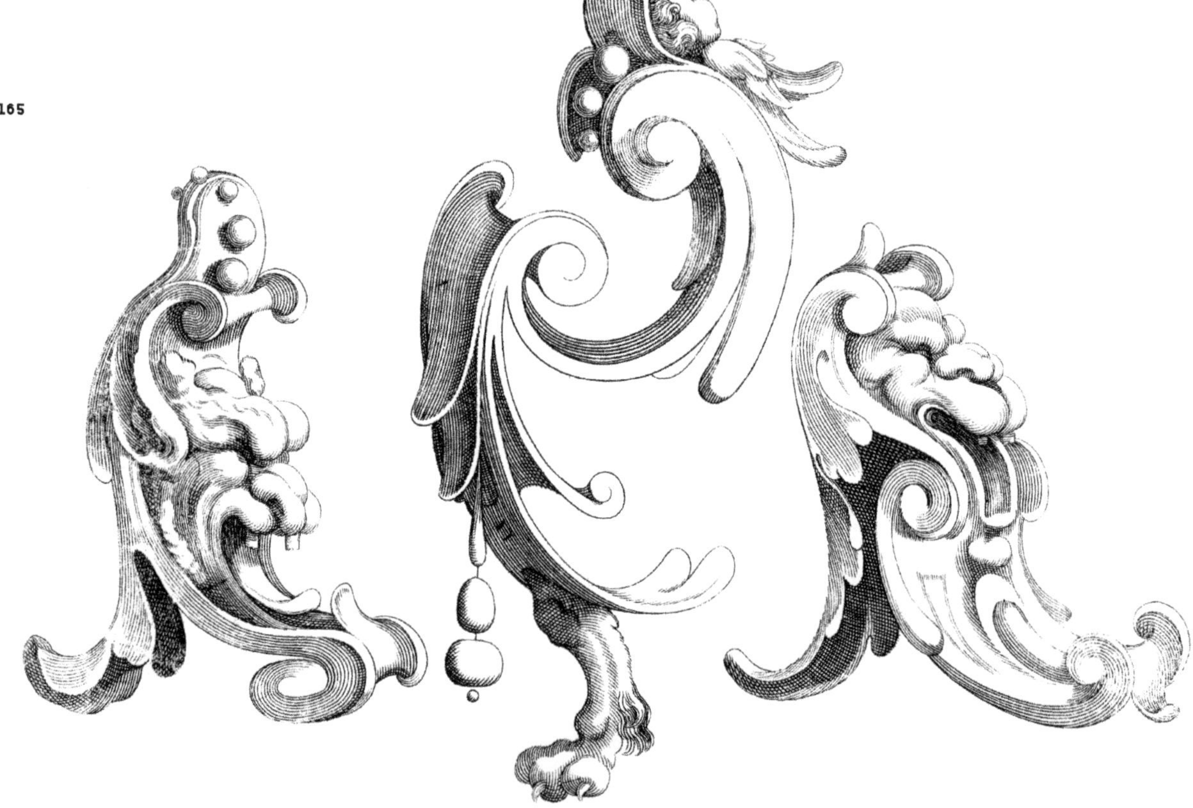

164: Grotesque ornament with a cherub, anonymous, after Arent van Bolten, c. 1604 – c. 1616.

165: Three ornaments with mascarons, anonymous, after Arent van Bolten, c. 1604 – c. 1616.

166

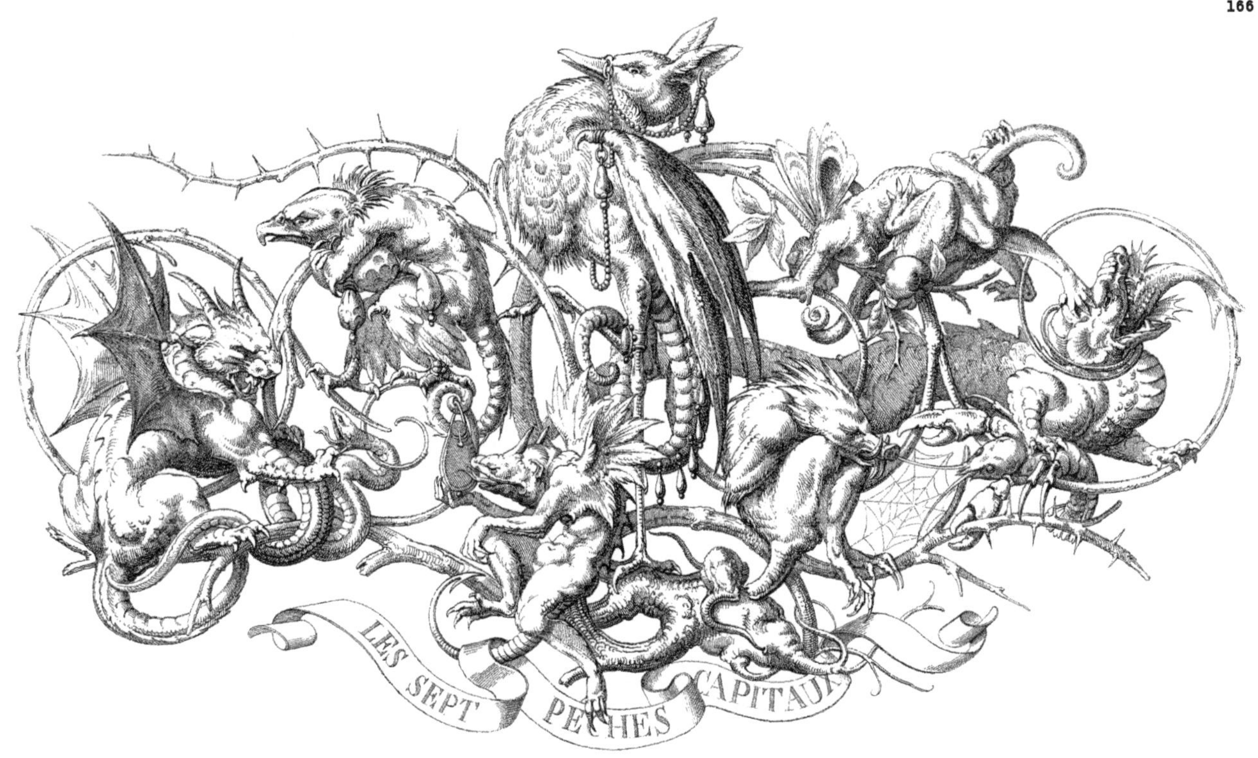

167

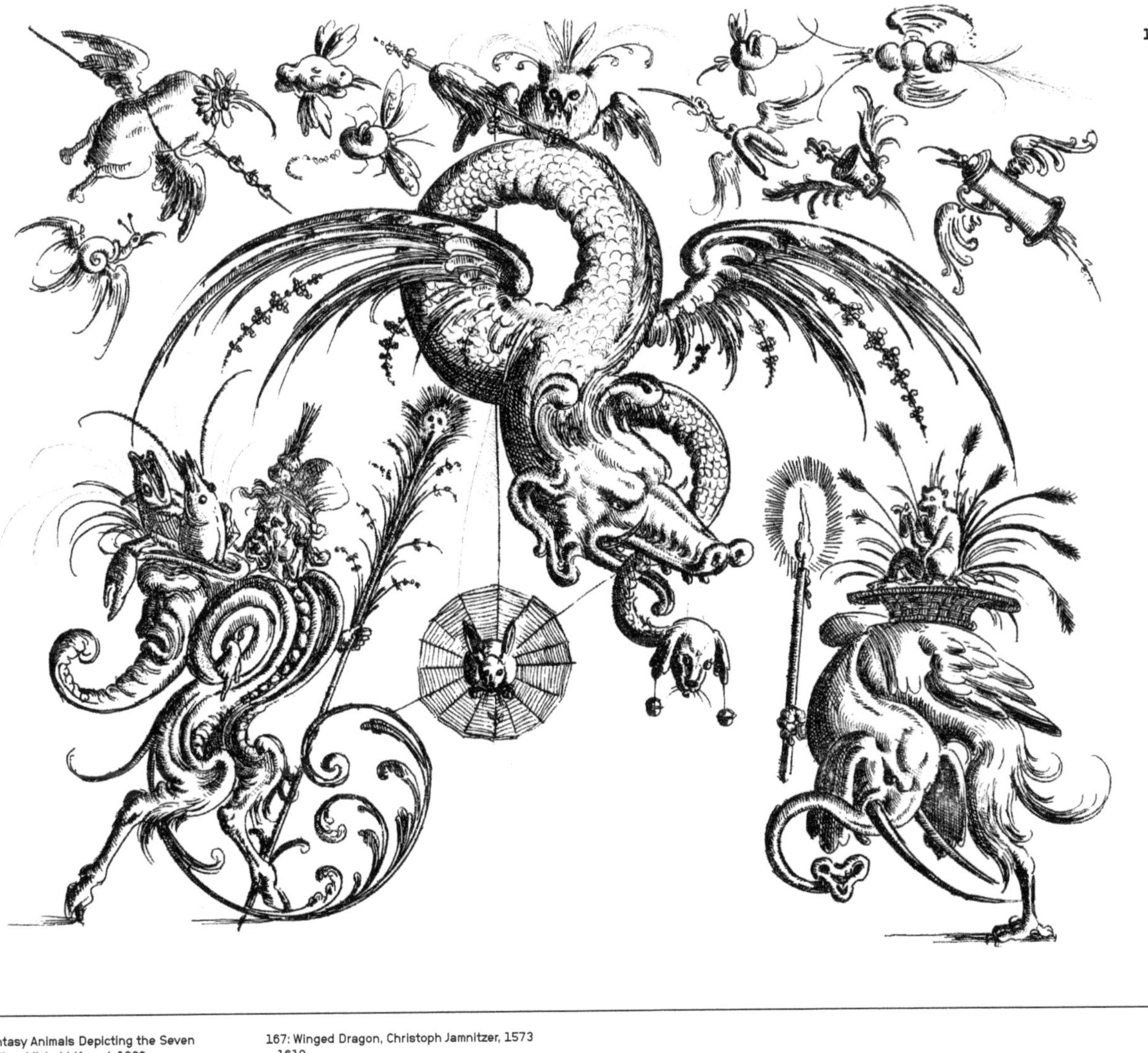

166: Fantasy Animals Depicting the Seven Deadly Sins, Michel Liénard, 1866.

167: Winged Dragon, Christoph Jamnitzer, 1573 – 1610.

168

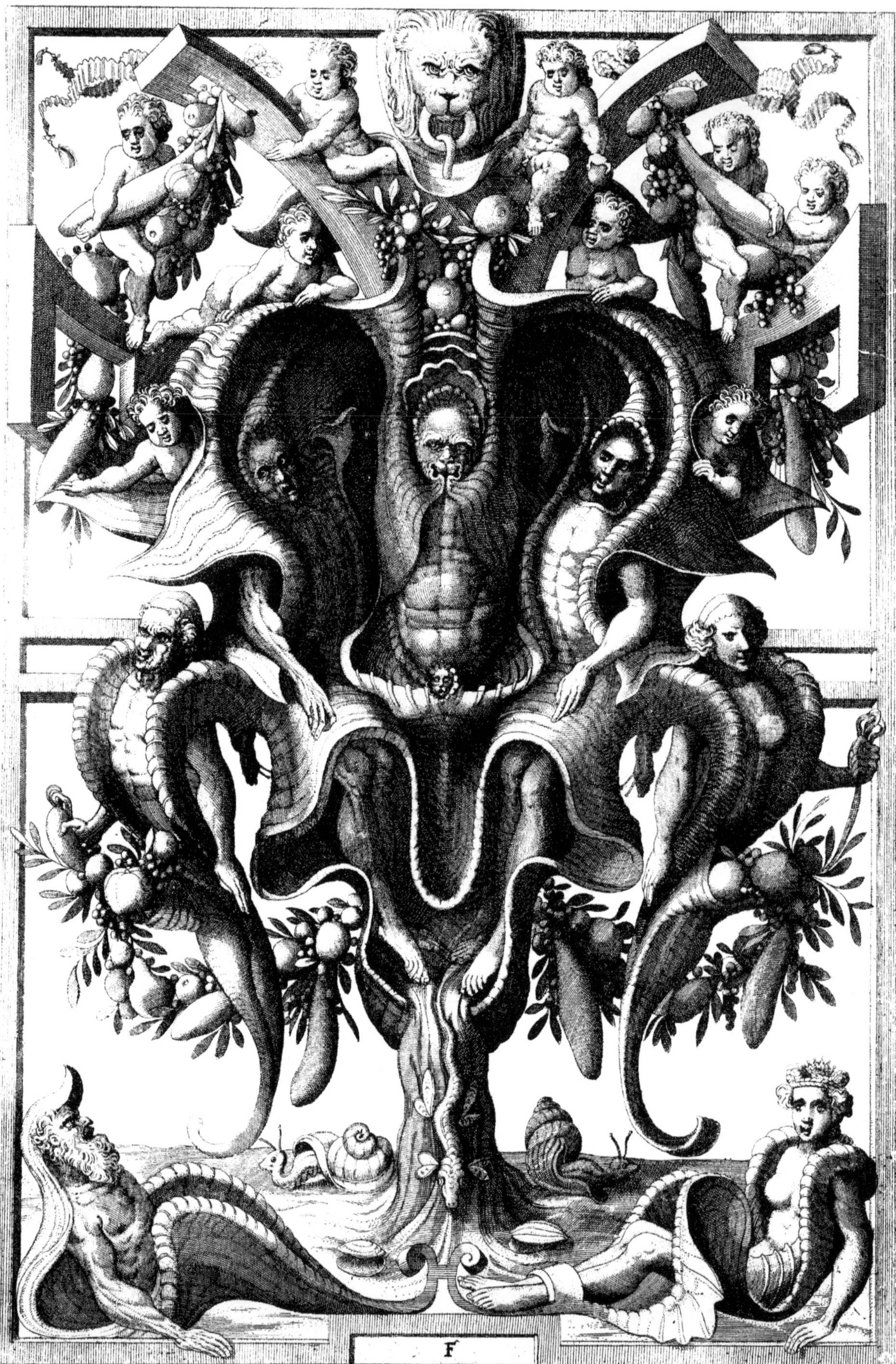

168: Shell-like ornament in which figures are trapped., Johannes or Lucas van Doetechum, after Cornelis Floris (II), 1556.

169

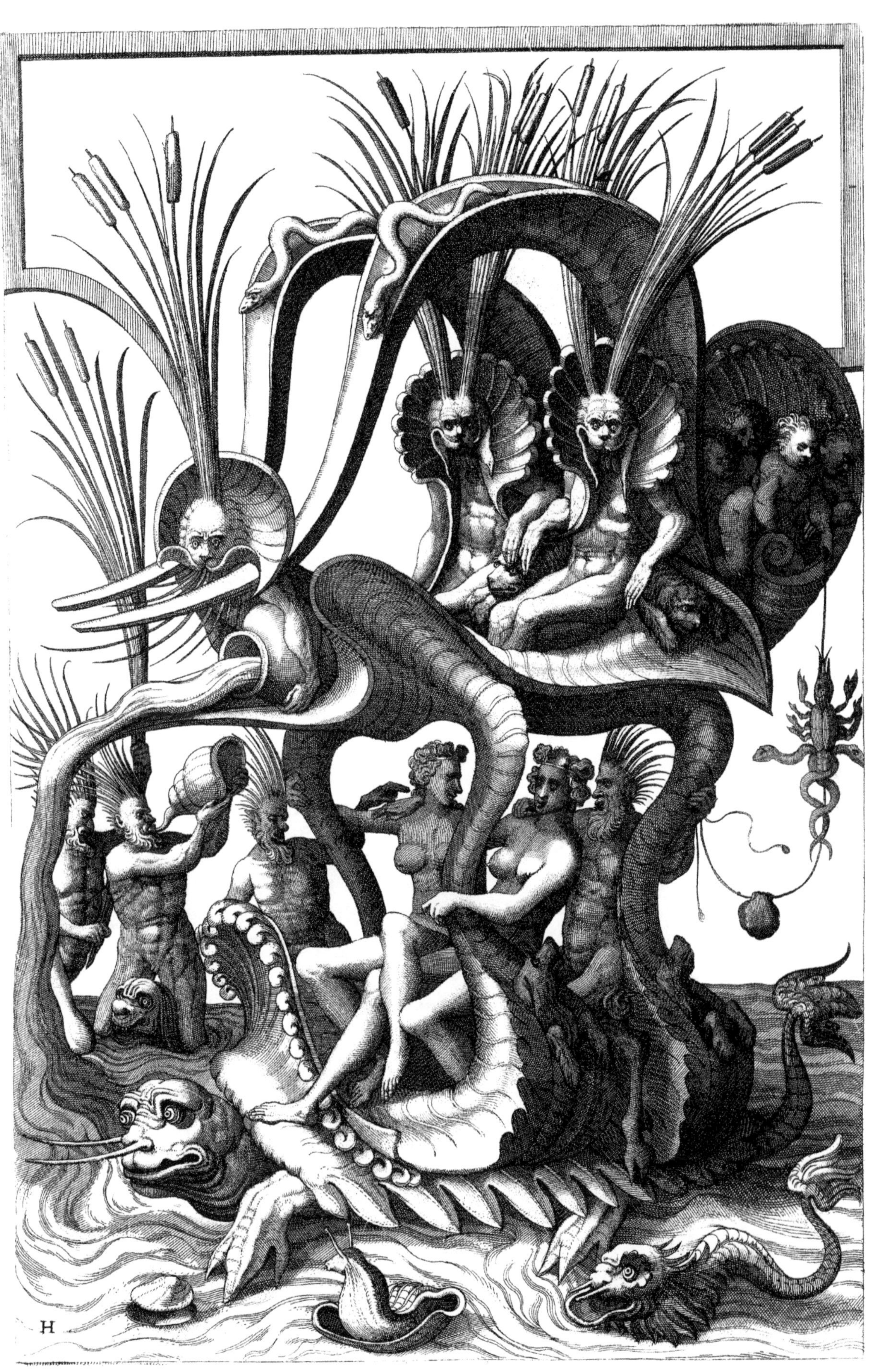

169: Fantastic water turtle carrying a cart on its back, Johannes or Lucas van Doetechum, after Cornelis Floris (II), 1556.

170

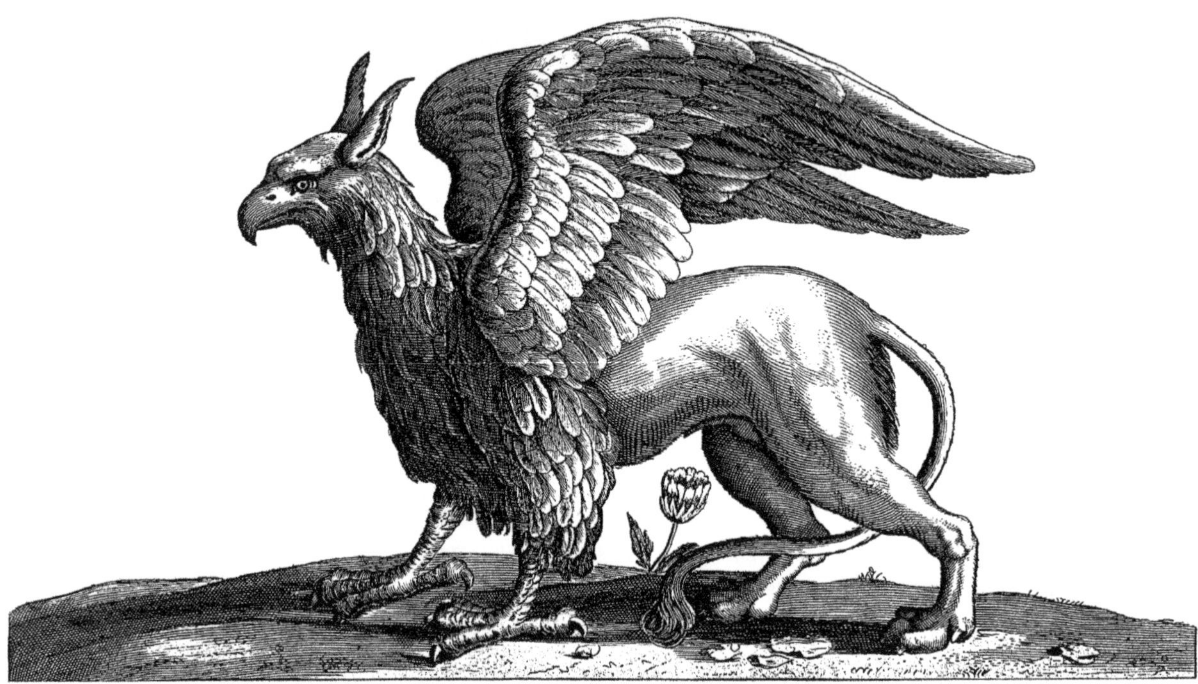

171

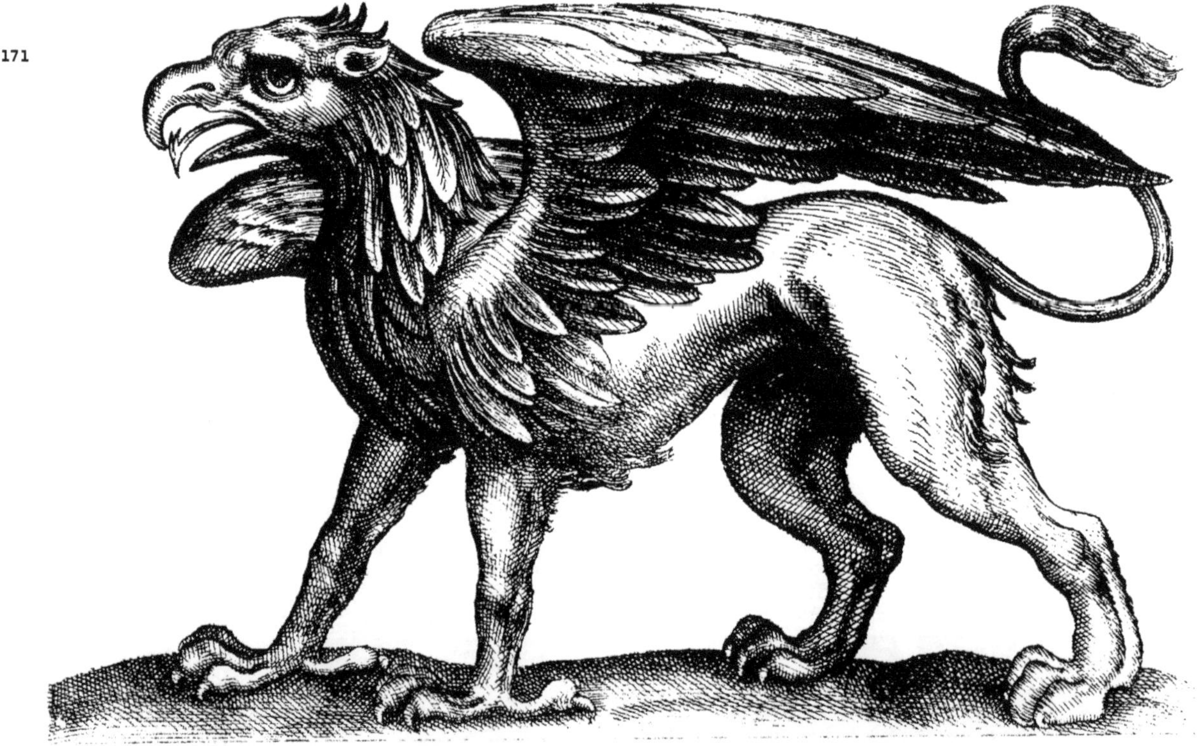

170: A griffin, Engraving by D. Loggan, 1663, after W. Hollar.

171: A Griffin, Antonio Tempesta, in or before 1650.

172

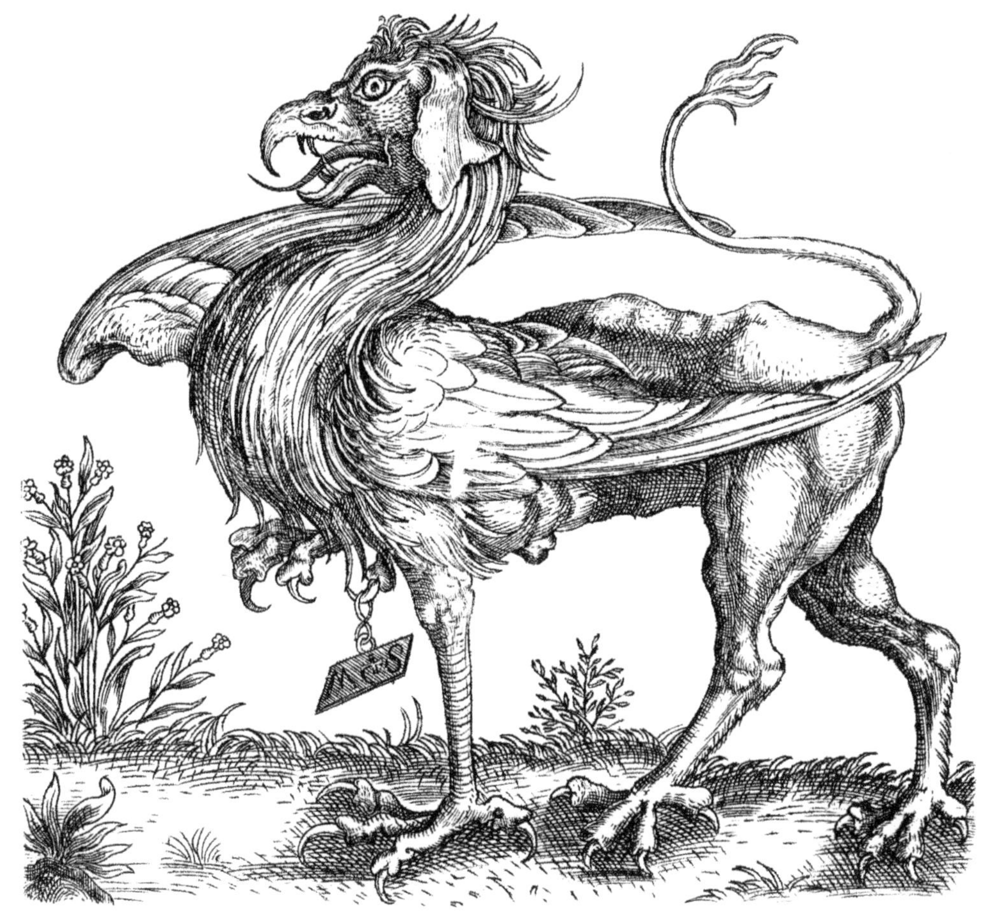

173

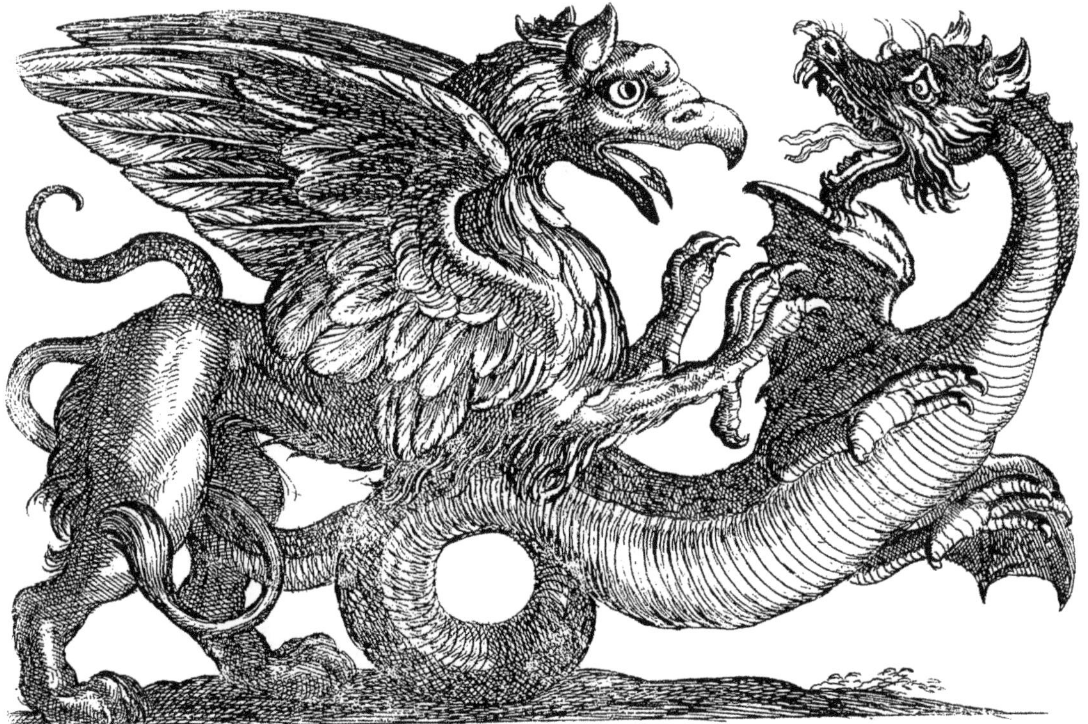

172: A Griffin, Martin Schongauer, 1500 – 1550.

173: Dragon and Griffin Fighting, Antonio Tempesta, 1600.

174

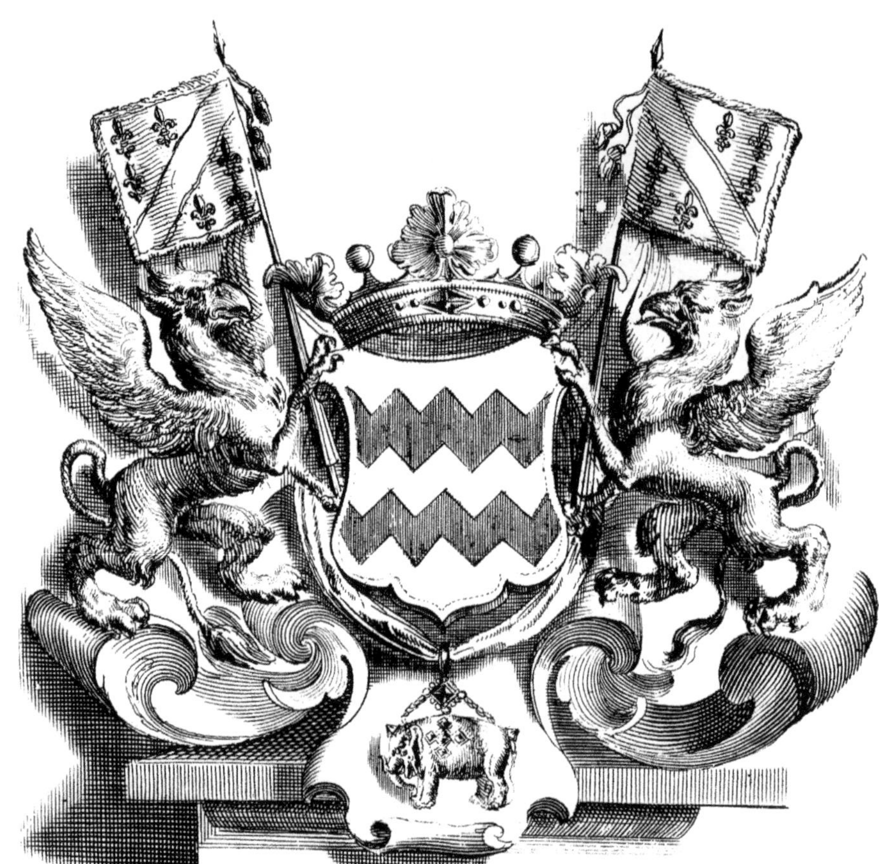

175

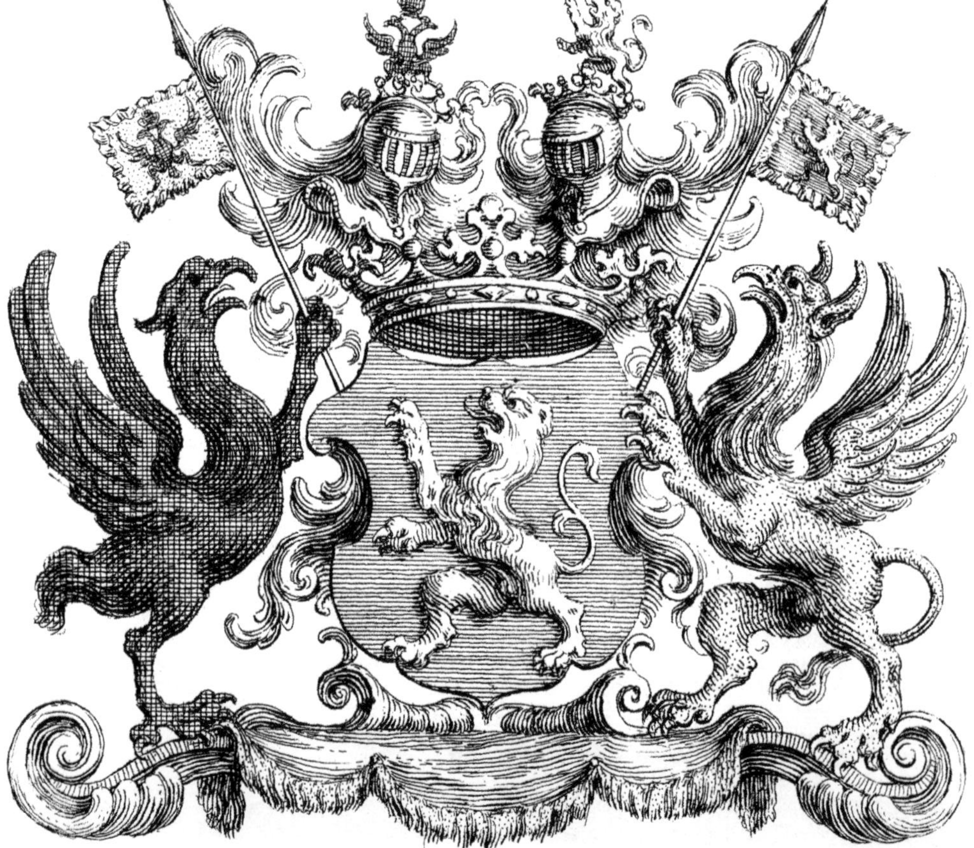

174: Coat of arms of Godard Adriaan van Reede, anonymous, 1660 – 1700.

175: Helmeted coat of arms with Dutch lion, Simon Fokke, 1776.

176

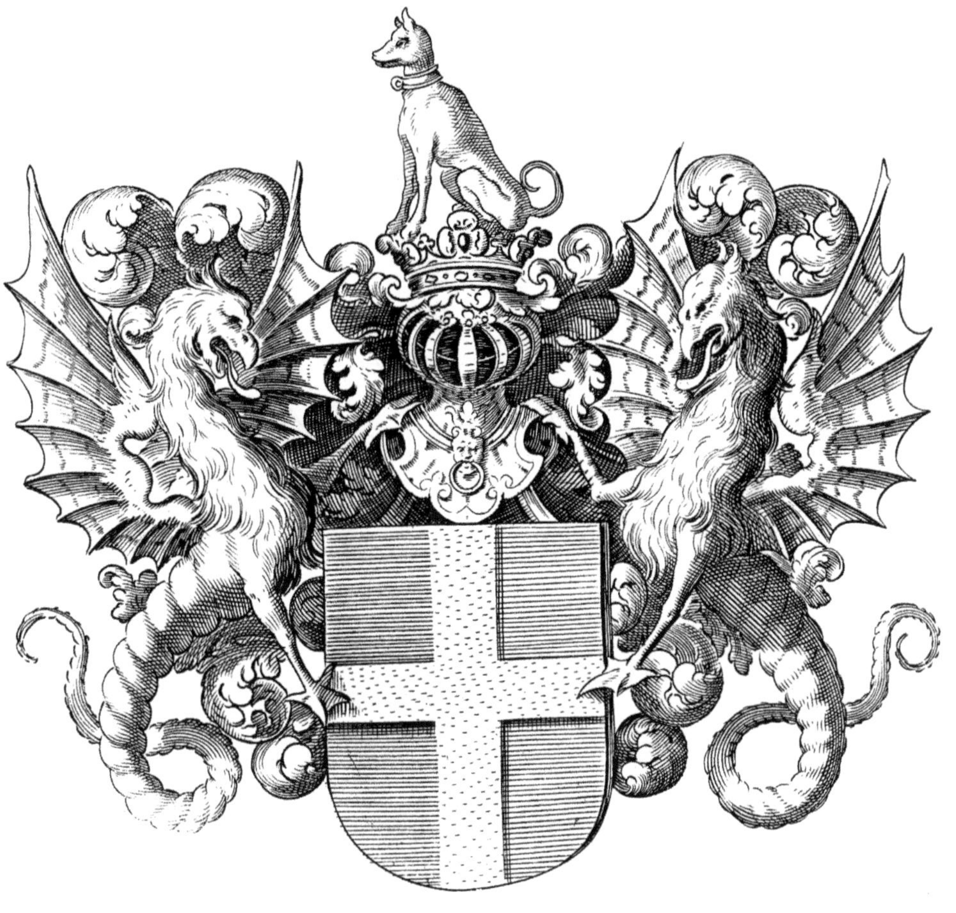

177

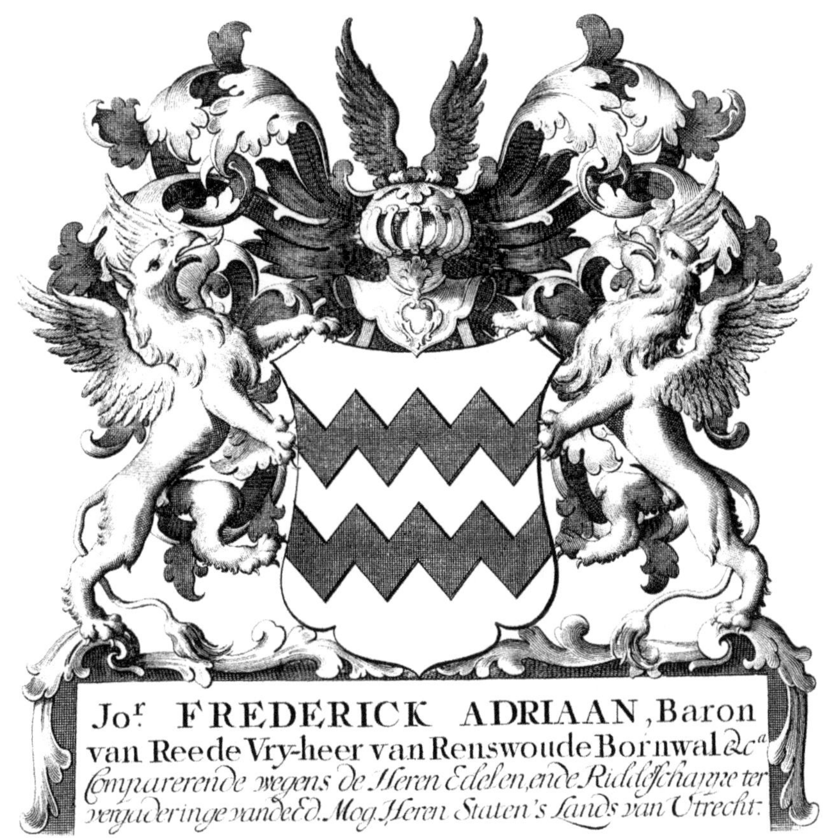

176: Coat of arms of Van Lynden, anonymous, 1600 – 1800.

177: Coat of arms of Frederik Adriaan van Reede, anonymous, 1659 – 1738.

178

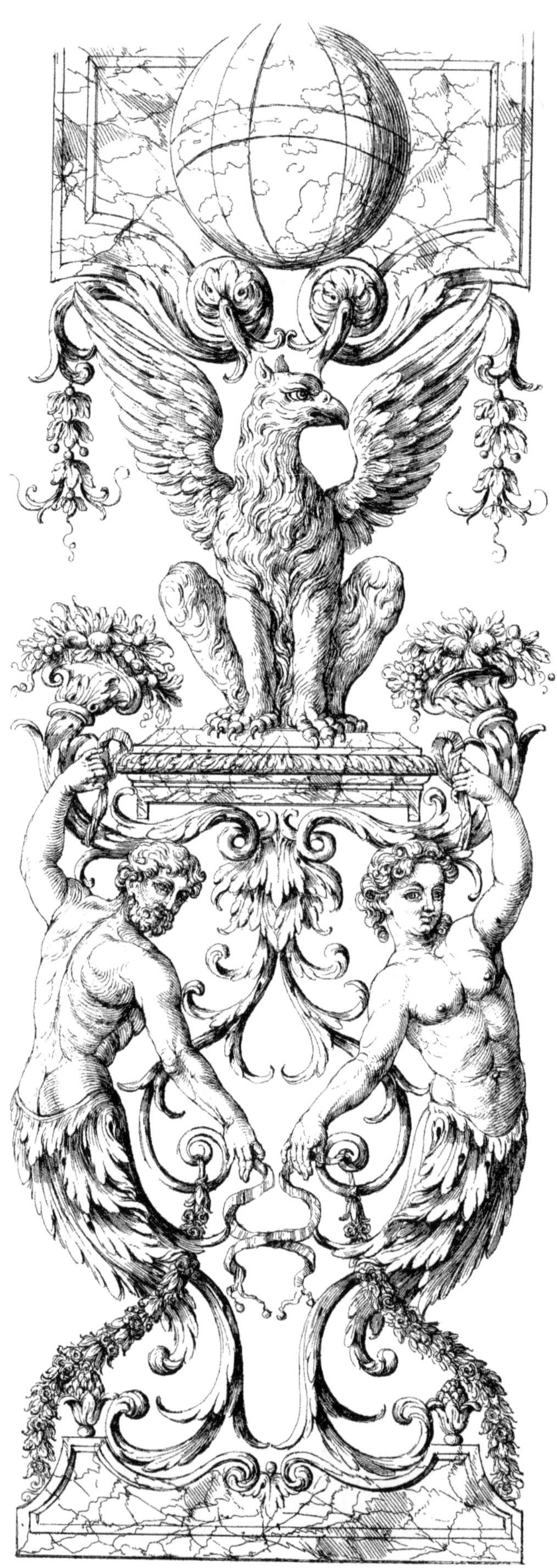

178: Two terms bear a pedestal with a griffin,
Paul Androuet Ducerceau, c. 1670 – c. 1685.

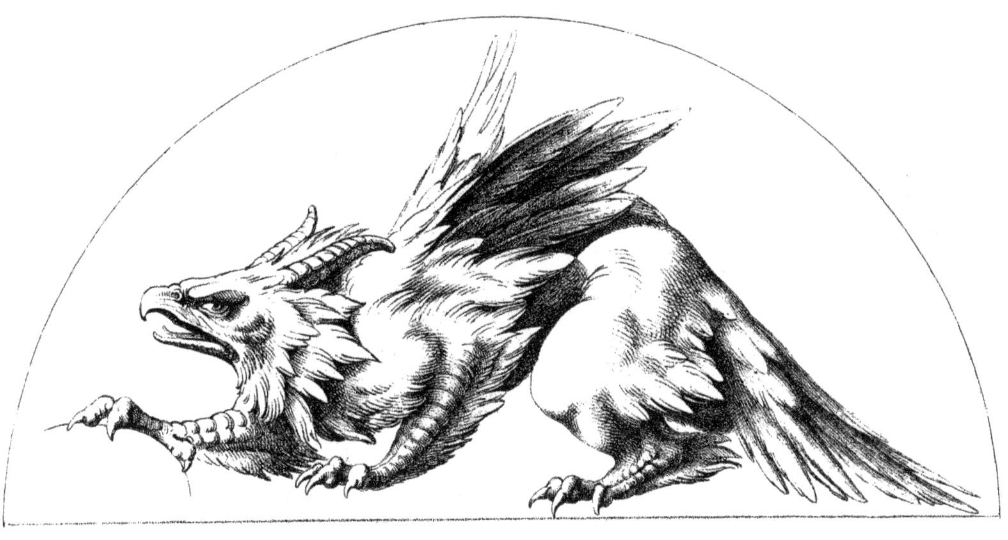

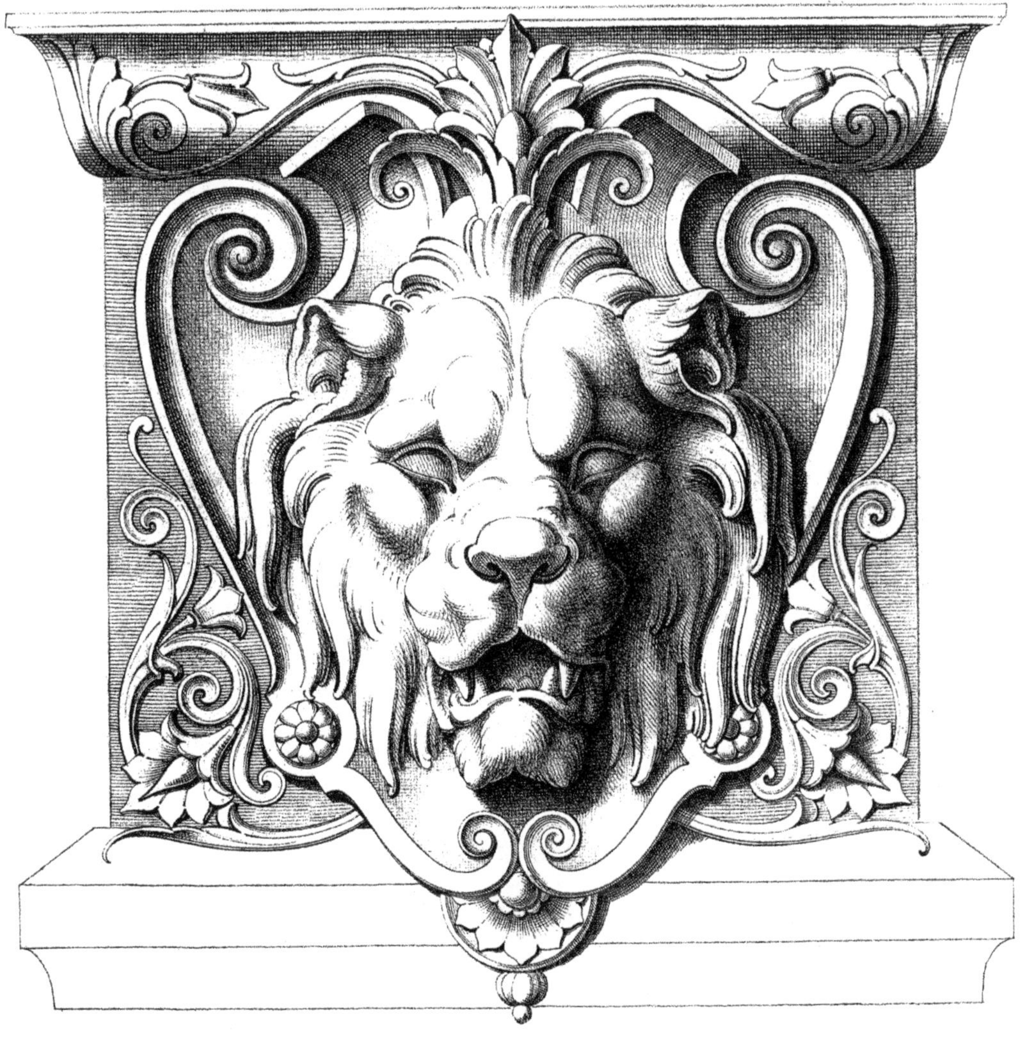

179: Griffin and shield with lion's head, Michel Liénard, 1866.

180

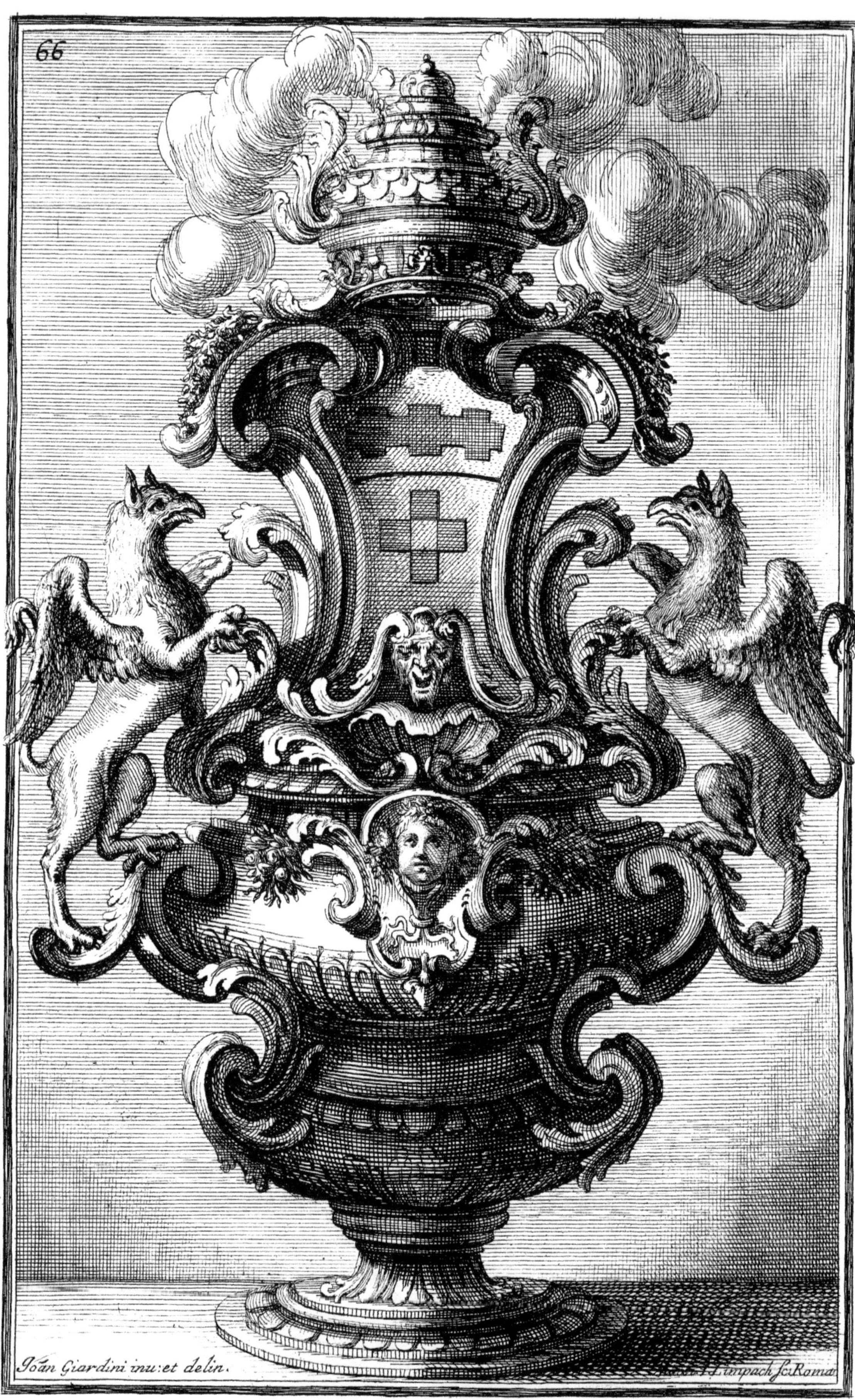

180: Incense burner with two griffins and a coat of arms, Maximilian Joseph Limpach, after Giovanni Giardini, 1714.

181

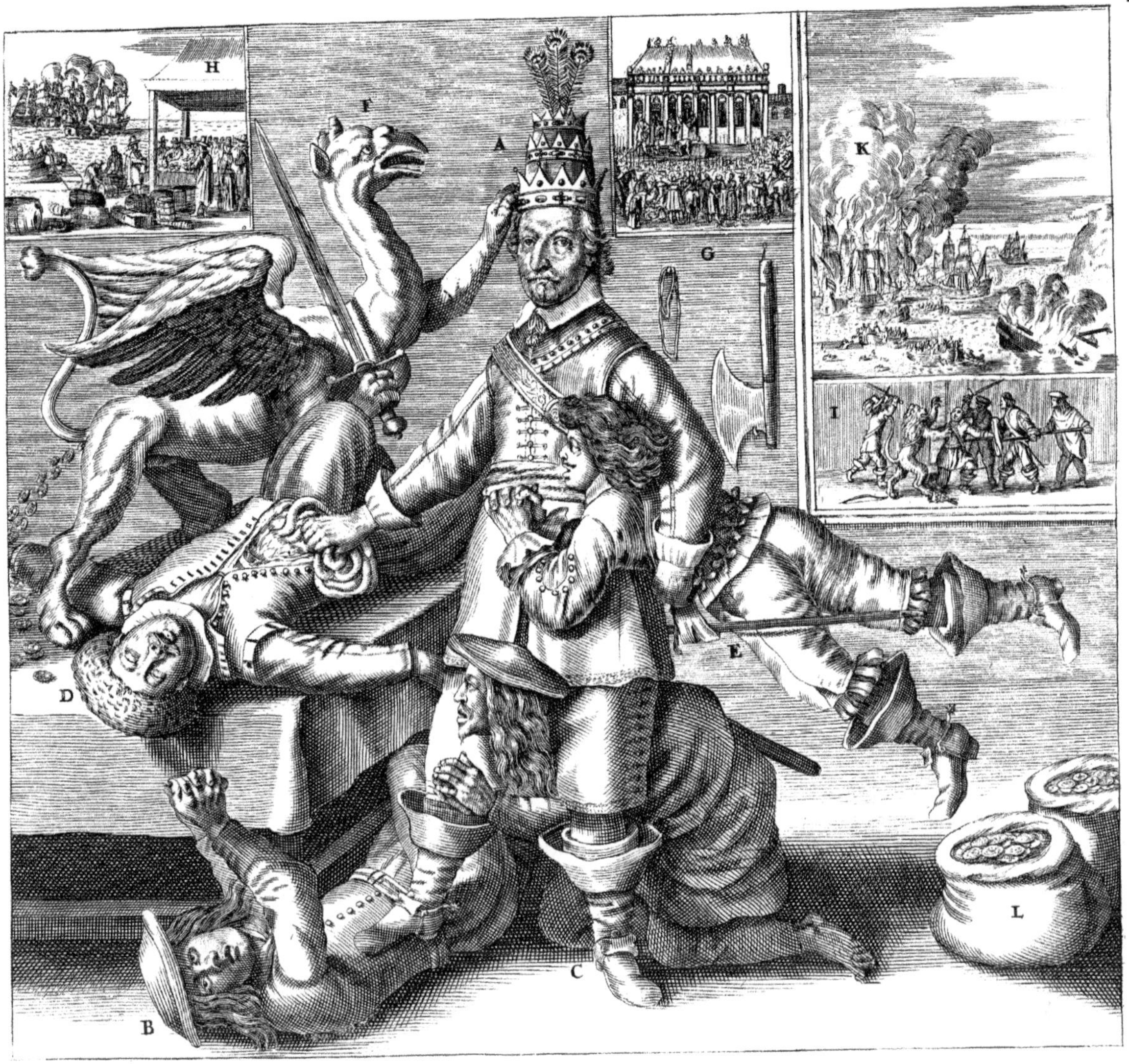

182

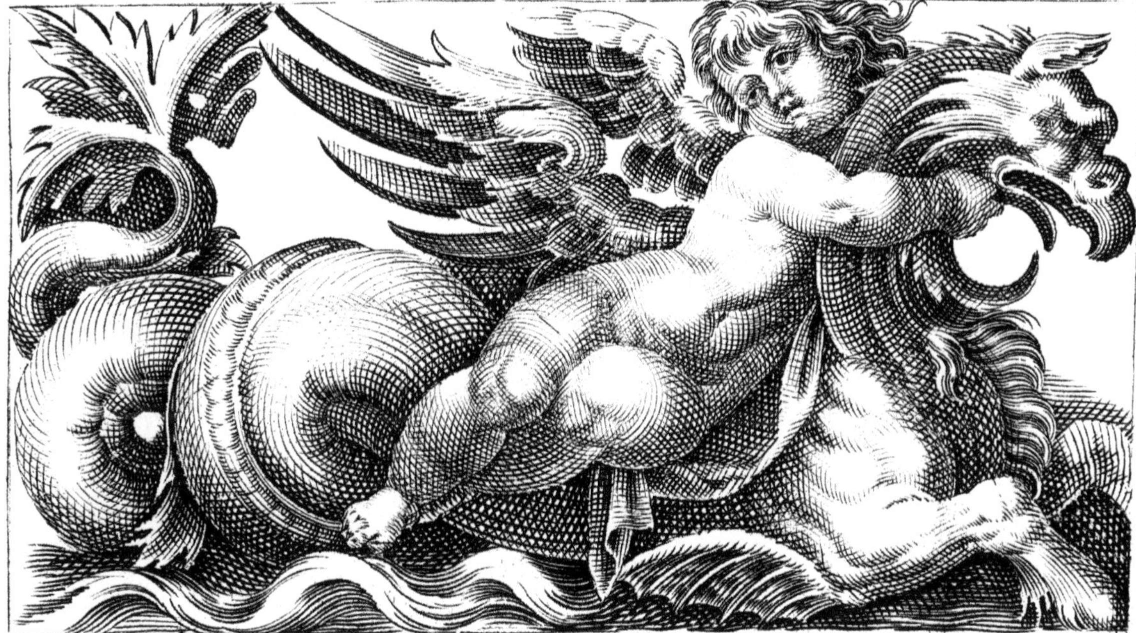

181: Allegory on Oliver Cromwell, Crispijn van de Passe (II), 1652.

182: Putto, seated on a sea creature with the head of a griffin, Adam Fuchs, after Giovanni Andrea Maglioli, 1526 – 1606.

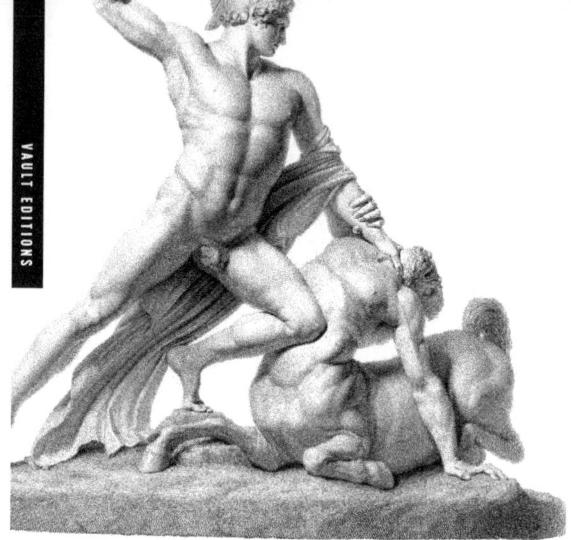

LEARN MORE

At Vault Editions, our mission is to create the world's most diverse and comprehensive collection of image archives available for artists, designers and curious minds. If you have enjoyed this book, you can find more of our titles available at vaulteditions.com.

REVIEW THIS BOOK

As a small, family-owned independent publisher, reviews help spread the word about our work. We would be incredibly grateful if you could leave an honest review of this title wherever you purchased this book.

JOIN OUR COMMUNITY

Are you a creative and curious individual? If so, you will love our community on Instagram. Every day we share bizarre and beautiful artwork ranging from 17th and 18th-century natural history and scientific illustration, to mythical beasts, ornamental designs, anatomical illustration and more. Join our community of 100K+ people today—search @vault_editions on Instagram.

DOWNLOAD YOUR FILES

STEP ONE

Enter the following web address in your web browser on a desktop computer.

www.vaulteditions.com/dmc

STEP TWO

Enter the following unique password to access the download page.

dmc38452fscrx2

STEP THREE

Follow the prompts to access your high-resolution files.

TECHNICAL ASSISTANCE

For all technical assistance, please email: info@vaulteditions.com

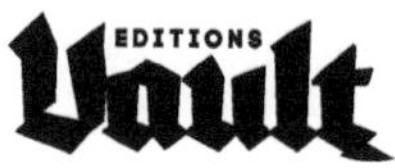

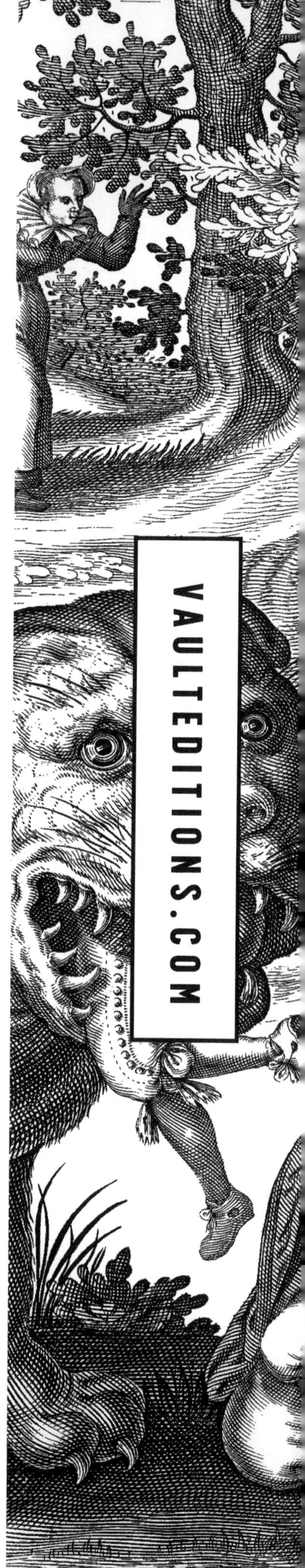

www.ingramcontent.com/pod-product-compliance
Ingram Content Group UK Ltd.
Pitfield, Milton Keynes, MK11 3LW, UK
UKHW051207260726
13967UKWH00011B/3147